Biblical Prophecy Real Talk

Correlating Predictive Prophecy to Current Times

—Higher Truth Unveiled—

By Jarvis "Jimmy" Ross

April 2026

Editor: Jarvis "Jimmy" Ross

Biblical Prophecy Real Talk (Correlating Predictive Prophecy to Current Times)

by Jarvis "Jimmy" Ross

Troutman, North Carolina

April 2026

Editor: Jarvis J. Ross @ jarvisjimmyrossauthor.com

About the Author and Work
Ross, Jarvis "Jimmy"

Biblical Prophecy Real Talk (Correlating Predictive Prophecy to Current Times)

This is an expository and persuasive work based on research. It is designed to explain, inform, and define subjects related to faith. It is not the intent of this work to dispute the claims of others. Rather, the intent is to elevate the Christian faith by means of persuasion by reason through induction and deduction of the sacred text of Scripture.

ISBN: 978-1-7351195-8-8

Cover design by Christina@diagonalleigh

CONTENT

EPIGRAPH

Living in the "Last Days": *Whether we recognize it or not, we are currently living in the "last days" that began at Pentecost as noted in Acts 2:17. However, these are not the same as the "end times." Our era is marked by significant prophetic events. Importantly, predictive prophecy does not focus on identifying any specific prominent political figure or historical character, except for Christ and the Antichrist. This is because the moral decline of human nature and the rise and fall of authoritarian rulers would persist regardless of who holds power. As such, we should not attribute the state of the world to any person. Instead of seeking answers in sensational news reports, we are encouraged to search the Word of God for true understanding.*

The Nature and Purpose of Predictive Prophecy: *Predictive prophecy is grounded in the context of the times, always aligned with Scripture and history, and revealed through God's providence. The events described in prophecy are determined beforehand, as God's foreknowledge encompasses the rise and fall of world leaders, all of whom are influenced by spiritual forces, whether good or evil. In His infinite wisdom, God foresees what will take place through the free will of humanity, yet He responds without ever infringing upon that freedom. In this way, God advances His redemptive plan, skillfully working around any opposition to His purpose. God's Kingdom is built through those who love Him and are willing to serve, and this is accomplished through acts of faith and a commitment to reaching the lost—a central theme of this book. The relevance of these truths extends across generations, emphasizing the ongoing importance of prophetic understanding in fostering hope, readiness, and preparation for what is to come.*

PROLOGUE

Introducing Spiritual Warfare

Taken from the show series, "Dune—Prophecy: "What holds more truth, history or prophecy?"

Mythology is a historical universal fantasy and aspect of all cultures about the existence of gods that hold sway and power over human life. Every country on Earth contains populations that engage with mythology, whether as part of religious belief, cultural tradition, or storytelling. This widespread engagement means that mythology is present in all nations.

During modernity, individuals may hold spiritual, folkloric, or neo-pagan connections to Greek, Norse, Celtic, and other pagan beliefs. In the US, folklore includes legends. Therefore, given our Judeo-Christian heritage, it is not unusual for large segments of the faith community and those outside of the faith community to believe in angels and demons. The consideration here is whether spiritual warfare exists between these angels and demons that play out on the earth through human channels. Buckle up as we go on an exhilarating journey of discovery.

The sacred prophetic text of Scripture confirms that we are living in prophetic times, marked by a noticeable increase in spiritual activity. Demonic forces have multiplied across the earth, led by Satan, who is called the "prince of the power of the air." He influences lies, conspiracies, and misinformation that circulate in the atmosphere. Ephesians 2:2 describes, before the birth of Christ, how people once followed the ways of the world, under the influence of this prince, obedient to a spirit that still operates in those who resist God's purposes.

The survey of Scripture has revealed that in the Old Testament and the New Testament, during the public ministry of Christ and His Apostles and disciples, and during the ministry of the Early Church, God's people confronted the spiritual forces and activities behind natural occurrences.

Concerning the Early Church, they didn't retreat from the challenge of spiritual opposition that was seen as persecution in the natural, but exercised the authority that Christ endowed the Church with at Pentecost, recorded in Acts 1:8: *"But you shall receive power (ability, efficiency, and might) when the Holy Spirit has come upon you, and you shall be My witnesses in Jerusalem and all Judea and Samaria and to the ends (the very bounds) of the earth."* The Greek word for "power" is "Dunamis," the source of the English word, "dynamite." Practically, it means explosive power for a bold witness. Dunamis power is released when disciples of the Lord and the collective community of faith launch out on the mission to reap God's harvest. I choose not to use contemporary-modern terms as synonyms for what Scripture describes as "reaping God's harvest." My reason is not theological or doctrinal. It comes from a practical analysis of God's Word.

Spiritual warfare involves combating oppression and evil through prayer, righteous deeds, and faith and action, rather than fighting fire with fire, because the battle takes place on higher ground. Believers are encouraged to avoid arguments with malicious opponents and trust in God's justice, which will ultimately prevail.

Spiritual warfare is essential for believers facing oppression rooted in fear, deception, and lies, and misapplied scripture. This life-giving work outlines how true followers of Christ should respond to persecution that is a fallout from spiritual attacks with faith, prayer, and good works rather than vengeance or argument, emphasizing reliance on God's justice to prevail and angelic protection.

The Oppression Tactics and Scripture Misuse and Confronting it through spiritual warfare: Oppressors use fear, deception with lies, threats, and violence to intimidate those considered of a lesser class labeled as "bad people." (Their struggles are due to inadequate, impoverished income that can lead to crime, violence, and immorality out of an instinct to survive. This is not an excuse for bad behavior, but points to a less-than-quality life that creates temptation to illicit behavior. At the other end of the spectrum, wealth associated with greed can also contribute to crime, violence, and immorality as the wealthy elevate themselves above the law and beyond repute.)

The Targets of Spiritual Warfare—Followers of Christ and the Poor: Satan targets low-moderate income people due to God's call to reach and care for the orphans, widows, and strangers who are poor. Christ's public ministry began with the poor to reach up to all people (Luke 4:18) and God's redemptive plan of salvation for them in the "last days." Satan knows that when they come to the Lord in the harvest of the "latter rain," his end is near. They have been unfortunately tagged with the historic, politically correct label of minorities that today fits anyone who does not fit the standard of the dominant culture of upper-middle-class affluent people who hold to their cultural values, religious views, and political policies above others. Most dominant cultures desire to dominate and control the poor and marginal income people (Read James 5:1-7). They often justify their actions as pseudo-Christians with misinterpreted and misapplied biblical passages like Matthew 11:12, which highlights false religious leadership that creates a false image of Christ and Christianity.

Believers' Response to Spiritual Persecution and Attacks: True believers should avoid vindictive retaliation by following Christ's example of rebuking evil without violence, and refrain from arguing with hateful "mean-spirited" people, as illustrated by His rebuke of His disciples in Samaria, recorded in Luke 9:54. Instead, the approach is by invoking God's rebuke as Archangel Michael did against Satan (Jude 1:9). Prayer and "good works" ("Letting your light Shine") are essential in this spiritual battle. Prayer combined with good works is vital since faith without works is dead.

God's Justice and Spiritual Warfare: Believers are urged to avoid personal vengeance, leaving judgment to God, who promises to repay wrongdoing. (Just as all men and women are *"appointed to die once and then face judgment,"* there is a day of reckoning coming to every individual where they will give an account before God, before they die, which can happen at any time and any place.

Christ coming as "a thief in the night" not only applies to the Second Coming of the Lord, but to a day in this life when people will reap what they have sown through divine reciprocity, which becomes self-imposed judgment based on those who blatantly reject the Lord. Meanwhile, spiritual warfare begins with prayer and righteous deeds to overcome evil because God's angelic forces have already defeated Satan's rebellion—we are living out the victory. "Don't wait for the battle to be over, shout the victory now."

In the final analysis, Christ defeated and destroyed the works of the devil on a cruel cross of capital punishment for humanity's sins, giving us the victory.

The Nature of the Conflict

Because confusion reigns about the real enemy, many find themselves "shadow boxing"—struggling against unseen forces, mistakenly directing attacks toward governments, political figures, religion, various movements, and influential, affluent voices that divide people. The true conflict, however, exists in the atmosphere and heavenly realms, where good spiritual forces of God battle against evil spiritual forces of Satan. Although it may sound like science fiction, the truth is "art imitates life." Practically, aside from Hollywood productions, art imitating life from a biblical perspective means to look at scripture not as some fantasy but as real life, which is revealed in these pages as the story behind the story. Spiritual warfare is a biblical reality that has played out through time and history.

Biblical Examples of Spiritual Warfare: A vivid example is found in Revelation 12:12, which recounts the devil's casting to Earth following his defeat in the heavenlies. Knowing his time is short, Satan's fury intensifies, and he persecutes believers with great force. This marks a period of heightened spiritual warfare and persecution for humanity, as Satan focuses his anger before his eventual judgment.

Revelation 12:12 belongs to a larger narrative (Revelation 12:7-17) detailing Satan's expulsion from heaven and his subsequent war against God's people. The scope of this passage spans the entire history of Christianity, with the woman (Mary) giving birth to Christ, and continues through Christ's ascension, the Church's persecution during the Apostolic and Middle Ages, the ongoing Church Age, and culminates in the final conflict before Christ's return, often referred to as the Tribulation period by scholars.

Spiritual Warfare in the Last Days: This work reveals how the "last days," which began at Pentecost, overlap and recapitulate with the "end times," when the final events of eschatology will signal the rise of the antichrist. Although we are not in those final times, our generation experiences signs that foreshadow what is to come.

Empowerment through Biblical Prophecy: "Biblical Prophecy Real Talk" serves as a guidebook, helping believers recognize spiritual opposition and oppression while equipping them to overcome. Romans 8:35-38 reassures that nothing can separate us from the love of Christ …Even when faced with death, believers are described as "sheep for the slaughter" because their martyrdom reflects the life of Christ. Yet, the passage emphasizes that amid all these hardships, we are more than conquerors, gaining victory through Christ who loves us. The assurance continues: neither death nor life, nor angels nor principalities, nor impending or threatening things, nor things to come, nor any powers can separate us from God's love.

The Spirit of Antichrist: The Focus of Spiritual Warfare

The "spirit of Antichrist" has traversed generations and appeared in the garden of delights as a beautiful dragon. That spirit has influenced human vessels of tyrannical monarchs and dictators throughout history as forerunners to the actual person. He will ultimately manifest as the key person to the operations of the "Beast" in Revelation during the Tribulation.

The spirit of Antichrist signifies opposition to Christ, masquerading as Christian, and a spiritual attack on foundational principles of Christianity (false doctrine), directed towards disciples of the Lord and God's harvest.

From the pages of the sacred text and other studies, the spirit of antichrist is equated to **divination** and **spiritism**, which signifies distinguishing the difference between spirituality and spiritualism.

The realm of divination imitates the Godhead and the three heavens to deceive seekers, the unchurched, and religious-political-minded Christians. This theme serves as a warning against influences or teachings that attempt to undermine or distort the true nature of Christ and the essence of Christian faith. The spirit of antichrist can be seen as a dictatorship through oppressive religious and political policies that exploit disadvantaged, downtrodden people. The poor in Scripture represent a major last-day target for salvation that will usher in "the restitution of all things," and end the reign of the devil, which is why they are attacked.

—*Recognizing the Antichrist Characteristics*—

Defacing Christ: Defacing Christ refers to actions or ideologies that diminish, distort, or misrepresent Jesus, particularly His divinity and the unifying power of His sacrifice—the efficacy of His blood to bring all ethnicities and cultures together as one. This truth is displayed vividly in the Book of Revelation, which is not merely for the "hear after," but for the "here and now." This distortion can arise from false teachings or misapplications of Scripture, leading believers away from an authentic expression of faith to what Scripture calls "another gospel"—depicted from an ethnocentric cultural perspective.

False Christian Narratives: False Christian narratives are stories or teachings that mislead, manipulate, or present untruths, especially today, in the form of conspiracy theories, which are essentially propaganda. Recognizing and rejecting these narratives is essential for maintaining the purity of doctrine and ensuring that faith is rooted in truth. Recognizing and discerning the evil intent behind these narratives, and rejecting them, is vital to maintaining integrity in the Christian life and finding peace and a sense of well-being.

Exploitation for Gain: Exploitation for gain addresses the malign of false prophets and false apostles who misuse Scripture for personal gain and control of gullible minds—an abuse of authority for personal benefit. This theme cautions against using religion as a means to achieve financial or social advancement, often to the detriment of others who are powerless. Upcoming tools are explored to easily recognize these false teachers by identifying motives and characteristics.

Vindictiveness and Vengeance: Vindictiveness and vengeance are on the rise due to desperate times and mutual anger and hate towards those who inflict hurt and pain wittingly or unwittingly. But vindictiveness and vengeance should not be part of the Christian life. Painful, harmful encounters and experiences reflect a desire for retribution or retaliation. It is a temptation to respond to wrongdoing with further wrongdoing. These attitudes stand in stark contrast to Christlikeness and the scriptural call to forgiveness, mercy, and the demonstration of grace. Aside from the methods of firefighters, fighting fire with fire only makes a bigger fire.

Fear and Deception: Fear and deception are identified as the primary characteristics and tools of the devil that he uses to lead seekers astray and hinder spiritual growth. This theme underscores the necessity of discernment and faith in overcoming misleading lies, conspiracy theories, and influences, enabling individuals to remain anchored in truth and continue their journey towards exponential blessings, spiritual freedom, and the transformative power of the gospel to deliver.

—Godly Responses to the Spirit of Antichrist—

Sowing and Reaping: Sowing and reaping, also referred to as reciprocity, is a biblical concept that emphasizes the consequences of words and actions. The concept teaches that whatever one invests in, whether positive or negative, will return to them. Good will be returned with a clear conscience filled with peace and gratitude. Evil will be returned with a burning conscience, but unrepentant because of the corruption of evil and hatred for God. Sowing and reaping evil as reciprocity becomes self-imposed judgment because they fight and violate God's revealed will in the human conscience.

Vengeance is in the Hands of God, who will deliver His people from the hands of those who fear retribution because of their injustices.

Spiritual Unity: Spiritual Unity is a calling echoed throughout Scripture and outlined in Ephesians 4. Spiritual unity stresses the importance of harmony and togetherness among believers. It calls for the breaking down of barriers and walls, encouraging the pursuit of oneness in faith and purpose—the cause of Christ, as a powerful means of rebutting evil. It becomes the means in the Body of Christ to defeat spiritual opposition and bring divine intervention into the affairs of life through prayers and petitions.

Spiritual Mobilization: Strategy for Authority in Spiritual Warfare

When you reach the chapter entitled "Waging Spiritual Warfare," the section on "Spiritual Mobilization" outlines a clear strategy for exercising authority in battling spiritual opposition. This strategy addresses the forms of oppression and suppression of human rights and freedoms that often manifest through human agents. However, it is important to recognize that the real battle does not target the human element itself. As emphasized in Ephesians 6:10-12, we are reminded that our struggle is not against flesh and blood, but against spiritual forces.

Instead of a direct approach through confrontation or protest, the approach is indirect through a network of disciples earnestly praying and proclaiming "good news" in the face of "doom and gloom." The prescribed approach is intercessory "prayer in the spirit." This type of prayer is characterized by non-protesting, humble supplication that seeks and welcomes God's presence to intervene in challenging circumstances. The foundation for this approach is found in II Chronicles 7:14, which calls for earnest prayer and seeking God's face as the means for transformation and healing in our "worlds."

Through this spiritual mobilization, those who are actively protesting for justice in the streets are covered and protected by God's angelic host. The act of intercessory prayer invites divine intervention because the Community of Faith serves as "Salt" and "Light" in the world as intercessors on their behalf, standing in the gap. Believer's efforts at spiritual warfare provide a spiritual shield against spiritual forces that influence people with evil intent.

Reflecting on the history of Old Testament Israel and the New Testament Church, we observe numerous instances where God intervened on behalf of His people. In both eras, God contended with their spiritual adversaries, which ultimately led to victory in the natural realm. These examples serve as a model for understanding how spiritual warfare, fought through prayer and reliance on God, brings about real change and triumph over opposition.

Summary: Understanding the Age & Responding with Faith & Action

Timeless Human Nature and Historical Parallels: This section underscores the idea that, apart from technological progress, the essence of the current age remains much like that of ancient times. From the era of Adam through the records of the Old and New Testaments, the reigns of monarchs and emperors, the Crusades, the Middle Ages, and the devastation of World Wars I and II, humanity has continually faced a world marked by evil, hatred, and violence among nations.

The prevailing condition of the human heart has not changed; moral struggles and the challenges of human nature persist through every era. Events such as wars, rumors of wars, sickness, disease, and social or political upheaval—including revolutions and insurrections—are not just features of history but are also present realities.

A Message for Disciples in the "Last Days"

In light of these times, the message addressed to the disciples of the Lord is both urgent and hopeful. The Body of Christ is entrusted with the Great Commission, and these challenging times present a unique opportunity: "where sin abounds, grace does much more abound." As the world grows darker, the chance to reach people searching for answers becomes brighter, and the answer remains Christ. Therefore, believers must acclimate to these prophetic times—not with anxiety or fear, but with confidence and adaptability. Fear is depicted as a real tool of the enemy, paralyzing individuals and keeping them from acting, while faith is the means by which the Lord enables His people to move forward through the power of the Holy Spirit.

Responding with Faith and Proactive Engagement: Ironically, instead of succumbing to fear, believers are encouraged to rejoice because the fulfillment of salvation is nearer than ever before. Christians are called to position themselves with the Lord, serving as His agents of redemption and reconciliation, impacting the lives of those weighed down by hostility and turmoil. This requires proactive involvement—engaging spiritually and practically before the full impact of coming challenges is realized. Much like playing chess, believers are urged to anticipate, prepare, and participate in spiritual warfare, as further explored throughout this book.

It is important here to note in conclusion that morality cannot be legislated with outward laws. Laws draw lines in the sand to enforce violent acts. Only the gospel can change the condition of the human heart that erases the lines that divide people without laws. The converse of Romans 4:15 and 5:13 is that where there is no sin, there is no need for law.

INTRODUCTION

New Age Governing Disorder

Order is evident throughout the universe, reflected in its arrangement and inherent beauty. This natural order demonstrates the intentional design created by God. When the universe deviates from this order, through manmade ecological disruptions and climate change, chaos results. Similarly, predictive prophecy serves to remind the church of the necessity for divine order. When the church strays from the order established by God—especially by engaging in activities or movements not rooted in Scripture—disorder and confusion can ensue.

The Apostle Paul concludes the fourteenth chapter of First Corinthians with a clear directive: *"But all things should be done with regard to decency and propriety and in an orderly fashion."* This instruction emphasizes the importance of maintaining order in all aspects of church life, including worship, fellowship, relationships between men and women, and the church's testimony to the world. Any involvement in chaotic activities or movements that are inconsistent with the character of Christ distorts the world's perception of the church and confuses the reality of Christ, which is the devil's disorder.

Scripture affirms that God is a God of peace, not confusion (I Corinthians 14:33). The church is therefore called to operate in divine order, which is realized through relationships, spiritual gifts, and callings that are accountable and aligned with biblical teaching. Such an order ensures that the church functions effectively, building up believers and serving as faithful witnesses for Christ. The central focus is on edification—being built up and strengthened in the Lord—along with preparation and readiness to bear witness.

A Warning for the Last Days: This serves as a preface to highlight a significant warning: in the "last days," there will emerge a "One World Government-New Age Order." This development will create turmoil in various parts of the world through conspiracy theories and new age philosophies. Such influences will foster chaos and confusion regarding faith in Christ and the authenticity of the church, seeking to replace true faith with a deceptive imitation.

—Predictive Prophecy—

Because all Scripture is prophetic, Predictive Prophecy Correlated to Current Times sets the church in order, like soldiers prepared for battle to stand against "spiritual wickedness." BPRT draws together the parallels of the past, present, and future to describe their commonality from generation to generation. Despite denominational distinctions and local church affiliation, the church is one and should not be divided by faith. Therefore, the language presented in this work, regarding the future, sounds like the times we are living in today. The rationale presents a complete picture of "prophetic times," in relevant descriptive words that bring the story behind the story of Scripture to life. Thus, the opening here:

Certain Christian communities believe in the concept of a "One World Government and New Age Order" that emerges from an age-old conspiracy theory that resembles "last day," "end times" tyrannical Monarchies.

Relative to the prophetic times we live in today, the formation of these governments will be run exclusively by a monarchial dictator, initiated by a secretive society that includes the wealthiest elites, corrupt politicians, tech giants, international corporate interest groups, and run by AI technology and cybercurrency. History has proven that we have seen a semblance of those types of governments, but the New Age/One World Government will be the apex of autocratic, totalitarian dictatorships that will include a one-party system.

Throughout history, and particularly in these modern times, they operate clandestinely "in plain sight" and are often alluded to as "the deep state." Allegedly, they are plotting the overthrow of fragile, vulnerable democracies. Their supposed goal is to advance totalitarian and authoritarian movements that would ultimately eliminate the democracy of sovereign nations and states.

The New Age Order: A Heretical Quasi-Christian Religion

It shouldn't be a surprise to the reader that all religions have sects that have broken away from the original to form a fabricated type for wealth, power, and control, that morph into cults. The "New Age Order" is seen as such—perceived as a deceptive movement that is intent on replacing traditional Christianity, as depicted in Scripture, with a new, syncretic-theocratic world religion. This ideology is seen as supporting a unified global geopolitical system founded on New Age ideology, but it doesn't include all world leaders and nations, which is important for believers to understand.

Ultimately, the ideological objective is a single world religion that would supplant established faiths, including non-Christian faiths—a hodgepodge conglomerate of amalgamation of faiths.

This false religion is interpreted by some as being prophesied in Scripture as an anti-Christian movement, which masquerades under the guise of Christianity. It is viewed as being orchestrated by Satan to usher in the End Times, culminating in his reign for seven years, divided into three-and-a-half-year increments.

Pathways to a One World Government

Supporters of this theory claim that the path toward a One World Government will come to pass through fabricated global crises such as climate-related natural disasters, ecological disruptions from exploiting natural resources on the earth, lab-manufactured pandemics, and covert terrorist attacks. However, as you shall see in further reading, divination becomes a source of the Antichrist movement to conjure up demonic forces, seen in the Book of Revelation as a cause of these catastrophic events, seen through the lens of science. These events are believed to be used to provoke civil unrest, incite protests, and riots to justify military intervention. The alleged aim is to oppress society's most vulnerable—the weak, poor, physically and mentally challenged, and those who do not conform to traditional gender roles—by portraying them as burdens and a blight on society, and by using political repression to control them.

Additional strategies, as perceived by proponents, include extensive surveillance and monitoring of financial systems to restrict economic involvement, which will be "unpacked" under the number 666, in further reading. As well, there will be efforts to take over the media, arts, sciences, and education. Through these means, the propaganda ideology (disseminated through "tickle your fancy" preaching and politics) will generate conformity to policies of dictatorship, depicted through computer AI religious-political imagery that is described in the Book of Revelation as the "Beast," which I shall show as a gigantic, monstrous computer.

Roots of the Conspiracy

The roots of the conspiracy go back to the expectations held by the Jewish Religious community of Judaism during the time of Christ, which anticipated a political-religious deliverer, but ultimately rejected Yeshua HaMashiach, the Chosen Anointed Messiah.

In the eyes of Jewish Rabbis, they rejected Christ as the Chosen Messiah who would come through the Patriarchs due to their misconstrued interpretations of the Tanakh, the Written Torah. Consequently, the Pharisees handed Him over to Roman authorities as a seditionist for execution by capital punishment, the cross of redemption. Here, let me qualify that Satan doesn't know everything about God's eternal plan of salvation. I Corinthians 2:8 points out his lack of knowledge of the work of salvation; otherwise, the "rulers of this age" (often interpreted as demonic powers or Satan, as well as human leaders) would never have crucified the "Lord of glory." They lacked hidden wisdom because they were spiritually blind. The verse indicates that the crucifixion was a fatal error on Satan's part, as it ultimately sealed his defeat. The devil can be outwitted when it comes to God's plan of salvation.

According to this theory about the Jews during Christ's time on earth, a similar society of Jews in the modern world will eventually accept a false political-religious messiah, who fits their mold, as the prophesied Chosen One and worship him as God, as detailed in further reading.

It is important to note that this theory is rooted in antisemitic narratives and also targets minority ethnic groups that are viewed with fear and distrust by its proponents because of the potential of their population growth.

Sceptics across religious circles see these conclusions as unproven assumptions and stress the necessity of supporting such claims with concrete evidence. However, for students of Scripture, like the Bereans in Acts 17:10-12, the primary evidence remains the Word of God for true believers.

When we analyze the mission of the Church ("Ecclesia, "the *"Called out Community of Faith"* known as the Body of Christ) from the pages of predictive prophecy, it will become clear that ethnic minorities living in Third World conditions and Third World Countries, and the ten lost tribes of Israel (the diaspora), are keys to the salvation of the worldwide Jewish community (Judea and Benjamin) and the return of Christ. Persecution against them is a futile satanic effort to prevent the return of Christ!

Scriptural Thesis: Isaiah 53:1-12

Isaiah 53:1-12 is presented as a call to examine the truth of these ideas through the lens of Sacred Scripture. The passage describes the rejection of the Messenger and the message of the Messiah, as well as His suffering as He bears the griefs, sorrows, and iniquities of humanity's sin.

Considering Christ's diverse heritage and lineage from biblical genealogy and growing up through his formative years in the low-to-moderate-income working-class community of Nazareth, it would appear that many outsiders from that culture saw him as too common for the role of a Messiah.

Note the public's common view of Christ from the following words in Mark 6:3, *"Is not this the Carpenter, the son of Mary and the brother of James and Joses and Judas and Simon? And are not His sisters here among us? And they took offense at Him and were hurt [that is, they disapproved of Him, and it hindered them from acknowledging His authority] and they were caused to stumble and fall."* Also, consider the remark from Nathaniel—"Can any good thing come out of Nazareth?"—when Philip announces that they have found the Messiah. It suggests that the Messiah was despised and rejected because He did not fit the misinterpreted image, status, or role expected of Him.

Despite being despised, afflicted, and unjustly punished, He remains submissive and silent, ultimately sacrificing His life for the transgressions of others. Through His sacrifice, many are justified and made righteous, as He intercedes with those regarded as sinners, the lost and marginalized, and even those considered deviants. This Scriptural account forms the foundation for understanding the nature of true faith and the enduring message of redemption.

The Search for Authentic Christianity

As we journey through the pages of this book seeking answers to the mysterious declarations of prophecy and hidden gems of truth regarding the past, present, and future, we begin here. We start here with a sharp contrast between what politicized Christianity looks like versus the origin of the Christian faith from the "Author and Finisher" (Hebrews 12:2) of the faith, portrayed in the Early Church. We answer the questions in comparison to the life of Christ about whether vindictiveness, retribution, vengeance, threats, violence, hate, fear, blame, and intimidation belong in the Christian life.

This comparison serves as a foundation for our exploration, guiding us to recognize the distinctions between cultural or political expressions of Christianity and the original teachings and example of Christ. It isn't a casual endeavor; it is an intentional quest to understand the core of the Christian faith and its profound implications for every era.

Questions for Reflection

As we proceed, we will address important questions by comparing them to the life of Christ. Through this comparative lens, we aim to clarify what truly belongs to the faith as demonstrated by Christ Himself.

The objective is Jude 1:3, *"Beloved, my whole concern was to write to you in regard to our common salvation. [But] I found it necessary and was impelled to write you and urgently appeal to and exhort [you] to contend for the faith which was once for all handed down to the saints [the faith which is that sum of Christian belief which was delivered verbally to the holy people of God]."* It's called "the faith," which is a basic saving faith that reaches out across ethnic and cultural lines to win the lost for Christ (Acts 1:8).

CHAPTER 1.

Examining Prophetic Interpretation

Theology, in its simplest form, can be described as humanity's concept of God, shaped by diverse perspectives rooted in individual experiences. People generally arrive at their understanding of God through one of two primary ways given their experiences in life. The first comes from affluent human experience as Transcendence, wherein God is perceived as existing above, beyond, and outside the bounds of human comprehension. In this view, approaching an understanding of God necessitates a careful, deliberate, and sequential process—known as liturgy—utilizing a theological framework to study and grasp His nature.

The second perspective comes from not-so affluent human experience as the Immanence of God, which emphasizes God's immediate presence in each person's life and circumstances. Although the two observations are from the Theism (Oneness) of God both represent God's omnipresence but are divided by faith. The only reliable means of recognizing and understanding these profound truths is through Scripture alone.

The Principle of Scriptural Interpretation

My approach to interpreting Scripture is fundamentally shaped by a well-known saying from a scholastic theologian: "If Scripture sense makes common sense, seek no other sense." This encapsulates my interpretive principle: when the plain reading of Scripture is logical and clear, there is no need to search for deeper or alternative meanings. This approach differs from fundamentalism, which often interprets Scripture on the surface level of translations, whereas my method seeks the plain truth beneath those translations. As a result, my teachings may sometimes appear unorthodox, especially to those who are more accustomed to traditional or orthodox interpretations. Nevertheless, my perspective remains anchored in a straightforward understanding of the meaning of Scripture.

Pragmatism in Teaching God's Word: When it comes to communicating God's Word, my understanding of pragmatism is grounded in making theology practical and accessible. My objective is to present theological concepts in a way that is understandable and relevant to everyday people. This method accommodates individuals across the educational spectrum, from those with little or no formal education to those with advanced academic backgrounds.

My philosophy aligns with the insight of a respected theologian who observed that "All false systems of theology begin with man and seek to work up to God. In all our thinking, we must begin with God and work down to man." Guided by this principle, I start with the higher truths found in the original languages of Scripture, then convey their meaning in ways that apply to daily life. I aim to make these truths accessible and practical within the real world—where people live, work, play, and engage in spiritual conversations, a context often referred to as "God-talk."

To fulfill this aim, I deliberately avoid using church jargon, clichés, or complex doctrinal terminology. Instead, I communicate in clear, plain language that resonates with everyone, regardless of their religious background, whether they are believers (the regenerate) or nonbelievers (the unregenerate). This ensures that the message remains meaningful and relatable to all.

Understanding Biblical Interpretation and Pragmatism: A casual reader of the Bible may naturally approach Scripture with a literal mindset. Nevertheless, literal interpretation often overlooks the deeper meaning found within the original languages of the biblical texts—namely, the Masoretic Hebrew, the Vulgate, and Koine Greek. For this reason, I do not adhere strictly to literalism in interpreting Scripture, but I do uphold the inerrancy of the transliterated text.

Transliteration is a process that provides a word-for-word rendering of the original texts, such as the Masoretic Hebrew, and is culturally neutral. In contrast, translations adapt the original text into other languages, following translation hermeneutics that are influenced by cultural interpretations. For example, the translation efforts that began with the King James Version in 1611 were shaped by the cultural and political context of the British Empire, resulting in versions that contain errors and omissions. By contrast, the Masoretic Hebrew and Vulgate/Koine Greek texts maintain the integrity of the original writings when transliterated, without error or omission. (On my website blog at jarvisjimmyrossauthor.com I wrote an extensive article entitled "Where is your Faith" that describes the rocky road of the descent of Scripture.)

Consequently, I do not subscribe fully to theological distinctives, which can be culturally biased and politicized to serve dominant cultural interests. Such interpretive approaches often foster division and separation among people. Conversely, the original texts of the Masoretic Hebrew and Vulgate/Koine Greek support a vision for Global Christianity and cultural parity, emphasizing universal discipleship.

The pragmatic approach shares similarities with inductive reasoning, which is considered a bottom-up method. This process begins with specific observations and gradually leads to a general conclusion, resulting in probable rather than certain outcomes.

Unlike deductive reasoning, where conclusions are guaranteed if the premises are true, inductive reasoning produces only likely conclusions, based on the available evidence. These conclusions remain open to revision if new, contradictory evidence comes to light. It is important that the most advanced theologian remain open to correction and change as their faith grows.

As you explore the chapters of this book, remember that God's Higher Truth is so authentic that it can be hard to accept. Lies often appear persuasive, yet the truth may seem stranger than fiction. This reality leads to confusion regarding politics, religion, and geopolitics, including matters of war. Living on the wrong side of history brings negativity and despair.

Predictive Prophecy Interpreted: Predictive prophecy in Scripture is not a secret code to be deciphered but rather is presented in plain language.

The key to interpretation relies on a pragmatic approach, examining the narrative that unfolds behind the surface of the biblical text—the story behind the story. By connecting significant prophecies, a sequential timeline of events emerges, illuminating the conditions that define the "last days" and "end times" across generations. Rather than predicting the future, predictive prophecy forthtells what has already been written correlated to current times. It defines "how" and "why" we came to where we are in the country and the world.

The God-talk: God-talk involves changing the narrative and the discussion by removing religious jargon and politically correct language to focus on the higher truth in Scripture. It then weaves spiritual truths found in the sacred text into everyday language so that the unlearned in theology and doctrine can grasp the meaning. This approach emphasizes the pursuit of a deeper understanding of spiritual teachings and what it means to be spiritual, encouraging believers to look beyond superficial interpretations and carnal, secular, alarming news. God-talk points out "good news" and hope for every generation.

Divine Calling Versus Natural Abilities: Natural abilities that individuals possess from birth are not the determining factors for those "gifted" in apostolic ministry. As you continue reading, you will see the difference between Apostles and Prophets in Scripture and those who claim the office today. When God calls someone to these ministries, their role becomes that of a Church Planter or Mission Developer. In this calling, God anoints them with the specific gifts and abilities necessary to fulfill the responsibilities tied to their ministry. Therefore, natural talents alone do not qualify someone for prophetic or apostolic service. While God may choose to enhance their innate abilities through spiritual endowment, the genuine capacity to serve comes from the Holy Spirit's empowerment, rather than from natural skill or talent.

Distinguishing Biblical Prophecy from Other Practices: Prophets and prophecy, as described in the Bible, are fundamentally different from psychic predictors, fortune-tellers, or clairvoyants. The ministry of prophecy is not akin to following astrological charts or receiving directives that control one's life based on such practices. Specifically, biblical prophecy is not about foretelling or predicting individuals' personal futures. Instead, it involves forthtelling—that is, declaring what God has already revealed and predicted in Scripture. Theologically, this is understood as predictive prophecy, further elaborated through the biblical narrative.

The Prophetic Spirit and Its Challenges

Despite the clear distinction from clairvoyance, those who are genuinely gifted and called to prophetic ministry possess a pronounced prophetic spirit. They are often highly intuitive, exhibiting deep awareness and understanding of people, circumstances, events, and global conditions. Typically, these individuals find themselves isolated in their ministry, facing opposition from established norms and enduring persecution through ridicule and blacklisting, largely due to the controversial nature of their messages, which frequently expose sin and corruption. This reality echoes John 16:2: *"They will put you out of (expel you from) the synagogues; but an hour is coming when whoever kills you will think and claim that he has offered service to God."*

Prophetic ministers are radical agents of transformation and advocates for the oppressed within society. Their ministry tends to resonate with and attract grassroots support, seeking common ground. When confronted with persecution and ridicule, they respond by defending the faith of the Bible, though at times, those endowed with the gift of prophecy may struggle to control its expression, leading to intense emotional responses.

The Essential Nature of Prophetic Ministry: The essential, exegetical, and biblical definition of prophecy is as follows: It is a supernatural ability to speak forth God's written Word into immediate situations, providing relevance, encouragement, and preparation for what lies ahead.

Prophecy—Natural and Spiritual Dimensions: As illustrated in 1 Corinthians 15, prophecy possesses both natural and ongoing spiritual dimensions. Significant events tied to prophecy—such as End Time occurrences—are preceded by the period known as the Last Days. The "last days" are understood to span from the Day of Pentecost until the onset of the "end times," which are associated with concepts like the "Latter Rain" and the emergence of the antichrist.

I do not propose to be a prophet, and neither am I an analytical thinker. Instead, I process information visually, seeing the big picture rather than focusing on individual parts. Because of this, I believe it is helpful to pursue a systematic study of Scripture to clarify the various views of the "last days" and "end times," ultimately narrowing them down to a single perspective of faith.

—The Systematic Approach to Scripture—

To gain the clearest understanding of the sequence of events related to the "last days" and "end times," a systematic and practical approach to interpreting Scripture is necessary. It is important to define what it means to be systematic in this context.

My pragmatic-systematic approach arranges doctrinal topics into groups, then they are laid out in chronological order, arranged under one topic. This method helps us comprehend the full teaching of Scripture by fitting individual doctrines together, forming a unified framework of thinking and faith.

Systematic theology is visual and descriptive, aiming to understand scriptural truth by building upon foundational distinctions of faith. The ultimate goal is to apply God's Word to everyday life.

The Role of Etymology and Spiritual Pragmatism: My pragmatic method begins with the etymology of the historical meanings and linguistic roots of sacred texts. This approach is neither secular nor strictly intellectual; it merges practicality with spirituality, connecting to natural life and reflecting Kingdom Concepts of a God who is both sovereign and empathetically engaged with humanity. Scriptural references such as Hebrews 4:15 illustrate the empathy of God, while Genesis 1:26-28 underscores the authority delegated to humanity's free will on earth. It means that the sovereignty of God becomes married to the human will to clearly see God at work in human affairs.

In this framework, for God's Word to influence human affairs, it relies on the "yielding" of free will and the "invitation" of individuals and groups. This does not suggest that God is incapable of intervening without human invitation, but rather that He chooses to act only when people yield to His will and invite Him into their lives. To do otherwise would contradict how God nurtures human beings and builds His kingdom, honoring the essential nature of divine love expressed through free will.

The term "pragmatism" is derived from the Greek word "pragma." The origin of the concept is traced back to human experience and the development of language, emphasizing practicality and relevance in communication. The related Greek term "practicus" means "fit for action," aptly summarizing my interpretive approach to scripture, faith in action.

In summary, I see pragmatic interpretation as the process of bringing higher truths into daily life—where people live, work, play, and, for believers, share their faith. Ultimately, God-talk is a call to action.

To further clarify, God-talk is best defined in practical terms: when I engage with others individually or in groups, I draw from my personal experiences—positive or negative, right or wrong to illustrate how good and evil right and wrong can operate through our lives, wittingly or unwittingly.

The Inductive Approach: To frame this discussion, consider an inductive reasoning perspective, drawing on the biblical concept of reckoning, defined as the mental assent of faith. Viewing prophecy through this lens encourages interpreting predictive passages in clear, practical, and common-sense language. Rather than treating these scriptural prophecies as obscure codes or mysterious messages requiring decryption, the preferred method is to adopt a pragmatic common-sense approach.

Summary of Sequential End-Time Events

In summary, the events of the last days and the end times should be interpreted and understood in straightforward terms. This method helps clarify the anticipated progression, ensuring that readers can visualize the order of events as described in the Book of Revelation, rather than certifying the timing of the events. By using common-sense language, the message and purpose of prophecy become accessible and relevant for preparation and readiness.

CHAPTER 2.

Biblical Prophecy's Inner Nature

Prophecy, according to its essential unpacked biblical definition, is the supernatural ability to proclaim God's written Word in response to immediate circumstances. This speaking forth carries relevance for the present while also encouraging and preparing believers for the future.

Biblical Context and Timeline: As described in I Corinthians 15, prophecy has both a natural occurrence and a continuing spiritual dimension. The progression of End Time events is preceded by the Last Days. Biblically, the "last days" span from the Day of Pentecost to the "end times." The transition into the end times is marked by the conclusion of the last days, the "Latter Rain," and the emergence of the Antichrist.

When exploring eschatology (the last things of time), this approach does not rely on Dispensational or Covenantal theology, unfamiliar to some readers, as a means of determining when predicted biblical events will unfold. (It's not the "when" but "be ready.") Scripture affirms that no one knows the precise timing of these events or of Christ's return. Even Jesus, during His earthly ministry, acknowledged in Matthew 24:36 that only the Father knows the exact day and hour. When considering the Hypostatic Union of Christ, the theological concept that Christ possesses both divine and human natures, united in one body, this union means that Jesus is fully God and fully man, without either nature diminishing the other. In that context, when considering Christ's words and actions, it is important to recognize that He sometimes spoke and acted from His human perspective, but not from making a false claim. At different moments, Jesus would choose to operate as a man, consciously limiting Himself to a sinless human state. This self-limitation involved setting aside His divine prerogative, called a "kenosis," of emptying Himself in Philippians 2:7—giving up His divine prerogative to act as God—so that He could fully experience and demonstrate identity with human life to complete salvation, while remaining without sin. In summation, that was the case for His utterance in Matthew 24:36, but within His divine nature in co-union with the Father, Christ knows the precise time.

As a pragmatic alternative, insights can be drawn from Biblical Demography—analyzing Scripture, historical data, statistics, biblical numerology, and distinguishing symbolism. This method highlights how societal trends and conditions intensify from generation to generation within the last days. In summary, world history is compared alongside biblical history to discern patterns and timelines.

The Central Focus of Prophecy

All prophecy in both the Old and New Testaments ultimately points to Christ's prophecy in Matthew 24. It is important to reiterate that biblical events can occur suddenly at any moment, according to the sovereign will of God. God may reveal His Son and the end of the age unexpectedly.

The suddenness of Christ's return is emphasized in Matthew 24:44: *"For this reason you also must be ready; for the Son of Man is coming at an hour when you do not think He will."* This is echoed in I Thessalonians 5:1-9, which warns that the day of the Lord will come as unexpectedly as a thief in the night. Believers are urged to remain alert, sober, and prepared, living as sons of light and day, but not afraid.

Preparation for Christ's Return: When biblical prophecies manifest in real life, they serve as critical signs and warnings for God's people. These signs call for preparation in the face of various environmental, social, religious, and political changes. The Christian response should be one of readiness and rejoicing in the nearness of redemption—not anxiety or withdrawal from society as with the Thessalonians.

Signs of the Lord's Return: II Thessalonians 2:1-4 underscores the importance of discernment regarding the coming of Christ and our gathering to Him. Believers should not be unsettled or deceived by claims that the day of the Lord has already arrived. A defining sign of Christ's return is apostasy—a significant falling away from the faith, denouncing and repudiating Christ as Lord, and accepting a false messiah. That higher truth is described in verses three and four of II Thessalonians 2.

The Apostle Paul, in Galatians 1:6-9, warns against "another gospel" that focuses on cultural norms, new age philosophies, or religious works rather than the true gospel of Christ. This warning is reinforced in Matthew 7:21-23, where Jesus cautions that not everyone who professes His name will enter the kingdom of heaven, but only those who do the will of the Father. Believers must avoid gospel teachings rooted in nationalist or cultural conformity, as their prevalence signals the regime of the Antichrist, the "lawless one" who will defy established laws for his own rule.

The major characteristic of this Antichrist will be his "delusional" nature, causing him to live in an alternate reality where he believes his lies are the truth. It will manifest as a deep-seated inordinate pride that is inherent, like the archenemy of God, Lucifer, before his fall (Isaiah 14:12-15; Ezekiel 28:12-17). There in Scripture, he ascends to heaven to overthrow the throne of God and become like the Most-High. Because of this, the Antichrist's mental and emotional state will be reflective of Malignant Narcissism, a severe personality disorder: antisocial, aggression, sadism, psychopathy, and a highly destructive personality, lacking empathy, and enjoying harming others. Contextually, his ambition will be to control the wealth of the world by ideological influence of the wealthiest nations.

As you progress through the pages of this book, you will come to a section where I highlight multiple characteristics of the Antichrist that are prevalent in dictators throughout history and the Pharisees during Christ's time.

Paul further discusses this concern in II Corinthians 11:4, mentioning the dangers of preaching "another Jesus" and a "different gospel."

The Twofold Process of Prophecy

Micro Events: Patterns Across Generations

Winston Churchill's famous warning, "Those who fail to learn from history are doomed to repeat it," illustrates the importance of heeding historical lessons. However, true repetition of history is scientifically impossible; rather, patterns from the past reemerge, especially when unresolved issues persist across generations.

In the context of biblical prophecy, warnings proclaimed in Scripture often catch up to the present when ignored. Therefore, prophecy begins at a micro level, with repetitive and similar events occurring in each generation and millennium. These recurring events serve as signs and warnings, preparing God's people for major, chaotic events that precede the culminating macro event.

Matthew 24:34 states, *"Truly I tell you, this generation... will not pass away till all these things... take place."* Within the Greek language, the word for generation, "Genea," can indicate infinity of time when repeated or used with another time word. Thus, the signs spoken of in Matthew 24 are repeated in successive generations, not as an assurance that Christ will return within a specific period, but as an ongoing call for Christians to be prepared for Christ's return in every generation.

The Macro Event: The Culmination of the Ages

The macro event refers to the ultimate fulfillment of prophecy as recorded in Revelation, chapters 20-22. These chapters outline the sequence of events that will accompany Christ's return, culminating in the end of the age as described in the biblical narrative.

Predictive prophecy is the practice of interpreting past predictions in Scripture and connecting them to both present circumstances and future events. Rather than simply foretelling what is to come, predictive prophecy foretells what God has already decreed, making it relevant for contemporary times. These divine declarations are preserved in sacred texts, and the role of the prophet is to proclaim them, illuminating their meaning for today and the days ahead.

The Role of Prophecy as a Spiritual Gift

According to biblical teachings, prophecy is recognized as an "Official Spiritual Gift" that serves the ongoing development of the Christian mission. This gift is intended not only to disclose the signs of the times but also to encourage and prepare the Christian community. Through prophecy, believers are reminded that the conditions and events occurring in the world are not merely random or of human origin. Still, rather, they are indicators of the ongoing struggle between good and evil spiritual forces. These revelations help the community to interpret current events within the framework of spiritual warfare rather than attributing blame solely to people.

Spiritual Conflict in the Last Days: The Christian community is urged to understand that the challenges and adversities they face signify the "last days"—a period marked by intense spiritual struggle. The battle is not limited to conflicts among individuals but is deeply rooted in the opposition between powerful spiritual entities. Believers are encouraged to find strength and empowerment through their union with the Lord, drawing on the boundless might that God provides.

Equipping for Spiritual Warfare: Scripture, specifically Ephesians 6:10-12, instructs Christians to "be strong in the Lord" and to "put on God's whole armor." This armor, likened to that of a heavily armed soldier that Paul witnessed in his rented prison apartment in Rome before his martyrdom (Acts 28:30–31), inspired him to use an analogy of a soldier's armor in his epistle to provide insight into a spiritual soldier's armor against all the strategies and deceitful tricks of the devil.

The passage emphasizes that the real struggle is not against human adversaries—"flesh and blood"—but against spiritual powers, including despotic authorities as in Daniel 10, world rulers of darkness, and wicked spiritual forces operating in the supernatural realm. Understanding this spiritual context calls the Christian community to be vigilant and prepared, relying on God's strength to face the challenges of the present age.

The gift operates in tune with the ongoing ministry of Church Planters to provide visionary direction, navigating spiritual strongholds and dismantling them. Further descriptions of the gift are described in passages like I Corinthians 12:10, I Corinthians 14:1-40, Romans 12:6, and Ephesians 4:11. These predictions, regarded as evidence of a higher power, are intended to reveal the true state of the world, offering guidance to the Covenant Community of Faith—both Jews and Gentiles—through challenging periods; ultimately, preparing the way for God's final harvest and the return of the Lord to Earth.

CHAPTER 3.

Prophets & Apostles—True & False

A traditional theological view, known as Cessationism, is rooted in translation hermeneutics—priests adding their spin on interpreting Scripture from Latin to congregants—and cultural interpretation.

Cessationism, originating from the teachings of Calvinism was embraced by Reformed Churches and some Baptist Churches. Cessationism asserts that the "miraculous" spiritual gifts—such as those given to Apostles and Prophets—ceased after the foundation of the Church was established and the Early Church Apostles had passed away. This cessation extended to gifts like speaking in tongues, prophecy, and healing, particularly after the canonization and closure of Scripture with the sixty-six books of the Bible.

While this traditional stance is influential, I personally, and exegetically, do not agree with cessationist theology concerning spiritual gifts. However, there is a parity with other views concerning the sovereignty of God. In examining the five "gifted offices" described in Ephesians 4:11-13, it is important to distinguish between the "gift" itself and the "office," seen as the ministry assignment.

Not everyone in our world who holds any of the five offices is necessarily called and anointed—or gifted—for that office; some are, and some are not. There is a poignant reference by the Lord in the gospels to wolves in sheep's clothing and false prophets that is further elaborated by the Apostle Paul as false apostles. This reference may be a reason why the office in most Christian circles is rejected. Therefore, it is essential to separate those who are divinely called from those who are self-appointed. Determining the authenticity of these ministries is not my call; rather, it is up to the church community, or "the sheep," to discern based on the fruit produced. They should know the "voice" of the Good Shepherd (John 10).

The Five Offices and Spiritual Gifts

I affirm the gifting and ministry assignment of all five offices mentioned in Ephesians, as the need arises and according to the purpose of calling. My emphasis is on the ministry assignment of the gift rather than the office.

I Corinthians 12 indicates that spiritual gifts are activated by God's Spirit, specific to calling and purpose, and thus, these gifts can be interchangeable. There is a relationship between the call and the gift. For instance, after "stirring up" the gift in Timothy, Paul encourages him as a Pastor to undertake the work of an Evangelist (II Timothy 4:5). One individual may possess more than one of the gifts, so the office does not always directly correspond to the gift as it does to ministry assignment. As stated in I Corinthians 12:7: *"But to each one is given the manifestation of the [Holy] Spirit [the evidence, the spiritual illumination of the Spirit] for good and profit."* Thus, indicating the gift serves the calling, and the specifics of the works in the calling can activate either of the gifts.

The Purpose of the Five Gifts

1. **Apostles:** Aside from the Early Church Apostles, the "gift" of an Apostle comes from the original word, "Apostolos," which means to launch out on a mission. In context, it navigates the terrain for places to plant churches, as we see with the Apostle Paul in the Book of Acts. It is a pioneering, foundational gift to provide oversight.

2. **Prophets:** The gift of prophecy is a supernatural ability to speak forth God's written word to immediate situations to inspire, encourage, and prepare for the future. It is a visionary gift for establishing the vision of the church. The gift functions toward repentance, correction, and guidance.

3. **Evangelists:** The gift of evangelism ("Evangelos") enables the individual to spread the gospel of "good news," win the lost, and lead people to Christ and disciple them, and to encourage the church to do the same.

4. **Pastors (Shepherds):** The role of the gift is to nurture believers in God's word, protect and guide them along the path of righteousness, and care for their whole person, spiritually, physically, mentally, emotionally, and relationally.

5. **Teachers:** The gift is intended to explain, clarify, and expound God's Word for practical application, leading to their walk of faith.

The five gifts clumped together are for building up and unifying the Christian Community into the Head of the Church, Christ, and the Great Commission of evangelizing and discipling from their respective bases of operation.

Reiterated from Scripture, the calling is further outlined in Ephesians 4:11-13, which describes Christ's intention in appointing some as apostles, prophets, evangelists, pastors, and teachers, establishing the foundation of the Church. This variety of gifts is meant for the perfecting and full equipping of the saints, enabling them to minister and build up the Body of Christ. The ultimate goal is that all believers attain unity in faith and mature into the fullness of Christ.

Function and Distinction of Gifts and Offices: The concept of the fivefold ministry is especially prominent in Charismatic, Pentecostal, and some Evangelical circles. While some groups, unaffiliated with these movements, may also recognize these roles as valid, the term "fivefold ministry" is especially associated with Pentecostal beliefs and "Word of Faith" movements. Some affirm the continued existence of charismatic gifts in the modern church, including the possibility of a "Latter Rain" outpouring of Holy Spirit gifts, while others uphold cessationist beliefs, holding that these gifts ceased.

Modern Day Apostles and Prophets

Some Christians assert that there are Apostles and Prophets today whom we should heed. However, again, it is crucial to distinguish between the "gift" of prophecy—defending and proclaiming the established Word of God—and the "office" of Prophet, which often involved delivering new revelations from God.

According to the canonization of Scripture, there are no new revelations, although there are extrabiblical sources, such as the Apocrypha, recorded in the Catholic Bible. Such sources may be studied, not for clarity of Scripture, but for substantiating that extrabiblical sources are not necessary to prove the validity of Scripture. Canonized Scripture is the primary guide. In that context, aside from gifts that run throughout history, all that God intended has already been revealed in Scripture. The gift of prophecy remains, but the office was foundational.

The same distinction applies to the gift and office of an Apostle today: while the office laid the foundation for the Church, the gift now enables believers to build upon that foundation of the Apostles and Prophets.

Ephesians 2:20-22 states, *"You are built upon the foundation of the apostles and prophets with Christ Jesus Himself the chief Cornerstone. In Him the whole structure is joined together harmoniously, and it continues to rise into a holy temple in the Lord ..."*

Qualifications and Purpose of Apostolic and Prophetic Ministry

Natural talents or abilities are not the qualifications for the ministry of apostles and prophets. When God calls individuals to these ministries, they usually become Church Planters or Mission Developers. God anoints them with the necessary gifts and abilities to fulfill their ministry duties, but the actual capacity to serve comes from the Holy Spirit, not from innate ability. God may enhance their natural abilities, but spiritual service is rooted in divine endowment, not human talent.

Contextually, Prophets and prophecy in the Bible are not akin to psychic prediction, fortune-telling, or clairvoyance, nor do they function like astrological charts that dictate one's life. Biblical prophecy is not about predicting individual futures; it is about forthtelling what God has already revealed and foretold in Scripture. Theologically, this is elaborated as predictive prophecy.

The Character and Experience of the Prophetic Ministry

Although biblical prophecy is distinct from clairvoyance, those called to prophetic ministry often possess a prophetic spirit and keen intuition—an untold knowledge and awareness about people, circumstances, events, and world conditions. Frequently, they work alone, face opposition from the established order, and suffer ridicule or blacklisting because their message exposes sin and corruption. As Jesus warned in John 16:2, *"They will put you out of the synagogues; but an hour is coming when whoever kills you will think and claim that he has offered service to God."*

Those who conduct prophetic ministry serve as radical transformation agents and advocates for the oppressed, often attracting grassroots support. Despite persecution and ridicule, they defend the faith of the Bible. Sometimes, those with the gift of prophecy struggle to control their gift and may be overtaken by strong emotions because they are confident and boldly confrontational, which is often perceived as arrogance.

Distinguishing Between the Office and Gift in the Church

Aside from the office, the spiritual gift of prophecy was set apart for many believers for the edification in mutual fellowship (I Corinthians 14:3). It is an enabling of a believer to speak forth God's word for encouragement and guidance. The gift does not equate to holding an office of prophet or apostle. Rather, it is an anointed spiritual ability for the common good within the fellowship of believers, distinct from a leadership role within the church.

True Prophecy as Divine Communication

True prophecy is recognized as a miraculous communication from God through human personality, imparted through the Spirit. This concept is grounded in Scripture, such as II Peter 1:20-21, which emphasizes that prophecy does not originate from personal interpretation or human desire. Instead, holy men spoke from God, carried and inspired by the Holy Spirit. Similarly, II Timothy 3:16 highlights that every Scripture is "God-breathed," given by divine inspiration, and serves various purposes: instructing, reproving, correcting error, disciplining in obedience, and training in righteousness. In that context, all Scripture is prophetic.

The nature of true prophecy is so deeply inspired that it surpasses human comprehension, and so true that it's hard to believe. The "verity" of predictive prophecy often leads to debate regarding its truth. Historically, true prophecy was met with resistance and disapproval. It exposed evil and corruption, resulting in the persecution and hatred of prophets, which is why the Lord stated, "You have killed the prophets" (Matthew 23:37; Luke 13:34). Consequently, true prophets, unlike Monks in a monastery, lived a solitary life away from the public as much as possible.

The Certainty and Manifestation of True Prophecy

A distinguishing feature of true prophecy is its fulfillment: it comes to pass precisely as predicted. Unlike vague or ambiguous statements, true prophecy is clear in its message, although the timing of its fulfillment may be unpredictable. Nevertheless, it will manifest, often when least expected.

The Purpose of Prophecy: The purpose of prophecy is not merely to foretell "doom and gloom." Rather, it is a supernatural event intended to inspire and encourage God's people. Often, this encouragement comes through calls to repentance and forgiveness, preparing individuals for the future. Prophecy serves as a call to change behavior and align actions with righteousness. In essence, prophecy is instructional, guiding people toward spiritually clean living, the opposite of "cleanliness is next to godliness," which is a pharisaic notion. Spiritually clean living is conformity with God's will in thought, purpose, and action.

Tests of Authenticity (Messenger and Message): True prophecy can be discerned through both the character of the messenger and the nature of the message. Matthew 7:15-20 warns believers to beware of false prophets who appear harmless but are, in truth, destructive. The passage teaches that prophets are recognized by their "fruits": just as healthy trees bear good fruit and diseased trees bear bad fruit, so do true and false prophets reveal themselves by the outcomes and virtues evident in their lives. Every tree that fails to produce good fruit is removed and destroyed, reinforcing the principle that authenticity is demonstrated by the fruit produced and false prophets and prophecies will corrupt and fail. These "fruits" are the virtues consistent with Christlikeness, as detailed in the fruit of the Spirit in Galatians 5:22-23: *But the fruit of the [Holy] Spirit [the work which His presence within accomplishes] is love, joy (gladness), peace, patience (an even temper, forbearance), kindness, goodness (benevolence), faithfulness, Gentleness (meekness, humility), self-control (self-restraint, continence). Against such things there is no law that can bring a charge.*

CHAPTER 4.

Confusing Spiritualism with Spirituality

From the portrayal of the spirit of divination in the Old Testament to the philosophical religion called spiritism, there is a close connection and description of the "spirit of antichrist" in the New Testament. Therefore, it is expedient that true believers distinguish predictive prophecy from Spiritism or Spiritualism, which requires careful comparison and analysis to discern the differences.

We should de-mystify (take the spooky out) what it means to be spiritual. Being spiritual is not spiritualism that will be clarified.

Spiritism, also known as Spiritualism, is a comprehensive doctrine that blends elements of *science, philosophy,* and *religion,* with its foundation laid by Allan Kardec in the mid-19th century. At its core, Spiritism teaches that spirits undergo moral and intellectual evolution through the process of multiple incarnations, guided by universal principles.

Spiritism's beliefs focus on a spiritual realm or parallel universe, which serves as the dwelling place for spirits after death. In biblical terms, this domain is associated with fallen angels, or demons. In the Spiritist worldview, these spirits are immortal beings created by God who continually evolve by living through multiple human lives. Jesus Christ is seen as a highly evolved spirit—reincarnated on Earth as a moral teacher and model for humanity. This moral framework closely resembles that of a deceptive form of Christianity.

Spiritists claim that souls repeatedly return to Earth in human form, learning and growing with each life. The living are said to communicate with these spirits—departed humans or evolved guides—via mediums, spirit guides, clairvoyance, trances, and séances, often seeking guidance or knowledge. The Bible condemns such practices and references them in Acts 16:16-18, where Paul rebukes a fortune-teller possessed by a spirit of divination that attempted to confuse his mission by proclaiming him a servant of the Most-High God. It implied that what he did was no more than what she did. It was designed by the devil to confuse the issue of salvation as no more than what she offered. Paul "cast" the spirit out, which led to persecution from those who profited from her abilities. According to this perspective, the goal of spiritism is to create confusion within Christianity.

The Nature and Danger of False Prophets: False prophets, described as spiritualists who conjure spirits through divination, are exemplified by figures like Balaam in Numbers 22-24. Balaam was hired by Balak, the Moabite king, to curse Israel, but God intervened—famously through a speaking donkey—causing Balaam to bless Israel instead. The biblical principle remains clear: "you cannot curse what God has blessed." However, the Book of Deuteronomy warns that people can choose curses or blessings based on their actions (Deuteronomy 11:26-29) and outlines the consequences of such choices in Deuteronomy 28. Despite these warnings, Scripture asserts that a true believer, walking in faith, is protected from curses.

Balaam's story continues in other biblical books—Deuteronomy, Joshua, Micah, II Peter, and Jude—where he is depicted as a prophet motivated by greed who led Israel astray into idolatry. False prophets are similarly described as those who serve money, not God. II Peter and Jude 1:11 cite Balaam as an example of false teachers who pursued unethical gain and caused others to sin.

The Deception of False Prophets and Spiritists: The predictions made by false prophets who tend to be in the "spirit of antichrist" are rooted in cunning and deliberate deception. These individuals stage events to make their predictions seem divinely inspired, but their forecasts are fabricated and ultimately do not align with true predictive prophecy. Spiritists believe in a single, supreme intelligence that governs the universe through divine laws—much like the concept of Karma—in which present choices shape future outcomes.

Spiritualism is an external practice of contacting spirits, and spirituality is an internal way of being and growing in Christ.

Spiritualist Imitates Christianity through the Pleiades Movement

The Esoteric Roots of Spiritualism: Spiritualism teachings are generally not taught in most churches. This focus means that most Christians are unfamiliar with certain concepts, such as the Pleiades, since they are not considered essential for mainstream doctrine and religious instruction.

Esotericism is the pursuit of specialized, hidden, or inner knowledge that is reserved for a select, initiated group rather than the general public. It covers a broad spectrum of spiritual, occult, and mystical beliefs, including Gnosticism, Alchemy, and Hermeticism. These traditions emphasize uncovering secret, deeper meanings behind reality and religion.

The term "esotericism" comes from the Greek word *esôterô* ("inner"), indicating a historical difference between "inner" initiated knowledge and "outer," uninitiated knowledge. Exoteric knowledge is public and accessible to all, while esoteric knowledge remains exclusive, requiring initiation or specialized study. The purpose of esoteric traditions is often to achieve a profound understanding of the divine, the universe, or the self, which is believed to be hidden or restricted.

—*The Unscriptural Nature of Secret Sects*—

Examples of groups or traditions that are associated with esotericism include the Freemasons, Rosicrucians, and various Hermetic or Gnostic teachings.

Studies vary concerning the modern-day secretive-anonymous movement called QAnon as a cult and quasi-Christian movement, but research into the characteristics is warranted for true followers of Christ.

The distinguishing factor for the followers of Christ is "transparency" and "integrity," because Christ has nothing to hide from His followers. John 15:15, *"I do not call you servants (slaves) any longer, for the servant does not know what his master is doing (working out). But I have called you My friends, because I have made known to you everything that I have heard from My Father. [I have revealed to you everything that I have learned from Him.]."*

The aforementioned movements are controversial, and it is not my role or responsibility to determine for the reader if they are right or wrong. It is up to the reader to weigh the characteristics of their cause and effects against Scripture.

Scripture makes it abundantly clear that God does not act without first revealing His intentions to His chosen messengers. As stated in Amos 3:7: *"Surely the Lord God will do nothing without revealing His secret to His servants the prophets."*

Throughout the sacred writings, it is evident that God does not withhold secrets regarding His purpose and plans for humanity. His precepts, counsel, and judgments are openly disclosed. The Book of Ephesians, for example, explains the "mystery" of God's will, revealing how He has made known His intentions for the fullness of time (Ephesians 1:9-10).

While God's wisdom is infinite and there are aspects of His understanding that surpass human comprehension—wisdom reserved for Him alone as expressed in Deuteronomy 29:29—He does not leave His followers in ignorance. Instead, He reveals necessary truths and mysteries, particularly through prophecy and the message of the gospel, as shown in Colossians 1:26 and Luke 8:10.

God chooses to share His secrets with His servants. He does not withhold them, but graciously discloses what is needed for humanity to understand His will and plan.

While some distinguish esotericism from mysticism and the occult, a close study reveals similarities that serve as a foundation for many spiritual and philosophical systems.

Historically, the Pleiades movement is referred to as the "Seven Sisters," a prominent cluster of stars within the constellation Taurus, or "The Bull," visible in the Northern Hemisphere. This tradition is practiced by astrologers and adherents of esoteric teachings; hidden spiritual, religious, and philosophical doctrines accessible primarily to select groups known as Initiates. These Initiates, often viewed as shamans, engage in New Age practices that involve spirit guides, connecting individuals with the energy and wisdom of the Pleiades star cluster.

Rooted in ancient mythology, the Pleiades appear as a small, misty dipper of roughly six stars but actually comprise over a thousand stars. Named after the daughters of the Greek god Atlas, these hot, blue, luminous stars are among the closest star clusters to Earth and can be located by following Orion's belt.

Focus and Philosophy of the Pleiades: The focus of the Pleiades movement centers on acquiring mystical knowledge beyond conventional understanding—exploring the nature of reality, consciousness, and divinity. Its influences appear in traditions such as Kabbalah, Hermeticism, Gnosticism, alchemy, and New Age beliefs. As we consider this philosophy, it is important to recall the discussion in the Prologue regarding "The One World Government/New Age Order." These teachings propose a parallel universe composed of the Astral Plane, Causal Plane, and the third, fourth, and fifth dimensions.

Metaphysical Planes and Dimensions: These concepts are not recognized by traditional Christianity or mainstream science as empirically validated realms. Instead, they are explored in metaphysics and mysticism as planes for the soul, emotions (astral), and destiny or karma (causal). Science regards these as metaphysical constructs, while esoteric teachings describe them as interconnected dimensions where consciousness evolves through varying densities of matter and spirit. In summary, science investigates the physical universe, whereas these planes describe a spiritual universe comprised of subtle energies and varying levels of consciousness.

The Astral Plane

The astral plane represents the domain of emotions, desires, and sensory experiences, often linked to dreams, out-of-body experiences, and the "subtle body"—a non-physical energy that bridges the material and spiritual realms. The term "astral" means "star-like," signifying its connection to celestial spheres.

The Causal Plane

The causal plane is connected to the law of karma, destiny, and the "causal body," where the blueprints for individual lives and personality patterns are believed to be stored. This realm is associated with concrete thought, spiritual understanding, and the effects of past actions. It is the plane where cause and effect (karma) are manifested, influencing experiences and evolution across lifetimes.

Discerning the Difference

When we consider the words of Scripture, it's easy to understand that Satan imitates the Godhead because his malignant narcissism craves being God. II Corinthians 11:14, *"And it is no wonder, for Satan himself masquerades as an angel of light."* Isaiah 14:14, *"I will ascend above the heights of the clouds; I will make myself like the Most High."*

So, the Pleiades try to imitate the three heavens. In mythology and metaphysics, these are considered the third, fourth, and fifth dimensions. There is a correlation between the universe and the spiritual dimension, distinguished by the fundamental difference between good and evil.

In Scripture, the first heaven corresponds to the earthly realm, the second to the stellar heavens, and the third to the heaven of God, beyond the stars. Esoteric traditions identify these as the third dimension (Earth), the fourth dimension (Stellar Heaven), and the fifth dimension (Heavenly Kingdom of God). According to II Corinthians 12:1-4, the Apostle Paul was "caught up"

(Greek: harpagésómetha; Latin: rapere, from which "rapture" is derived) to the third heaven. Paul could not discern if this was a vision or an out-of-body experience, but he heard inexpressible mysteries. Pleiadian philosophy describes similar experiences, with practitioners channeling messages from enlightened extraterrestrial beings believed to communicate spiritual wisdom from these dimensions. However, it is crucial to distinguish between the three heavens in Scripture and the metaphysical dimensions described in these teachings.

The Third Dimension—Material Existence: The third dimension represents the state of human existence and consciousness—the material world, or the atmospheric heaven in which we live.

The Fourth Dimension—Realm of Spiritualism and Darkness: The fourth dimension is associated with spiritualism and is considered the kingdom of literal darkness—the astral plane where dark forces reside among the stars, also known as the stellar heaven. It is viewed as the domain of evil, the origin of fear, deception, and lies—powerful tools of the devil. There is a belief that UFOs are, in fact, angels in disguise, intended to mislead humanity into believing in other beings comparable to God.

Fear and deception are said to attract negative energy from dark auras and demons. All material objects and humans are believed to be made of energy by the Creator, dust, radiating either positive or negative energy in both spiritual and natural realms. True faith, characterized by righteousness and justice, is devoid of negativity.

The fourth dimension is described as a world of illusion, accessed by some through meditation, chanting, and visualization—often without awareness of its dangers. This dimension is believed to act as a barrier between individuals and critical, life-altering prayers, as illustrated in Daniel 10, while also being the realm through which breakthroughs in spiritual warfare can occur.

Within the fourth dimension, demonic forces may masquerade as angels of light, seeking to prevent believers from reaching the throne of grace in the heaven of heavens in Scripture with their view of the fifth dimension. (Complicated) It is also identified as the source of prophecy for false prophets who pose as Christians but are, in reality, deceivers. This realm leads individuals—including some Christians—to attribute blessings and benefits to universal laws rather than to God, resulting in materialistic idolatry. In the Kingdom of God, there is no neutrality or compromise, which is why repentance is the remedy for delusion.

Additionally, the fourth dimension is the sphere of divination (seeking knowledge of the future through supernatural means), soothsaying (predicting the future), necromancy (communicating with the dead), fortunetelling, and astrology. All these practices focus on foretelling the future. Authentic biblical prophecy, by contrast, is not about predicting individual futures, as these are already revealed in Scripture and the Gospel; obedience to God's Word is the determining factor.

Those who serve as channels or mediums for these forces may call themselves prophets, psychics, or seers, declaring false visions and even operating within Christian circles. This dimension encompasses parapsychology (supernatural inquiry), hypnotism, spirit guides, spirits of witchcraft, familiar spirits, and spirits of shamanism. These entities may grant temporary wishes to deceive individuals.

The fourth dimension interacts with the third, with demonic forces able to enter the earthly realm through invitations from humans, including through false doctrine that promises health, wealth, and prosperity based on universal laws.

Once in the third dimension, these forces can influence or demonize people and manifest in various forms. They are organized within the stellar heaven and orchestrate attacks on Earth as described in Ephesians 6:10-12.

The Fifth Dimension—Realm of Light and Divine Authority: The fifth dimension is described as the Kingdom of literal Light. In scientific terms, this aligns with the nebular theory, which posits that our solar system formed from clouds of gas and dust. The "Big Bang" theory and the concept of quasars—

distant, intensely bright sources of light surrounded by black holes—are also referenced. The black hole is seen as the entryway into the fourth dimension, positioned between the fourth and fifth dimensions.

In Scripture, their version in the fifth dimension represents the heaven of heavens, but the heaven of heavens in Scripture is the true source of spirituality, blessings, and covenant benefits from the Lord of Glory, Jesus the Christ. This is where believers go when their soul departs their body when they die. Hebrews 12:22-23, *"But rather, you have come to Mount Zion, even to the city of the living God, the heavenly Jerusalem, and to countless multitudes of angels in festal gathering, And to the church (assembly) of the Firstborn who are registered [as citizens] in heaven, and to the God Who is Judge of all, and to the spirits of the righteous (the redeemed in heaven) who have been made perfect."*

The Godhead reigns as Sovereign Ruler over all realms. The fifth-dimension duplicates faith, attracting positive energy from the bright auras of believers and the angels of light.

Caution: The Danger of Deception

Blessings and benefits originate from the heaven of heavens (Light). But the fourth dimension seduces people seeking God to think that blessings and benefits come from their version of the fifth dimension when, in reality, it is the delusion of the fourth dimension (darkness).

The fourth dimension imitates the works of God found in the fifth dimension. Scientifically, Christ's journey—His incarnation, miracles, death, resurrection, ascension, and return to His throne—mirrors phenomena described in these terms, and Satan seeks to replicate these actions to deceive humanity.

A fine line exists between the works of God and those of Satan, who imitates divine acts. For example, Pharaoh's magicians in Exodus were able to duplicate Moses' miracles using magic derived from the fourth dimension. This should not surprise believers, as "Satan is transformed into an angel of light" (II Corinthians 11:14).

Magic is real only to those who permit it in their lives. Discerning the difference between divine and deceptive acts requires spiritual discernment. The key is to observe the "fruit" produced. Scripture equates fruit with loving character. Miracles performed by those whose character and behavior deteriorate are not from God but from the fourth dimension. Conversely, if character and behavior improve, despite personal flaws, the source is the heaven of heavens.

Entities and human agents operating in the fourth dimension are real and can imitate, to an extent, the works of God. This is a tactic used to distract seekers from the true and living God. The influence of the fourth dimension becomes real in a person's life only if they allow it. Therefore, all forms of dark arts, black magic, paranormal activity, and spiritualism must be repudiated, denounced, and renounced. As stated in II Corinthians 4:2, believers have renounced disgraceful and underhanded ways, choosing to openly speak the truth and commend themselves before God and others.

CHAPTER 5.

Spirituality's Superpower

Spirituality isn't merely a means of walking by faith as a disciple of the Lord. There are remedial benefits of spirituality.

Spirituality offers a powerful means of managing stress. To capture your immediate attention, it is important to recognize that embracing spirituality or adopting a spiritual mindset can serve as an effective stress reliever. Spirituality helps cleanse the conscience of toxicity and negative thoughts. Through spiritual practices, individuals can address and release negative emotions, allowing for a healthier mental and emotional state. Thus, from the viewpoint of Scripture, spirituality can be seen as a "superpower." This superpower operates through the human will within the God-conscious, indwelt by the Spirit of God. In this way, spirituality becomes not only a source of relief but also a transformative force that empowers individuals to confront and overcome stress.

Spirituality as a Discipline for the Whole Person

As a discipline process for the body, soul, mind, and emotions, spirituality brings impulses that cause unwanted and undesired activity and behavior under the control of the human spirit, indwelt by the Holy Spirit. It is the Spirit of God within our temples, the body, that enables believers with grace to manage their lives for their greater good and God's glory.

The Stress-Relieving Power of Spirituality: Spirituality is a powerful, evidence-based stress reliever that helps manage anxiety, frustration, and disappointment because it instills God's purpose for all that an individual goes through. It keeps the individual within the will of God. It provides a framework to find meaning in difficult situations, which reduces anxiety and helps people recover faster from trauma. It reduces cortisol and increases "feel-good" chemicals in the body, like dopamine and serotonin.

"Cortisol is a steroid hormone produced by the adrenal glands, often called the " stress hormone " for its critical role in the body's "fight-or-flight" response. It acts on nearly every organ to regulate metabolism, blood sugar levels, blood pressure, and immune function ..."
(https://www.webmd.com/a-to-z-guides/what-is-cortisol)

Spiritual Practices and Their Benefits: From a biblical perspective, spirituality helps to foster hope, purpose, and community, including such spiritual practices as meditation, deep breathing, prayer, and the awareness of God in nature. It enables coping mechanisms for adversity, enhances resilience, and can lower blood pressure as the individual learns to relax and exercise calmness. These practices emphasize forgiveness, gratitude, and compassion, which reduce emotional stress.

Spiritual Intimacy with the Lord

Spirituality, within the Christian faith, is the human experience of forming an intimate relationship with the Lord. This close relationship originates from the Hebrew concept of the "Shema," which is further developed in Christian teachings. As stated in Deuteronomy 6:4-5, *"Hear, O Israel: the Lord our God is one Lord [the only Lord]. And you shall love the Lord your God with all your [mind and] heart and with your entire being and with all you might."* This passage emphasizes the call to love God wholly and completely.

Engaging in spirituality involves a pursuit of deeper meaning and purpose in life. Unlike asceticism, it is marked by a journey toward spiritual transformation, aiming to become more Christlike in one's character and actions. For many believers, spirituality is closely tied to experiencing inner peace, sensing a connection with God through His creation, and interacting with others in a way that reflects Christ's service and love.

While often linked to religious practices, the experience of spirituality can exist independently of organized religion. At its core, spirituality centers on personal growth and the exploration of life's larger questions. This journey may include practices such as meditation, reflection, or acts of service, all of which foster a deeper relationship with God and an enriched sense of purpose.

Spiritual DNA and Individual Growth

To "be spiritual" is to embrace an identity rooted in spiritual DNA—a divine heritage and lineage that aligns with Christ, literally deposited in the human spirit as a "seed." The Scriptures affirm this connection: Acts 17:26 emphasizes that God made all nations from a common origin and bloodline and determined their appointed times and boundaries. Galatians 3:29 proclaims that those who belong to Christ are Abraham's offspring and spiritual heirs according to the promise. Additionally, I John 3:9 asserts that those born of God possess a new nature that resists habitual sin, for God's nature ("sperma") remains within them.

Spiritual DNA identifies believers with Christ-like character, which each person seeks as spiritual maturity. This journey toward spiritual maturity is highly individual; believers progress at different rates in their faith, much like fingerprints or snowflakes— no two are alike. Spiritual maturity is not about conformity to any particular religious standard but about unique growth in Christ, and these differences should not be judged as religious shortcomings. For this reason, some spiritual believers may not attend church regularly, distinguishing their spiritual identity from mere church membership by saying, "I'm not religious but spiritual."

Fellowship Beyond the Church Building: The biblical admonition in Hebrews 10:25 to gather together is not a command to attend a specific church building because dedicated church buildings were not constructed during the time of the writing. The early Christians—the ekklesia, or "called-out ones"—met in homes, marketplaces, catacombs, and public places, even by riversides, and mountainsides, just as Christ did. The purpose of gathering was to maintain edifying fellowship that becomes worship, as illustrated in I Corinthians 14.

Understanding Spiritual Maturity and Identity in Christ

Stages of Spiritual Maturity: The Apostle Paul, in his epistles, draws a distinction between immature and mature believers by using the metaphors of "milk" and "meat." Immature believers require "milk," or the basic teachings of faith, while mature believers seek "meat," the deeper truths that foster growth into Christlikeness. This teaching highlights that spiritual development occurs at varying rates for each individual, with every believer following a unique journey of faith within the broader faith community.

Chronological development and spiritual maturity are closely connected. As individuals progress through life—from childhood to old age—each stage presents an opportunity to discover personal identity. For example, if someone does not find their identity as a maturing adult during adolescence, it is unreasonable to expect them to display spiritual maturity by the age of thirty. Spiritual growth contributes to and enhances natural maturation. This relationship is reflected in traditions such as the age requirement of thirty for the priesthood and Bar Mitzvah, a rite of passage for boys at twelve or thirteen, coming of age.

Spirituality as Identity with Christ: Believers are given a new spiritual nature that mirrors Christ's own nature, yet they maintain their distinct human individuality. The Holy Spirit works in a personal and unique manner with each Christian, shaping them into the image of Christ through their individual walk of faith. Spiritual believers are not shaped by a religious cookie-cutter to look and act like others.

Shifting from Religion to Spirituality: Theologian Harvey Cox observes a significant transition in the Christian experience: spirituality is gradually replacing traditional religion. This shift is evident as Christianity moves from an "Age of Belief," where creeds and hierarchical structures dominated, to an "Age of Spirit," where personal spirituality takes precedence over formal religious practices. Cox explains that belief is a matter of intellectual agreement with doctrines, while faith represents a profound orientation of one's entire life. In contemporary times, people are increasingly hesitant to accept authority without firsthand experience. As Cox asserts, "Religion without relationship is life without Spirit!" Many individuals are weary of being told how to live by others and prefer to encounter Christ in their everyday lives—where they live, work, and play.

Being the Church: Living Out Spirituality

The central message of this section emphasizes a foundational mantra for spiritual believers: Rather than simply "doing church," they strive to "be" the church. While "doing church" can often refer to attending Sunday services or participating in routine religious activities, sometimes described as "Sunday go to meeting Churchanity." "Being Church" means actively living as a disciple of Christ in all aspects of life, whether at home, at work, or in leisure. This perspective encourages believers to engage in genuine fellowship, where diverse views are exchanged, and important questions are explored. These questions include: Where is God in my life? What is He up to? Where is the Church in all this? What is my Purpose?

Personal Relationship with Christ: Spirituality, according to this understanding, is not a blind leap of faith. Instead, it is rooted in a trusting and personal relationship with Christ. The Bible teaches that a spiritual person can perceive God's purpose and plan unfolding in their life, even if others do not recognize it. As explained in I Corinthians 2:15, while the spiritual person can discern and examine all things, their unique perspective is not always fully understood and judged by others. In practice, this means that spiritual individuals can often understand people and circumstances deeply, but their own actions and motivations may remain unclear to those who do not share their spiritual outlook.

Expressions of Spirituality: Spiritual Christians regularly practice meditation on God's word, seeking to align their thoughts with divine truth. They engage in acts of kindness and love, live with intention and purpose, and earnestly seek truth in their daily lives. Such practices foster inner peace, contentment, self-awareness, compassion for others, and a sense of meaningful living.

Three Biblical Principles of Spirituality

Spirituality is built upon three primary biblical principles: Maturity of Relationship, Having the Mind of Christ, and Following the Voice of the Lord.

Maturity of Relationship: Maturity of relationships enables believers to address life's challenges from a higher perspective. For example, when Samuel felt rejected by Israel's desire for a king, God assured him, "…they have not rejected you, but they have rejected me…" Spiritual believers learn not to take life's problems too personally. They accept growth and maturity through the difficulties they face. Mature disciples of Christ can hold differing views and engage in meaningful debate without damaging their relationships. They embody the sentiment expressed by John Wesley: "If it doesn't strike at the root of Christianity, we think and let think."

Having the Mind of Christ: Having the mind of Christ is about thinking in alignment with God's word and applying it to daily living. Paul, in Corinthians, contrasts spirituality and carnality, observing that carnality is thinking without the mind of Christ, while spirituality is thinking with the mind of Christ—interpreting experiences and choices within the context of God's word.

Following the Voice of the Lord: Finally, following the voice of the Lord means acting promptly and obediently when God speaks to one's consciousness—a quality referred to as spontaneous obedience. This readiness to respond to God's guidance is a hallmark of true spiritual maturity.

Spirituality Versus Carnality

In Westernized Christian heritage, classical ideology and traditionalism have often defined spirituality in terms of morality, good works, and the outward appearance of being a good person. This view has also positioned spirituality as the direct opposite of carnality. However, to truly understand these concepts, it is important to examine what scripture says about them.

Carnality in Scripture: Carnality, according to Scripture, primarily refers to the state of non-Christians—those who are unregenerate. The Greek word "Sarkikos" is used to describe unregenerate human nature, or "flesh," human nature. Another related term, "Sarx," is associated with spiritual immaturity. The Apostle Paul reflects on his own carnality in Romans 7:14, stating, *"We know that the Law is spiritual; but I am a creature of the flesh [carnal, unspiritual], having been sold into slavery under [the control of] sin."* This scriptural reference highlights carnality as a condition of spiritual lostness and separation from God.

Spirituality in Scripture: In contrast, spirituality is understood as the opposite of carnality. It primarily signifies a personal relationship with Christ and, secondly, spiritual maturity. The Greek word "pneumayikos" means supernatural or regenerate, and it forms the basis for the theological term "Pneumatology," which is the study of the person and work of the Holy Spirit. Paul describes the Christian's supernatural, regenerate, and glorified state in I Corinthians 15:44: *"It is sown a natural (physical) body; it is raised a supernatural (a spiritual) body. [As surely as] there is a physical body, there is also a spiritual body."*

Additionally, spirituality is linked to maturity as a disciple of Christ. Paul refers to this in I Corinthians 3:1: *"However, brethren, I could not talk to you as to spiritual [men], but as to nonspiritual [men of the flesh, in whom the carnal nature predominates], as to mere infants [in the new life] in Christ [unable to talk yet!]."*

Based on these scriptural insights, carnality can be seen primarily as the "lost" state of the unregenerate, whereas spirituality refers to the "found" state of the regenerate. This leads to the question: What does it truly mean to "be" spiritual in our understanding of the Christian life? The answer lies in recognizing spirituality as a personal relationship with Christ and a journey toward spiritual maturity, rather than merely outward moral behavior or good works.

Living and Walking by Faith: The Spiritual Believer's Journey

Faith Over Rules—The Spiritual Way of Life: Spiritual believers are distinguished by their commitment to living and walking by faith, rather than adhering strictly to religious rules and regulations. The guiding principle for such believers is "The Golden Rule," which serves as a concise summary of the "Moral Law." This law is rooted in loving God, oneself, one's neighbor as oneself, and extending love to all people. The apostle Paul, in Romans 13:8-10, emphasizes that walking in love is the fulfillment of each of the ten commandments. In essence, love is the ultimate standard by which spiritual believers measure their actions and attitudes.

Nature and Purpose of Faith in a Spiritual Person's Life: Scripture identifies one kind of faith from which the benefits of faith originate. The first aspect of this faith is known as "saving faith." Saving faith serves two distinct purposes, both stemming from the same foundational word.

The initial faith is received through God's provision of grace. As stated in Ephesians 2:8: *"For it is by free grace (God's unmerited favor) that you are saved (delivered from judgment and made partakers of Christ's salvation) through [your] faith. And this [salvation] is not of yourselves [of your own doing, it came not through your own striving], but it is the gift of God."*

The Greek word for faith is "Pistis," which means to rely on another for salvation, commonly referred to as "saving faith." From this basic saving faith, a second form emerges—grace provision—that is based on "being persuaded." This is often described as "beneficial faith." Beneficial faith anoints and enables the recipient to accomplish their assigned tasks. Scripture records this in I Corinthians 12:9: "To another [wonderworking] faith by the same [Holy] Spirit," which is also known as enabling faith.

Grace, Charity, and the Gift of Faith: In Ephesians 2:8, the term "grace" comes from the Greek word "Charis," which is the root of the English word "Charity." Charity, derived from Charis, means unmerited, unearned, and undeserved favor. This grace is closely linked to Pistis or saving faith. The passage states, "We are saved by grace through faith…" The conjunction "and" in this context implies that faith itself is a gift. The verse continues, "We are saved by grace through faith, and that (faith) is not of ourselves. It (faith) is the gift of God lest any man should boast…" This clarifies that salvation is not acquired through good works. Rather, grace—God's unmerited, undeserved, and unearned favor—is demonstrated through Christ's work on the cross and trusted by those who believe.

Beneficial Faith and Its Role in Ministry: The second form of faith, referred to as "beneficial faith," enables the believer to participate in ministry. To fully understand its purpose, one must consider the context of the spiritual gifts described in I Corinthians 12:4-12. In verses 4-6, Paul explains the workings of the Godhead in a life dedicated to serving the Lord. He notes that while there are various "gifts," they all originate from the same Spirit. It is God's Spirit who distributes and anoints individuals with gifts, the Lord who assigns callings and ministries, and the Father as Creator who brings about the results.

In summary, the manifestations observed in ministry are the collective work of the Godhead, provided by grace so that no one can boast about their achievements—God alone is to be glorified. Paul further states in verse 7, *"But the manifestation of the Spirit is given to every man to profit withal,"* which illustrates the concept of beneficial faith. Every believer is equipped by the Spirit to contribute to the common good and to fulfill their calling.

The Attributes and Virtues of God: Foundations for Christian Living

The relationship between theology and the nature of God is often misunderstood, both by newcomers and seasoned traditionalists. A quote from my years as a professor stands out: "The essence of theology is man's concept of God." This statement highlights that regardless of who develops theological frameworks, their ultimate purpose is to help humans comprehend God. However, while theology aids understanding, it is the attributes and virtues of God that are meant to guide our daily lives.

As followers of Christ, we are directed by God's Word and Spirit, which illuminate His nature through commandments, different from principles and laws that become rules and regulations. For believers, one central rule prevails: the "Golden Rule," which shapes our relationship with God (vertical) and with others (horizontal) through love. Love, in fact, is the very essence of God's nature.

The Kingdom of God—Built on Love, Not Regulations: The Kingdom of God is not established through theology, doctrine, dogma, or external rules and regulations. While these elements come to us from outside, love originates from the heart. The Kingdom operates based on God's attributes and virtues, which are imparted to us by His Spirit. Everything God does flows from His nature, characterized by His attributes and character. He desires that His followers also shape their lives according to His revealed virtues, as described in Galatians 5:22-23.

- Holy: God is spiritually pure and untouched by sin.

- Just/Righteous: God is upright and bases our lives on the righteousness of Christ. This justice transcends human fairness, as seen in Christ's sacrifice for sinners—the innocent dying for the guilty.

- Loving/Good: God is kind, magnanimous, benevolent, and full of favor.

- Faithful/Truthful: God is consistent, reliable, trustworthy, and always keeps His promises.

- Merciful/Gracious: God is kind, empathetic through Christ, and compassionate, withholding deserved punishment.

- Forbearing: God is long-suffering and patient.

- Forgiving: God forgives all sin except "blasphemy of the Holy Spirit," which is defined as unbelief.

- Gentle: God cares for His children as a loving father, providing tender care, discipline, and tough love.

- Nurturing: God raises us as His own children.

- Peaceful: God calms the turmoil within the heart.

CHAPTER 6.

Demonically Targeted Attacks

Coming from the "Prologue," the question of whether angels and demons truly exist is not merely rhetorical—it demands thoughtful examination, correlating both science and Scripture. If these spiritual beings are real, their existence serves a distinct purpose and reason.

Are Aliens Fallen Angels in Disguise: While I am neither a scientist nor an astronomist, I am aware that the existence of aliens has never been definitively proven. Although there have been reports of sightings, no conclusive evidence has surfaced. For instance, Area 51—officially recognized by the CIA in 2013 after the Freedom of Information Act—has long been the subject of conspiracy theories.

Many have claimed that the base houses alien spacecraft and extraterrestrial bodies, but the government considers such theories to be false. The reality is that Area 51, also known as Homey Airport or Groom Lake, is a legitimate Air Force base in southern Nevada. Its primary mission has been to test experimental aircraft and weapons systems, which led the government to deny its existence, unintentionally fueling further conspiracy theories and UFO folklore. Test flights involving high-altitude, unusually shaped aircraft contributed to these suspicions. In fact, some Department of Defense reviews have revealed that certain UFO conspiracy theories were deliberately planted by the Pentagon in the 1980s to conceal highly classified weapons programs, which only heightened public intrigue. Despite all the speculation, there has never been credible evidence of alien life or technology in Area 51.

This leads to a critical question for true believers: whom should you trust—God or the government? There is a balanced perspective that doesn't resolve the issue; rather broadens the thinking about this dilemma, noting that this isn't a conclusion. The conclusion is up to those of faith and students of Scripture. The answer is the "possibility" that aliens and UFOs are, in reality, fallen angels in disguise.

Demonically Disguised Attacks on Faith in Christ: Exploring this concept helps to clarify why spiritual warfare is real, as are the angels and demons behind these spiritual battles. These forces manifest as spiritual attacks on Christ's disciples, often originating from corrupt governing bodies and permeating society at large. It is intentional to reference disciples rather than "the church," for reasons that will become apparent as you continue reading.

Attacking the Mission

Institutions are typically manmade regardless of the name attached, which refers to religious systems formed around various doctrines, comprised of members who may be divided by race, politics, culture, theology, or doctrine. In contrast, the Body of Christ is a universal collection of believers—united by the mission of Christ—to spread the Gospel of the Kingdom of God. This Body has no official or episcopal leaders; Christ Himself is the only head. These believers, both Jews and Gentiles, are grafted together into one unified body.

If you have come this far, you likely recall the previous chapter, "Spirituality's Superpower." In summary, the Body of Christ consists of disciples who actively follow the Lord in their daily lives. These individuals do not abandon their Christian witness at the church door after the benediction but carry their faith into every aspect of life. Although scattered across different institutionalized religions and some uncommitted to church membership, they remain connected by their commitment to Christ and the mission.

Concerning spiritual warfare, some steeply institutional organizations, due to their cessationist stance, do not entertain engaging in spiritual warfare as a form of ministry, but Scripture does. Instead, they tend to maintain the status quo—neither advancing nor retreating, much like military personnel awaiting orders (mocking time), referred to as "standing," when in fact, the order was already given with the Great Commission.

The Great Commission is the primary outreach mission ministry of the Body of Christ, and it is a biblical fact that when believers are engaged in evangelism and discipleship, they will encounter demonic resistance to reaching God's Harvest. The biblical reality is that God has called the church to confront spiritual resistance when it impedes the gospel. Note the latter part of Matthew 16:18, *"And I tell you, you are Peter [Greek, Petros— a large piece of rock], and on this rock [Greek, petra—a huge rock like Gibraltar] I will build My church, and the gates of Hades (the powers of the infernal region) shall not overpower it [or be strong to its detriment or hold out against it]."* The latter part reads, *"...be strong to its detriment or hold out against it."* The literal language is not about a docile church, cowering in a corner, biting its nails, worried about the devil's attacks. Instead, the church holds a proactive position and advances towards overthrowing the gates of hell that represent holding God's harvest hostage as POWs.

In contrast, disciples within these congregations, whether leaders or lay members, serve as Salt and Light within their churches and communities. They embody God's call to reconcile the world to Himself and to one another. As "Salt," they help preserve society from God's judgment; as "Light," they guide people toward Christ. Because they are motivated by the Great Commission, it is the Body of Christ and its mission that comes under spiritual attack.

There is coming a time in the "last days" when these scattered disciples will be united across networks to engage in evangelism and discipleship, reaping God's harvest.

Spiritual Attack Against Disciples: The concept of spiritual attack highlights the ongoing struggle between good and evil, with the Body of Christ as the central target. These attacks are not simply directed at humanity, but specifically at those engaged in fulfilling the Great Commission. The aim is to undermine faith and divert potential believers from Christ.

Such attacks often seek to disrupt the order within government, churches, families, and society as a whole.

The Order of Angels and Demons: To understand spiritual warfare, it is important to examine the roles of angels and demons (fallen angels), both in the heavenly realms and on earth.

Angels and demons are often perceived through visions and have the capacity to take on human form. Consider the first fallen angel, Lucifer, who appeared as a beautiful dragon—that some surmise as a serpent—in the Garden of Eden. (The comparative language of a dragon comes from Revelation 12) Drawing from Isaiah 14:12 and Ezekiel 28:13, 15, it is reasonable to conclude that Lucifer's appearance in the garden reflected his status as an archangel-cherubim—attractive and deceptive.

Another example is found in Genesis 6:4, where the "sons of God" saw that the daughters of men were beautiful, married them, and produced offspring known as the Nephilim—giants who became renowned warriors. This occurred during a period of widespread corruption, prompting the flood, and these Nephilim are considered predecessors to giants like Goliath. Additional appearances include the theophanic visit of two angels and the Lord to Abraham in Genesis 18. There are many such instances but let us now turn to angelic visions.

One notable example is Jacob wrestling with the angel in Genesis 32:22-32. In both Old and New Testament accounts, angelic appearances are typically visions experienced only by the individual involved and not visible to others. For instance, Ezekiel's vision of "a wheel in the middle of a wheel" (Ezekiel 1) was a Cherubim moved by the Spirit of God, providing providentially for God's people. In natural life and to the reader, this vision could be viewed as a gyroscopic spacecraft. While there are numerous other examples in Scripture, this overview establishes the foundation for understanding the purpose of angels and demons in spiritual warfare.

The Descending Order of Demonic Forces

To gain a clear understanding of the order of fallen angels, we begin by examining Ephesians 6:11-12, employing an exegetical approach and comparing it with relevant passages in Scripture, particularly those involving Michael the Archangel in the Book of Daniel.

Spiritual Armor and Its Purpose: Ephesians 6:11 states, *"Put on God's whole armor [the armor of a heavy-armed soldier which God supplies], that you may be able successfully to stand up against [all] the strategies and the deceits of the devil."* The idea here is to protect their mind from false doctrine and unfounded conspiracy theories. Therefore, Paul admonishes believers to equip themselves with spiritual armor from verses 13-17 that covers vital areas of their physical anatomy, which can be seen metaphorically but applies to spiritual protection and preparedness to withstand spiritual attacks from the devil, emphasizing God's provision for spiritual warfare rather than physical fighting.

Each piece represents a spiritual virtue of TRUTH: the Belt of Truth (Strength), the Breastplate of Righteousness (Heart), Gospel Shoes (Peace), Shield of Faith (Dispelling Error), Helmet of Salvation (Protecting the Mind), and the Sword of the Spirit—Word of God (Offensive Weapon). It closes with "Prayer in the Spirit" in verse 18, the offensive weapon petitioning God to authorize His army of angels to combat the demon forces.

Comparing this with II Corinthians 10:4-5, we see that spiritual armor is necessary because *"the weapons of our warfare are not physical [weapons of flesh and blood], but they are mighty before God for the overthrow and destruction of strongholds."* This means that spiritual battles occur in the minds of Christ's followers. II Corinthians 4:5, *"[Inasmuch as we] refute arguments and theories and reasoning and every proud and lofty thing that sets itself up against the [true] knowledge of God; and we lead every thought and purpose away captive into the obedience of Christ (the Messiah, the Anointed One)."* John

Melton once said, "The Mind is its own place and can of itself make a heaven of hell or a hell of heaven."

These are not worldly or physical conflicts but are instead fought with divine power to dismantle strongholds of false teachings and to bring every thought captive to the obedience of Christ, as stated in Hebrews 12:2, by focusing and concentrating on Christ, the Author and Finisher of our faith.

The Nature of Demonic Forces: Scripture describes a hierarchy among demonic forces descending from the stellar heavens, also referred to as the second heaven.

It is important to remember that neither Satan nor his angels possess divine attributes such as omnipotence, omniscience, or omnipresence. God limits their power, and they must gain God's permission, as in the Book of Job, to attack believers through accusations before God about some form of unfaithfulness. We see that scenario in Job 1:8-9, where Satan, as "the accuser of the brethren" (Revelation 12:10), accuses Job of serving God, not because he loved God, but because of the material things he received, and challenged the Lord to take them away, and Job would repudiate the Lord.

However, the caveat is that Satan is aware of our weaknesses throughout our history and targets the vulnerable areas of our lives. This is why our strength should be perfected through weakness—strengthening the weak areas of our lives through the "Fruit of the Spirit" (Galatians 5:22-23).

Those spiritual forces do not know our thoughts but attempt to influence them—thus, "prayer in the spirit" is emphasized—and they cannot be everywhere at once. However, in matters of divination, they communicate through a telepathic network, similar to radio waves. Their activity is evident in the Book of Job (1:7; 2:2), where Satan tells God he has been "going to and from in the earth, and from walking up and down in it." This illustrates how demonic forces move throughout the earth, seeking to accuse or tempt people, like a troll, a patrol, or a prowling adversary. While there is no empirical proof of this theory, it is a matter of faith and the study of Scripture.

The Hierarchy of Demonic Forces

The First Order—Principalities: The primary purpose of spiritual armor is to dismantle spiritual strongholds that resist the Gospel. Jesus refers to such strongholds as the "strongman" in Mark 3:27, Matthew 12:29, and Luke 11:21-22. In these passages, He explains Satan's influence and the mission of the Lord's servants to free those under demonic control, stating that the strongman must be bound before his house—his geographical stronghold—can be plundered, meaning rescuing those held captive. This concept is illustrated in Daniel 10:13, where Daniel's prayer is delayed by a "strongman" called "the prince of Persia," the spiritual entity behind Persia's king, until Michael the Archangel intervenes. This passage demonstrates that God's angels engage in cosmic warfare on behalf of His people, referencing the spiritual entity behind the human ruler. In Ephesians 6:13, this strongman is cross-referenced with "Principalities," which the Amplified Classic Version of the Bible describes as despotic rulers. This points to both physical rulers and the spiritual forces operating through them, as seen in Daniel.

The Second Order—Message Runners: The passage continues, "… against the powers …" These "powers" can be understood as messengers, or what can be termed "runners." Their role is to transmit orders from Satan through strongmen to the next level, the rulers of the darkness of this world.

The Third Order—Rulers of Darkness: Ephesians 6:12 further references *"… against [the master spirits who are] the world rulers of this present darkness, against the spirit forces of wickedness in the heavenly (supernatural) sphere …"* The "rulers of the darkness of this world" refer to social orders of demons. Please note that all illnesses and sicknesses associated with the human condition aren't inflicted by demons. Some conditions are hereditary or associated with the environment. However, unlike deliverance ministries, I think there is a place for spiritual gifts within our faith communities to develop practical certified ministries that help people get free from negative spiritual influence. During a season of pastoring, I developed a ministry among the Elders called "Breaking the Yoke" that dealt with deeply personal issues anonymously. I know that's a lot to ask, but God's help in our world is warranted.

These social orders of demons can promote false doctrine, sexual immorality, addiction (the Book of Revelation refers to "pharmacy," or "Pharmakeia" as drug use inducing hallucinations), insanity, sickness, disease, conflict, hate, fear, violence, and other afflictions of humanity, even depression and suicide. But I acknowledge that I'm preaching to the choir.

Modern Context: The Spread of False Narratives

The advent of the 21st century brought a proliferation of social media platforms, which have become significant sources of information. These platforms often disseminate opinions without a factual basis, creating false narratives about Christianity and the Christian faith.

Prophetic Insight—The Last Days and Information Overload: Daniel 12:4, a key prophecy about the "last days," states, "many shall run to and fro, and knowledge shall increase." Daniel is told to seal the book until the end of time, a period marked by increased travel and a surge in knowledge facilitated by technological advances such as computerized algorithms and artificial intelligence. These developments "run" along the internet, the so-called information highway. The sealing of the book may indicate that the true meaning will be revealed only at the appointed time, during which strong delusion and deception will prevail.

Paul warns, *"But understand this, that in the last days will come (set in) perilous times of great stress and trouble [hard to deal with and hard to bear]."* He describes people as being lovers of self (narcissistic), lovers of money (greedy), proud, arrogant, abusive, disobedient to parents, ungrateful, unholy, lacking natural affection, relentless, slanderous, intemperate, uncontrolled, fierce, haters of those that are good, treacherous, rash, conceited, and lovers of pleasure rather than God. Although they may appear religious, their actions betray reality, having a form of godliness. Paul instructs believers to avoid such people.

Among these are those who *"worm their way into homes and captivate silly and weak-natured and spiritually dwarfed women, loaded down with [the burden of their] sins [and easily] swayed and led away by various evil desires and seductive impulses."* These individuals are vulnerable to the evil characteristics of the "spirit of antichrist." (Birds of a feather flock together.) They are always learning from sources that "tickle their fancy" but avoid the truth and are never able to grasp the knowledge of the Truth. Think of this text in modern terms, with a sense of Ecclesiastes, "nothing new." It is implicit of sex trafficking, which is as old as prostitution.

CHAPTER 7.

Spiritual Activity in the Universe

God's Oneness with the Universe: God, as the Creator, is intrinsically united with the universe, and the universe is equally united with God through God's omnipotence, omniscience, and omnipresence, His infinite eternal nature.

The universe serves as both the expression and means of communication for God's presence. This profound connection is emphasized in Scripture, as seen in Romans 1:19-20, where Paul, through revelation knowledge shares the awareness of God through human conscience and the display of the universe.

"For that which is known about God is evident to them and made plain in their inner consciousness, because God [Himself] has shown it to them. For ever since the creation of the world His invisible nature and attributes, that is, His eternal power and divinity, have been made intelligible and clearly discernible in and through the things that have been made (His handiworks). So [men] are without excuse [altogether without any defense or justification]." This passage reveals that behind every law governing nature stands the Lord of nature. Colossians 1:16-17, *"For it was in Him that all things were created, in heaven and on earth, things seen and things unseen, whether thrones, dominions, rulers, or authorities; all things were created and exist through Him [by His service, intervention] and in and for Him. And He Himself existed before all things, and in Him all things consist (cohere, are held together)."*

If the Lord were to withdraw the word of His power by which He spoke our world and our known universe into existence (Genesis 1), the world would disintegrate by the same holy fire that will renew the earth in the restitution of all things (Acts 3:21). That period between time and eternity will occur when the very throne room of God will come to the earth as the New Jerusalem, where Christ, the offspring of David and the Bright and Morning Star will rule forever.

Aside from the idea of nature worshippers, God's presence permeates all aspects of creation—He is found in the sun, the moon, the stars, the sky, the trees, the earth, and the water. Consequently, to disregard or disrespect global concerns such as global warming, climate change, and environmental protection is, in effect, to disrespect God. Such disregard can lead to catastrophic environmental consequences that we will review in the book of Revelation. However, while God is present in all these elements, reducing Him solely to these components is considered idolatry.

God's Omnipotence: God does not merely possess power; He embodies power itself. His essence is found within the laws of physics, relativity, science, and technology. God exists as energy, molecules, electrons, cells, protons, neutrons, and the particles that fill the air, in the Person of Christ. Every aspect of goodness in creation is a reflection of God's omnipotence. Genesis 1:31a, *"And God saw everything that He had made, and behold, it was very good (suitable, pleasant) and He approved it completely ..."*

God's Omnipresence: God is present everywhere throughout the universe, the world, and even history, simultaneously. Standing above the constraints of time, He exists in the past, present, and future all at once. God's presence is even reflected in quantum physics, illustrating that the universe—God's creation—is all around us. As believers, we are blessed in heavenly places and encouraged to embrace this reality.

God's Omniscience: God possesses complete knowledge, knowing the end from the beginning. His foreknowledge determines and proclaims the destiny of His redeemed people. Our destiny rests in God's hands because He knows our thoughts even before we conceive them—even though He grants us free will and options for making choices. Every wrong decision will ultimately be made right within the circle of God's love—Romans 8:28. While the decisions we make may require varying lengths of time to reach fulfillment, delayed blessings are not denied blessings; each choice leads us, in His timing, toward our destiny. Romans 8:28, *"All things work together for good ..."*

The Three Heavens: A Biblical Perspective

Scripture describes three distinct heavens, each representing a different aspect of creation and spiritual reality. This understanding is rooted in both biblical text and Jewish tradition, which interprets references to "heavens" as indicating separate layers within God's creation, ranging from the physical realm to the divine.

The First Heaven: Atmospheric Heaven

The first heaven refers to the physical material world and the Earth's atmosphere—the sky immediately above us. This is the realm where clouds form, birds fly, and the air we breathe circulates. It is the most familiar and tangible of the three heavens, encompassing all that is accessible to our physical senses.

The Second Heaven: Celestial or Stellar Heaven

The second heaven encompasses outer space, extending far beyond the Earth's atmosphere. It includes the sun, moon, stars, planets, galaxies, and all celestial bodies. This vast cosmic expanse is sometimes associated with spiritual warfare, as some teachings suggest that battles between spiritual forces can occur in this realm.

One example is seen in the Book of Job 1:6, where it speaks of Satan coming among the "Sons of God," to give an account of their stewardship before God, and Satan comes among them. (Sons of God in Scripture were the one-third order of angels that rebelled with Satan in eternity. The fact that Satan came among them stipulates that even Satan and his demons are accountable to God. That should be reassuring to believers.) He accused Job of serving God selfishly for what he could get from God.

The idea of "coming before God" is not the literal presence of God because Satan and his angels were banned from entering the heaven of heavens, the throne room of God. So, their positioning would logically be between the threshold of the heaven of heavens and the celestial heavens, among the stars. From there, Satan railed out accusations against Job, initiating a spiritual attack on Job's life as a test of his faithfulness to God.

The Third Heaven: God's Literal Dwelling Place

The third heaven as God's dwelling place is an oxymoron because the heavens are His throne and the earth His footstool. The third heaven is better seen as the control room of the universe.

The third heaven is the spiritual, eternal dimension that serves as the throne room of God, angels, and divine realities. It exists beyond the limits of physical perception and is described in Scripture as the location of God's throne, where He presides over the universe and all creation. This realm is also called the "heaven of heavens," signifying its supremacy and eternal nature.

Scriptural Reference to the Third Heaven: In II Corinthians 12:2-4, the Apostle Paul recounts an extraordinary experience: *"I know a man in Christ who fourteen years ago—whether in the body or out of the body I do not know, God knows—was caught up to the third heaven. And I know that this man—whether in the body or away from the body I do not know, God knows—was caught up into paradise, and he heard utterances beyond the power of man to put into words, which man is not permitted to utter."*

This passage is often interpreted as Paul having an "out-of-body" experience in which his spirit was taken up in a vision to God's eternal throne. In this place—paradise—Paul witnessed and heard things so profound that they could not be expressed in human language.

Spiritual Significance of the Three Heavens: Understanding the concept of the three heavens helps Christians gain insight into the nature of spiritual warfare and prayer.

Spiritual battles are believed to sometimes take place in the second heaven, while deep communion with God and access to

His presence occur in the third heaven. This perspective emphasizes that life's challenges are not only physical but also have spiritual dimensions, requiring believers to seek divine wisdom and power to overcome them.

Spiritism's Conflict with the Three Heavens

This section delves into the deceptive nature of spiritism's parallels to the three heavens of Scripture. Building upon the earlier discussion in chapter four concerning "The Deception of Spiritism," I will examine the metaphysical sources associated with spiritism, which have gained popularity among individuals who identify as spiritual, often without distinguishing between "being spiritual" and engaging in "spiritism."

As previously established, the distinction between these concepts is as clear as the difference between night and day, or light and dark. In certain cases, the deceptive elements of spiritism have infiltrated church communities, leading followers away from foundational principles of faith toward alternative forms of the gospel. The broad category encompassing this spiritual movement is known as Pleiades, as noted in chapter four.

Misconceptions Shaped by Hollywood: The Antichrist and Heaven

Hollywood has played a significant role in shaping public perceptions of religious themes, particularly those surrounding demonic possession, apocalyptic scenarios, and children portrayed as embodiments of evil. Notable films such as The Omen, Rosemary's Baby, The Devil's Advocate, End of Days, The Day of the Beast, Heredity, and Left Behind have become classic examples that center on the concept of the Antichrist and related biblical ideas.

Distortions of Biblical References: These cinematic portrayals have often led to distorted interpretations of what Scripture actually says about heaven and the Antichrist. Rather than reflecting the true biblical narrative, Hollywood productions tend to sensationalize and dramatize these figures, resulting in widespread misconceptions among audiences.

Imaginary Depictions of Heaven: In addition to misrepresenting the Antichrist, movies and popular culture frequently depict heaven as an ethereal place located somewhere in the clouds. Such imaginary images have contributed further to misunderstandings about the nature of heaven, steering people away from what is actually recorded in Scripture.

Clarifying Scriptural Truths: This work aims to clarify these misconceptions by highlighting the differences between Hollywood's depictions and the accounts found in Scripture. It will emphasize the natural elements present in life on earth and demonstrate that the reality described in religious texts is quite distinct from the dramatized versions seen on screen.

CHAPTER 8.

Identifying the "spirit" of antichrist

The Origin of the Antichrist: While some suggest that Asia Minor may be the region from which the antichrist will arise, Scripture does not explicitly state his origin. It does, however, indicate that he emerges from the "sea," a symbolic reference to the masses of people. This suggests that the antichrist will gain prominence through widespread popularity. Revelation 17:15 explains, *"And [the angel further] said to me, The waters that you observed, where the harlot is seated, are races and multitudes and nations and dialects (languages)."* Waters in the text symbolize for people. Revelation 13:1–11 describes the first beast (the Antichrist) coming out of the sea, while a second beast (the False Prophet, spokesperson for the Antichrist) arises from the earth (13:11), signifying that he will be someone well-known on earth.

The true identity of the Antichrist will remain hidden until the prophesied event known as the "abomination that makes desolate." This pivotal moment is referenced in Daniel 9:27, 11:31, 12:11; Matthew 24:15; Mark 13:14; and Luke 21:20. According to these passages, the event will take place after the temple is rebuilt and a peace agreement is established in the Middle East. At this time, a holographic or artificial intelligence projection of the Antichrist may emerge from his stronghold in the Turkish region, described in Revelation 2:13 as "Satan's seat." From this location, he will orchestrate peace. Three and a half years after the treaty, the Antichrist will make an appearance in Jerusalem, break the peace agreement, and offer a "swine" on the altar—an act identified in prophetic scripture as the "abomination that maketh desolate" that is sacrilege to the Jews. Subsequently, he will demand worship as God and initiate severe persecution against Jews and Christians who refuse to conform to his agenda.

Characteristics of the Antichrist Matched with the Pharisees

A parallel can be drawn between the "spirit of Antichrist" and the conduct of the Pharisees during the time of Christ. These leaders, both religious and political extremists, consistently opposed Christ and His teachings at every opportunity.

As fervent traditionalists, the Pharisees substituted God's commandments with their own traditions. They manipulated the law for personal advantage while neglecting to uphold the very standards they imposed upon others. Much like adherents of a cultic religion, they were accused of secret immoralities, held disdainful attitudes toward women, and displayed xenophobia toward outsiders. Collectively, these behaviors contribute to a general outline of the "spirit of Antichrist."

Moreover, the "spirit of Antichrist" is characterized by bigotry, as it exalts the leader's ethnicity as dominant. He will seek to subjugate, segregate, and purge society of anyone opposed to his policies.

This spirit presents itself as Christian, undermining true faith by denying the sufficiency of Christ's divinity and the power of His sacrifice to redeem humanity and unite all people. Thus, the "spirit of Antichrist" does not wage open war against Christianity; instead, it operates through deception, subtly opposing Christ's divinity under a guise of faith. This is the essence of apostasy: abandoning the biblical faith for another, all while claiming to remain Christian.

The profile of the Pharisees offers a revealing look into the characteristics associated with the "spirit of anti-Christ." These traits appear in practical, everyday ways but are believed to intensify and become fully personified in the eventual rise of the actual anti-Christ, marked by greater oppression and intensity. The following sections outline these characteristics as observed in the Pharisees.

A God Complex: The most defining trait of the spirit of antichrist is the presence of a god complex, which warrants a thorough explanation. A god complex closely resembles the psychological condition known as malignant narcissism, but it should be noted that it is not classified as a clinical diagnosis.

A god complex is characterized by an unshakable and intense belief in one's own infallibility, superiority, and entitlement. This mindset often manifests as extreme arrogance and a lack of consideration for the perspectives or well-being of others. Individuals exhibiting this trait see themselves as above rules and regulations, believing they are immune to criticism or accountability. Their conviction in their own lies is so strong that their lives become indistinguishable from their falsehoods—they essentially become a living lie. They are convinced they possess exceptional, almost divine, knowledge and abilities. As a result, they demand special treatment and believe their supposed superiority entitles them to privileges denied to others.

Those with a god complex are often controlling and may respond with anger or frustration when events do not unfold according to their wishes. They generally lack empathy and seldom take into account the feelings or needs of others. Although they might exhibit charisma, it is typically coupled with an attitude of condescension. Such individuals blame others for their own shortcomings and failures.

Lack of God-given Spiritual Inspiration: The Pharisees' religious system originated during a period known as the 400 years of silence—a time when there was no open revelation from God. Consequently, their practices and doctrines were not divinely inspired but rather developed independently of spiritual guidance. In the same way, the antichrist will be entirely devoid of godly inspiration and will misuse Scripture for his own ends.

Desire for Control through Politics and Religion: The Pharisees actively sought to control their society by merging political power with religious authority, establishing a theocratic system of governance. Their drive for domination influenced both their interactions with others and the way they managed religious life.

Pride and Arrogance: Pride, egotism, arrogance, and self-centeredness were prominent features among the Pharisees. Their attitudes frequently reflected a form of narcissism, as they perceived themselves to be superior to others.

Rigid Traditionalism and Legalism: As staunch traditionalists, the Pharisees took extreme approaches in interpreting and applying the law. They often twisted and misrepresented the moral code for their own benefit, enforcing strict rules that ultimately served their personal interests.

Bigotry and Sense of Superiority: The Pharisees demonstrated clear bigotry, believing themselves superior to Samaritans and Gentiles. This conviction was rooted in their belief that they were God's chosen people, set above all others.

Hypocrisy in Actions: While the Pharisees preached high moral standards, their actions often contradicted their own teachings. Their sense of privilege led them to justify their wrongdoings, assuming that their elevated status exempted them from accountability.

Deceitfulness and Repetitive Lies: The Pharisees were skilled in lying, with their falsehoods described as coming from the devil (referencing John 8:44). Repeating lies can effectively deceive others, a concept known as the "illusory truth effect," where information repeated often enough is perceived as true, regardless of its actual validity. This condition also employs "reverse psychology" to distract from the truth by accusing others of the very faults they themselves possess. Closely linked to propaganda, this is encapsulated in the phrase, "Repeat a lie often enough and it becomes the truth," also known as the "Big Lie." In other words, the truth may be stranger than fiction, but a lie can be more compelling.

Suppression of Human Rights and Civil Liberties: The Pharisees worked to suppress basic human rights and civil liberties, which are defined here as the God-given power to make personal decisions without harming others or violating moral law. This suppression severely limited individual freedom and autonomy.

Secret Sexual Deviance: Throughout Scripture, it is revealed that religious sect leaders not associated with Christ engaged in sexual perversions in their private lives.

These behaviors were carefully concealed from public scrutiny. Christ exposed their hidden sexual deviance in John 8:7 when they accused a woman of adultery. Their personal guilt of accusing her came out when Christ wrote with His finger on the ground. I imagine that it was a reckoning of the "handwriting on the wall" that pointed out the possibility of a Pharisee copulating with her because the law demanded both the man and woman to appear before the tribunal. When Christ said, "Let him without sin cast the first stone," the conviction was so deep that they all walked away.

Disrespect for Women and Misogyny: The Pharisees did not respect women, reducing them to the status of "legal non-persons." This attitude is reflected in biblical references, such as Daniel 11:37, which implies that the antichrist will show no regard for the desires of women or any other god, choosing instead to elevate himself above all.

Persecution of Christ and Christians: The Pharisees actively persecuted Christ and his followers, justifying their actions by appealing to their religious beliefs and their understanding of God.

The onset of the Great Tribulation is marked by a wave of persecution, as prophesied by Jesus in Matthew 24:15. He warns that when the "abomination that makes desolate" is seen in the Holy Place, a period of severe persecution will begin, especially targeting the Jews.

The Spirit of the Antichrist and Racism: A Human and Divine Perspective

Counterfeit Messiah and Deceptive Policies: The Antichrist will not immediately appear as an overtly evil figure. Instead, he will be perceived as a counterfeit messiah, possessing a deceptive charm reminiscent of the serpent in the Garden of Eden. His policies will be characterized by a facade of inclusivity, focusing on loyalty to his name. While he may not outwardly display racism or prejudice, his underlying actions will ultimately reveal his true intentions.

Racism as a Spiritual and Demonic Issue: From the 1990s through 2016, racial reconciliation discussions often emphasized that racism transcends being merely a social issue, instead carrying a demonic aspect. Drawing upon scriptural principles and theological insights, many recognized the "spirit of the antichrist" as one who embodies evil, manifesting through words and deeds that foster division, destruction, and inequality. The characteristics and outcomes of racism, bigotry, and supremacist ideologies closely mirror this antichrist spirit.

Some theologians argue that racism is both satanic and demonic, as it outright denies the equal value and dignity of every human being—each created in the image of God. By rejecting this fundamental truth, racism stands in direct opposition to God's purpose for humanity.

The Antichrist's Goal—Division within the Body of Christ: A central aim of the antichrist spirit is to create division within the Body of Christ. By promoting disunity—especially along racial lines—this spirit weakens the church and spills over into society. Historically, racism has served as a powerful tool to establish and maintain such divisions.

Historical Doctrines and the Distortion of Unity: The historical development of doctrines of racism began with the justification of slavery enforced by Catholicism during Exploration under the pretext of civilizing the heathens, then enforced by most mainline churches in colonial America. Thus, justifying slavery, such as those claiming Aryan descent as uniquely favored by God and superior to inferior people of darker skin. Doctrinally, it exemplifies human attempts to create ideologies for economic benefits. These ideas have, at times, been likened to the narrative of the Israelites conquering lands to instill their values. However, Christian theology, as articulated in Galatians 3:28 ("in Christ, there is neither Jew nor Greek"), underscores that all believers are unified in Christ. Consequently, any ideology that elevates one group over another is fundamentally opposed to the Gospel and inherently racist, as the assertion of superiority is the core of racism.

Racism as a Tool of the Antichrist Spirit: Some notable theologians maintain that racism reflects the satanic and demonic essence of the antichrist spirit, as it undermines the inherent worth of all people. The spirit of the antichrist seeks to disrupt the unity of the Church, using racism as a primary means to cause division within both the Church and broader society.

Theologically, the Gospel transcends all distinctions, including those of ethnicity and race, affirming the equality of all individuals in Christ. Therefore, any doctrine or ideology that promotes the superiority of one group over others stands in direct conflict with the core message of the Gospel.

The Antichrist's Goal—Division and Control: Scripture presents the antichrist as a figure who demands absolute worship and submission. Although he may incite racial tensions to achieve his goal of division, his ultimate objective is to unify the world under his authority. In pursuit of this control, he may not openly promote racist ideologies but will manipulate racial hatred against certain groups to further his agenda. The greatest deception of the antichrist lies in his effort to draw all people under one centralized power.

Such ideologies distort biblical truths about human dignity and diminish the significance of the cross of Christ, which stands as the ultimate testament to equality and unity.

Summary

In conclusion, while the Bible does not explicitly state, "the Antichrist will be a racist," prevailing theological perspectives suggest that racism is a significant component of the Antichrist's agenda and spirit. Racism serves as a strategic tool for dividing humanity and undermining the unity central to the Christian message. Those who spread such ideologies do so with the intent of maintaining power and control.

The proper attribution for racial hatred is Satan, not individuals. Satan employs racism not to elevate any particular race because his motive is rooted in hatred for all people, regardless of their race, ethnicity, culture, or socio-economic status.

The Concept of Race: A Biblical and Historical Perspective

The Biblical Perspective on Human Identity: Scripture does not refer to the terms race, racial, or racism. Instead, the Bible identifies groups of people as nations. This designation serves as the primary way in which the text distinguishes among different peoples.

The Origins of the Idea of Race in America: The concept of race as it is understood today did not originate from Scripture, but rather developed over time in Western Europe and the United States. The emergence of this idea is rooted in a long and complex history, shaped by various influences including science, government, and culture. These historical forces have played significant roles in forming modern perspectives about race.

The Origins of Racial Hate: All racial hatred has its roots, like sin, tracing back to the story of Cain and Abel. Cain's animosity and violence toward Abel stemmed from the fact that Abel's offering to God was "righteous" in God's eyes. Abel's sacrifice—a lamb—prefigured Christ and was what God required (Genesis 4:3-8), while Cain offered the fruits of his labor (the works of his hands), which did not meet God's requirements. Abel's offering served as a substitute for his sin, aligning with God's demand for a blood sacrifice—a foreshadowing of Christ's vicarious suffering on the cross as a substitute for humanity's sin. When we consider the embedded consciousness of racial disdain, it reveals that racism is a heart condition rather than a mental state. It means that racial hate isn't removed by mere legislation and laws. Instead, laws place safeguards against the damaging effects of racism in the mind. But racial hate as a heart condition can only be removed by the gospel that penetrates the heart.

The Role of Eugenics and Race Science in American History

This section is dedicated to the followers of Christ's example and those who seek the truth about race relations.

During the Great Depression, certain racial scientists advocated for the idea that economic and social inequalities were rooted in genetics. They claimed that characteristics such as criminal behavior, work ethic, and intelligence were determined by race and inherited through one's genes. According to this perspective, poverty, criminality, or lower intelligence were seen as consequences of genetic inheritance rather than the result of social or economic circumstances.

The Rise of Eugenics in American Policy and Society: This belief system laid the foundation for the eugenics movement, which became a driving force behind institutionalized racism. Charles Davenport, the director of the Eugenics Records Office, was a prominent advocate who promoted these ideas. The influence of eugenicists was significant—expert testimonies from these scientists who helped persuade Congress to pass the Immigration Act of 1924. Furthermore, the social framework established by eugenics was later adopted by Nazi Germany.

Eugenics—Definition and Historical Impact: Eugenics refers to a group of beliefs and practices that aim to enhance the genetic quality of the human population. This was attempted by encouraging the reproduction of those considered "fit" and discouraging or preventing those labeled as "unfit" from having children. Historically, eugenics was used to rationalize racism, ableism, and forced sterilization. Although modern forms of "new eugenics" focus on using genetic selection or modification to reduce diseases, the practice remains ethically controversial due to persistent risks of perpetuating inequality.

The "One-Drop Rule" and Its Lasting Legacy: The "one-drop rule" was a racist legal and social doctrine in the United States that defined anyone with even a single ancestor of African descent ("one drop of black blood") as Black. This rule originated in the American South as a tool to uphold white supremacy and sustain the system of slavery. By defining racial identity in this way, the one-drop rule restricted rights and enforced racial segregation, relying on social constructs rather than biological evidence. The legacy of this rule persists in various forms to the present day.

The "Spirit of Antichrist" Comparative Nature

The term "tyrant" aptly describes the Antichrist and those in every era who embody the "spirit of Antichrist." Tyrants are despots who believe they possess supreme authority, even over God Himself. They use wealth and power to dominate others, often through the unjust abuse of their positions. Synonyms for "tyrants" include autocrat, dictator, totalitarian, and fascist. The Antichrist will fulfill prophetic descriptions found throughout Scripture, especially in Revelation chapters 4 through 21, and will be the most ruthless tyrant of all.

In the Book of Revelation, the Antichrist appears as the "Messiah." He is described as having a multi-ethnic Jewish heritage and claims to be the political deliverer that Christ was not. Presenting himself as the Messiah whom orthodox Jews previously rejected, he will be accepted by them as the redeemer who will restore Israel's position among world powers. Thus, he will initially masquerade as a Messianic Christian, but will later betray both Jews and Christians, leading to their persecution. The Antichrist will be a counterfeit Jewish Christian, and this deceptive pattern is repeated by all who operate in the "spirit of Antichrist."

The Antichrist's Rise to Power

The Antichrist will rise to power, propelled by widespread popularity among the masses. In Revelation 17:3, the Apostle John, in a spiritual vision, finds himself in the wilderness where he observes a woman seated upon a scarlet beast. This beast is adorned with blasphemous names, each exalting the beast as God. The woman is arrayed in purple and scarlet—colors symbolizing a fusion of royalty and priesthood—, and she is surrounded by immense material wealth, represented through the most valuable natural resources. In her hand, she holds a golden cup, which serves as a symbol for intoxicating substances that enhance lewdness and sexual immorality.

Written on her forehead is the title: *"Babylon the Great, the mother of prostitutes (idolatresses) and of the filth and atrocities and abominations of the earth."* She is depicted as being intoxicated with the blood of the saints and martyrs, signifying her involvement in their persecution and death. In Revelation 17:8, an angel explains the mystery of both the woman and the beast, which has seven heads and ten horns and emerges from the bottomless pit, a place of perdition. The beast is described as one who "once was, now is not, and yet will come," meaning the Antichrist comes from eternity. The seven heads represent seven hills or kings, possibly indicating the location of the churches; five of these kings have fallen, one is currently reigning, and the seventh is yet to arrive. This period marks the organizational phase of the Antichrist's rule.

The beast is categorized as the eighth ruler, and intriguingly, he is one of the former seven. Knowing which kingdom the seven represent will narrow the location from whence the Antichrist came. The ten horns represent separate kingdoms that have not yet been granted royal authority by the woman (the harlot), but they will receive power for only a brief period—"one hour"— alongside the beast, which alludes to their simultaneous destruction during Armageddon. These kingdoms are fiercely loyal and will willingly transfer their power to the beast. Ultimately, the Lamb (Christ) and His army of the redeemed will defeat them, with God's angels overcoming the evil influences behind their actions. In the final turn, the ten horns and the beast will betray the harlot and destroy her with fire, which may symbolize a catastrophic event, such as a nuclear explosion.

Two key scriptural considerations highlight the brevity of the Antichrist's reign. First, Christ's own words: *"A kingdom divided against itself cannot stand"* (Matthew 12:25). Second, II Timothy 3:13 states, *"But wicked men and impostors will go on from bad to worse, deceiving and leading astray others and being deceived and led astray themselves."* These passages suggest that the administration of the Antichrist, comprised of wicked and egotistical individuals, will ultimately turn on itself due to their mutual desire for power. Their loyalty to the Antichrist will be fleeting.

A primary sign will be widespread apostasy, which will bring about severe persecution of Jews and Christians—those who uphold God's promise and refuse to join the Antichrist's movement.

Interpreting Predictive Prophecy Concerning the Geographical Area of the Rise of the Antichrist

A significant principle in interpreting predictive prophecy is found in the Lord's rebuke to the church in Pergamum in Revelation 2:14. Here, the church is warned not to follow the harmful teachings of Balaam, which led to idolatry and sexual immorality. Pergamum, located in modern-day Turkey near the town of Bergama, is referred to as "the seat of Satan" (Revelation 2:13)—a symbol of a center of evil influence. This city was known for emperor worship, a key point in understanding the rise of the Antichrist, whom predictive prophecy suggests may emerge from the region of Turkey.

The Antichrist will claim descent from the House of David, citing the prophecy that "the scepter of kingship will remain in the lineage of David" (II Samuel 7:12-16), which points to a Davidic dynasty. While this prophecy ultimately refers to Christ, the "Seed" of Abraham and David who will reign forever in Christ, the Antichrist will attempt to subvert the Gospel with a counterfeit message. He will act as a diviner, aided by a spirit guide, and may journey from the region of Turkey to Jerusalem, performing signs and wonders through advanced technology and artificial intelligence. (See the last chapter for greater details.)

[Explaining the Possible Rise of the Antichrist from the Region of Turkey]

Turkey has a population of approximately 87.7 million people, which makes it the 18th most populous country in the world. This large population reflects the country's vibrant and complex demographic makeup.

Ethnic Composition: The population is characterized by a rich ethnic mix. It includes Turkish migrants from East Asia, indigenous Anatolian groups, minority Kurds, and Balkan communities who have gradually assimilated over centuries. This diverse background is a result of extensive cultural exchange and cohabitation, contributing to Turkey's unique social face.

Religion and Cohabitation: The majority of Turkey's residents are Muslim, including both native Muslims and refugees. The country has experienced significant miscegenation, with crossbreeding and blending among various populations, such as Southern Europeans, Middle Easterners from the Caucasus Mountains, Iranians, and Mediterranean peoples. This blending has led to a wide variety of appearances among the population.

Cultural Integration: Turkish culture is an ethnic blend that generally does not distinguish or discriminate based on ethnic backgrounds. This inclusive attitude has fostered a society where cultural differences are embraced within the broader community. Contrary to the opinion that the Antichrist advocates racial domination, his regime will be all-inclusive of various ethnicities to identify with the Christ of Scripture. Instead, his regime will elevate the rich and subjugate the poor.

Minority Communities: Within Turkey's diverse society, there is a small population (14,000-16,000) of Sephardic Jews (A major Jewish ethnic group whose ancestral roots trace back to the Iberian Peninsula—Spain and Portugal) residing in Istanbul. This is an example of the diaspora, multiethnic Hebrews, scattered around the world. Notably, this community represents the largest Jewish diaspora in the Muslim world, further highlighting Turkey's multicultural identity. There is some indication that

some of the ten lost tribes will come from this location.
Continue reading ....

CHAPTER 9.

Engaging Spiritual Warfare: Authorization Phase I

Understanding Spiritual Assault—Lessons from Job: Scripture highlights a crucial awareness regarding spiritual attacks on the lives of disciples who follow the ways of the Lord along the paths of righteousness. In military terms, disciples are positioned on the front lines, making them the first to face assault.

The life of a true disciple poses a genuine threat to the devil's schemes, resulting in a spiritual "target" being placed on their backs; the enemy seeks to strike from behind, concealing his assailants. This understanding of spiritual attack is drawn from the Book of Job. When compared to real-life experiences and proactive ministry beyond church walls, it becomes clear how Job's trials mirror the challenges faced by every disciple. Extracted from Job chapters 1 through 3, there are six essential areas where attacks are targeted at disciples' humanity, aiming to weaken, hinder, and obstruct their walk of faith and their mission to dismantle spiritual strongholds and reach God's harvest with the gospel. Here, we begin our awareness of spiritual warfare as "good soldiers" of Jesus Christ, prepared for combat against spiritual wickedness by learning to recognize the following signs of attack. These signs are accompanied by a sense of good news: spiritual attack signifies that the devil fears the power of the Lord within you.

Recognizing the Signs of Spiritual Attack

Attack on Your Finances: Job endured a form of ancient bankruptcy, illustrating how attacks on finances can drain the resources needed to fulfill one's mission. Such financial hardship also introduces worry, which can undermine faith.

Attack on Your Family: Job's sons and daughters were lost when a storm destroyed their home as they celebrated together. This loss leads to grief and uncertainty, prompting questions about God's purposes and momentarily halting progress until God's intentions become clear in hindsight.

Attack on Your Health: The enemy may use natural occurrences to inflict physical pain through sudden illnesses. Job suffered from painful "sore boils" that appeared serious and debilitating. Such health challenges can pause one's journey temporarily, until the Lord brings progressive healing.

Attack through Friends and Associates: This type of attack can be particularly painful, akin to a "Judas Kiss." Friends may turn away or betray, as Job's three friends ridiculed and criticized him, suggesting he must have done something to deserve his suffering.

Attack through Your Spouse or Potential Spouse: Job's wife demeaned and seemed to abandon him, perhaps in response to his loss of material possessions and inability to provide. This behavior hints at materialistic values and adds to Job's burdens.

Attack on Reputation: Proverbs 22:1 teaches the importance of maintaining a good reputation, stating, *"A good name is rather to be chosen than great riches, and loving favor rather than silver and gold."* This verse highlights that personal integrity, and respect of others are far more valuable than any material wealth.

The adversary, often working through his emissaries, is compared to a "roaring lion" that prowls about, seeking those he can destroy by damaging their reputation (I Peter 5:8). He is also described as the "accuser of the brethren" (Revelation 12:10), constantly attempting to undermine the character and witness of believers.

This strategy is evident in how Job was accused by his friends of harboring hidden sin despite his uprightness. Similarly, the religious leaders falsely accused our Lord of blaspheming God.

These examples show that attacking one's reputation is a primary objective of the enemy, aiming to weaken or destroy the testimony and witness of the faithful.

The "Good News" is that one's reputation and purpose can be restored. Ultimately, Job's perseverance through trials led to restoration and greater blessings.

Job 42:10 states, *"And the Lord turned the captivity of Job and restored his fortunes, when he prayed for his friends; also the Lord gave Job twice as much as he had before."* The lesson for disciples is that spiritual attacks allowed by God provide opportunities for revelation and growth. In hindsight, these trials reveal their purpose, elevating one's life to greater blessings and empowering victory over the enemy. With this understanding, the process of "waging spiritual warfare" begins, starting with the first phase.

—Getting Started—

Before one can actively participate in spiritual warfare, engagement is necessary. This is similar to moving a car from neutral into drive. Believers must first be inwardly prompted by the Spirit of God and motivated, driven by a conviction of expediency. The apostle Paul, in I Corinthians 6:12 and 10:23, discusses the concept of expediency, which means choosing actions that are profitable and beneficial as priorities, especially those that build up others and promote their freedom. Spiritual warfare centers on liberating individuals from spiritual bondage from both the penalty and the power of sin. In summary, the purpose of spiritual warfare is to reach God's harvest.

Jesus also underscores the necessity of expedience in John 16:7, stating the importance of His departure so that the Holy Spirit could come. The Spirit of God empowers those who receive salvation, equipping them to serve as witnesses for the Lord. Acts 1:8 declares, *"But you shall receive power (ability, efficiency, and might) when the Holy Spirit has come upon you, and you shall be My witnesses in Jerusalem and all Judea and Samaria and to the ends (the very bounds) of the earth."*

Often, Christians search for their purpose, yet Scripture narrows it to one: being a representative for the Lord where we live, work, and play.

The Drive: The drive for reaching God's harvest comes from obeying the Great Commission and a burden of concern. Matthew 28:18-20: *"Jesus approached and, breaking the silence, said to them, All authority (all power of rule) in heaven and on earth has been given to Me. Go then and make disciples of all the nations, baptizing them into the name of the Father and of the Son and of the Holy Spirit, Teaching them to observe everything that I have commanded you, and behold, I am with you all the days (perpetually, uniformly, and on every occasion), to the [very] close and consummation of the age. Amen (so let it be)."*

The Burden of Concern for the Oppressed

The call for deep concern among God's people is clear: believers are to care (with a sense of empathy) especially for those who endure unnecessary suffering and hardship due to the oppressive actions of the wealthy and powerful. This theme is powerfully emphasized in the Book of James, notably in James 5:1-8, where the apostle delivers a solemn warning to the rich.

James directly addresses the wealthy, urging them to "weep aloud and lament over the miseries" that await them. He vividly describes the decay of their possessions—their garments becoming moth-eaten, their gold and silver corroding—as a symbol of the fleeting nature of material wealth. This imagery echoes Christ's parable of the rich fool, illustrating that wealth accumulated without regard for others is ultimately useless in the face of death. At the time of judgment, the treasures amassed by the wealthy are redistributed to the oppressed during the restitution of all things (Acts 3:21). The corrosion of riches, James explains, will stand as a testimony against the wealthy and will consume them like fire (a burning conscience) which is the reality of eternal separation from God, because they have hoarded treasures for the last days.

Retribution and Divine Justice: Human guilt and shame entertain the potential for retribution from those who have been oppressed, suggesting the possibility that the downtrodden may rise above their oppressors. However, the predictive prophecy perspective does not present this as the outcome. Instead, Scripture teaches that retribution will come as a form of self-inflicted judgment for the wealthy—a direct result of ignoring God's command to restore and care for the poor.

This principle of retribution is rooted in the biblical law of sowing and reaping. An example is found in I Timothy 6:10, where believers are warned that the love of wealth leads to corruption, described as "the root of all evil." Then, in verses 17-19, the text further encourages the rich to avoid pride and arrogance, not to place their hope in uncertain riches but in God, who generously provides for all. The wealthy are exhorted to do good, to be rich in good works, and to be generous and willing to share. In doing so, they lay up for themselves lasting riches—a solid foundation for the future, enabling them to experience true life.

James identifies a particular injustice: the fraudulent withholding of wages from laborers who have toiled in the fields. The cries of these oppressed workers have reached the ears of the Lord of hosts—Sabaoth, the God of Battles. James further condemns the rich for their pursuit of luxury and self-indulgence, likening their actions to fattening themselves for the day of slaughter. He accuses them of condemning and murdering the righteous, who do not resist their oppression.

Despite these wrongs, James urges his readers to be patient. He encourages them to wait for the coming of the Lord, using the metaphor of a farmer who patiently waits for the land to yield its valuable crop, enduring until both the early and late rains arrival. This image symbolizes the "latter rain," representing the reaping of God's harvest in the last days. In this way, believers are called to strengthen their hearts and remain steadfast, for the coming of the Lord is near.

Scriptural Examples of Bearing the Burden: The burden of concern for those who suffer is not unique to James. In Jeremiah 9:1, the prophet expresses profound sorrow for his people's suffering. Likewise, Paul reveals his anguish for his fellow Israelites in Romans 9:1-3. Most notably, Jesus Himself embodies this burden, weeping over Jerusalem and its people as recorded in Luke 19:41-44. This passage includes the shortest verse in Scripture, powerfully capturing the depth of Jesus' compassion and sorrow.

Personal Application: This personal burden of concern for the downtrodden has been a driving force throughout my ministry career. At times, it has also brought conflict with those who did not share the mission of helping the poor, underscoring the challenge and necessity of advocating for the oppressed.

Basic Training for Believers: Living for Christ

Living for Christ—Unselfish Motivation and Blessing: Scripture teaches that living for Christ involves a fundamental shift in motivation. Instead of focusing on personal gain, believers are called to live unselfishly, prioritizing the needs and well-being of others. This selfless attitude is intended to start within the family, where daily actions and sacrifices reflect a genuine commitment to Christ.

Bearing One's Cross: The practical expression of bearing one's cross is seen in the willingness to sacrifice selfish desires. By putting others first and letting go of self-centeredness, individuals follow Christ's example and fulfill His call to discipleship. Such sacrifices are not merely symbolic; they manifest in everyday choices, especially within family relationships.

Reciprocal Blessings: According to Scripture, God rewards those who live unselfishly with reciprocal blessings. When believers bear their cross and serve others, God compensates their sacrifices with spiritual and practical rewards. This cycle of blessing reinforces the importance of living for Christ by serving others, beginning at home.

The Church is not merely a body of believers waiting to go to heaven. The Church should be actively engaged in bringing others with it to heaven. As such, the Church is God's agency through whom the Spirit of God works to bring about the Kingdom of God on Earth. For that to happen, there is a simple strategy that God has given believers called commandments. Reaching others for Christ hinges on one word, commandment. When we obey God's word, God honors His word with results. A good analogy is of a good soldier obeying the commands of the commanding general to press forward in spiritual battle, "storming the gates of hell" and rescuing Satan's POWs.

Every person who joins the military must first complete basic training, a process designed to determine if they are fit to serve as a soldier. Similarly, believers must undergo their own spiritual basic training. The Apostle Paul writes in II Timothy 2:3-4, *"Take [with me] your share of the hardships and suffering [which you are called to endure] as a good (first-class) soldier of Christ Jesus. No soldier when in service gets entangled in the enterprises of [civilian] life; his aim is to satisfy and please the one who enlisted him."* This passage highlights the importance of focusing solely on one's spiritual calling, without becoming distracted by worldly concerns and compromise.

No soldier, when in service, compromises by dividing his attention between the church and worldly activities. In church terminology, this would be described as being "on the fence," or undecided in commitment—living like the world when around unsaved people and living like you are saved around saved people. That is called hypocrisy. James 1:6-8 explains that a sound, made-up mind is necessary: *"Only it must be in faith that he asks with no wavering (no hesitating, no doubting). For the one who wavers (hesitates, doubts) is like the billowing surge out at sea that is blown hither and thither and tossed by the wind. For truly, let not such a person imagine that he will receive anything [he asks for] from the Lord, [For being as he is] a man of two minds (hesitating, dubious, irresolute), [he is] unstable and unreliable and uncertain about everything [he thinks, feels, decides]."*

Discipline in Basic Training

For believers, basic training is ultimately about discipline. Scripture presents discipline as a twofold process:

- Bearing Our Cross: This means sacrificing selfishness and putting God's will first.

- Bringing "Self" Under Christ's Authority: This requires submitting our desires and actions to Jesus Christ.

The practical outcome of bearing our cross and submitting to Christ's authority is an adjustment of lifestyle. When we revisit II Timothy 2:3-4, we see that basic training for a believer means living for Christ.

Living for Christ might sound narrow or restrictive to those who have not explored God's word deeply, but in reality, it is quite the opposite. Jesus promises "an abundant life," as stated in John 10:10: *"The thief comes only to steal and kill and destroy. I came that they may have and enjoy life, and have it in abundance (to the full, till it [b]overflows)."* Living for Christ means experiencing a full and overflowing life, marked by exponential blessings that come from faithful stewardship and service to God. These blessings provide resources and enable a better quality of life, but they are contingent on living for the Lord.

Importantly, living for the Lord is not about religious rules, legalism, or self-righteousness. I reiterate that it is about loving God, loving ourselves, loving our neighbors, and loving all others. Romans 13 teaches that walking in love fulfills all ten of the Moral Law Commandments. That is all the Lord requires, and His requirements are not burdensome.

Christ's Invitation to Rest

In Matthew 11:28-30, Jesus extends an invitation to everyone who feels weary and burdened:

"Come to Me, all you who labor and are heavy-laden and overburdened, and I will cause you to rest. [I will ease and relieve and refresh your souls.] Take My yoke upon you and

learn of Me, for I am gentle (meek) and humble (lowly) in heart, and you will find rest (relief and ease and refreshment and recreation and blessed quiet) for your souls. For My yoke is wholesome (useful, good—not harsh, hard, sharp, or pressing, but comfortable, gracious, and pleasant), and My burden is light and easy to be borne."

Learning Life Lessons Through Faith and Challenge

Basic training for believers is about discipline, commitment, and adjusting one's lifestyle to live for Christ and experience the fullness of life that He promises.

Adjusting one's lifestyle can be a difficult and often painful process. I learned this lesson firsthand through my own walk of faith with the Lord. For thirty-three years, I committed myself wholeheartedly to living for the Lord and serving in ministry. However, in 2007, my relationship with the church was severely tested. I became deeply disillusioned due to what I perceived as unjustified criticism and persecution directed at me and a disdain for reaching the poor. I expressed my faith perspective as spiritual and not religious and experienced more criticism. This experience led me to resign from the pastorate and step away from church attendance altogether for five years.

Experiencing Hardships and Spiritual Attack: During those five years away from the church, I encountered what I felt were unnecessary and unprovoked hardships. In reflection, I recognized that I had opened myself up to spiritual attack by distancing myself from the church body. Despite these challenges, I never placed blame on God for the actions of others. Instead, I recognized my need to repent for my attitude toward the church. Through repentance, the Lord delivered and renewed me, allowing my life to get back on track through involvement with churches via consulting.

The Danger of Divided Allegiances: This experience taught me the importance of wholehearted commitment in my faith journey. When we try to balance having one foot in the church and one foot in the world, we make ourselves vulnerable to the enemy's attacks. This was a lesson I had to learn the hard way. We can choose to learn difficult lessons by living in a way that is not pleasing to the Lord, or we can choose the easier path—living a life that honors Him.

The Role of Conscience and Spiritual Guidance: Determining what is pleasing to the Lord often comes down to the convictions of our conscience. When we act against our conscience, especially when it warns us against wrongdoing through God's Spirit, we experience negative consequences—the hard way. Alternatively, by following the guidance of our heart, inspired by the Spirit of God, we can respond positively: saying "Yes" to the Lord when our conscience affirms that we are on the right path, and "No" when we are headed in the wrong direction.

I John 3:19-23: *By this we shall come to know (perceive, recognize, and understand) that we are of the Truth, and can reassure (quiet, conciliate, and pacify) our hearts in His presence,*

Whenever our hearts in [tormenting] self-accusation make us feel guilty and condemn us. [For we are in God's hands.] For He is above and greater than our consciences (our hearts), and He knows (perceives and understands) everything [nothing is hidden from Him].

And, beloved, if our consciences (our hearts) do not accuse us [if they do not make us feel guilty and condemn us], we have confidence (complete assurance and boldness) before God,

And we receive from Him whatever we ask, because we [watchfully] obey His orders [observe His suggestions and injunctions, follow His plan for us] and [habitually] practice what is pleasing to Him.

Inviting and Yielding: Welcoming the Lord into Every Area of Life

Inviting the Lord into our hearts as our personal Savior and Lord is foundational to Christian faith, as referenced in Revelation 3:20. However, this invitation extends beyond our initial commitment; it also means welcoming God into the everyday circumstances and decisions that shape our lives. Unlike human interference, which can be intrusive, God's involvement is characterized by wisdom and compassion. He is fully aware of our situations and works to protect us from adversity and restore our dignity, doing so discreetly without exposing our personal matters to others.

Beyond our individual lives, Scripture encourages us to invite God into the broader affairs of government, politics, religion, and society, especially during times of widespread oppression or heaviness over the land. This invitation is outlined in the call of II Chronicles 7:14: *"If My people, who are called by My name, shall humble themselves, pray, seek, crave, and require of necessity My face and turn from their wicked ways, then will I hear from heaven, forgive their sin, and heal their land."* This passage emphasizes several distinct actions: humility, seeking God's presence, turning away from wrongdoing, resulting in answered prayer, forgiveness, and healing for the community.

Yielding to the Lord's Guidance: Yielding to God involves ongoing choices about what influences our hearts. Scripture often refers to the heart in two senses: as the "soul," which is the seat of our passions, emotions, desires, and will—the self-conscious part of our being; and as the "spirit," the God-conscious part, where we commune with God through the indwelling of the Holy Spirit. This distinction creates a tension within us, as described in Galatians 5:17, where the desires of the flesh (human nature) and the Spirit are set in opposition. The passage highlights that these forces are antagonistic, resulting in an internal conflict that challenges our freedom to simply do as we wish. Ultimately, it is the believer's responsibility to choose whether to yield to the "old nature" or the "new nature" shaped by the Spirit.

Scriptural Instruction on Yielding: Romans 6:13 offers practical guidance for followers of Christ regarding yielding: *"Do not continue offering or yielding your bodily members and faculties to sin as instruments (tools) of wickedness. But offer and yield yourselves to God as though you have been raised from the* *dead to [perpetual] life, and your bodily members and faculties to God, presenting them as implements of righteousness."*

Through the empowering work of God's Spirit—referred to as "Dunamis," the power and ability of the liberating gospel in Romans 1:16—believers are equipped to resist the pull of the flesh and instead yield to the Spirit. This empowerment means that we are without excuse in our ability to live according to God's will. Romans 1:16 declares, *"For I am not ashamed of the Gospel (good news) of Christ, for it is God's power working unto salvation [for deliverance from eternal death] to everyone who believes with a personal trust and a confident surrender and firm reliance, to the Jew first and also to the Greek."*

A Practical Analogy: Yielding to the Lord can be compared to approaching a yield sign while driving. This signals us to slow down and be prepared to stop if necessary. In life, when we sense that something is approaching that could lead us into difficulty or danger, we are wise to slow down, stop, and invite God's grace to guide us—allowing Him to help us change direction and avoid trouble. This practical approach to yielding underscores the importance of being attentive to God's presence and promptings in every situation, allowing Him to direct our paths for our good and His glory.

Benefits of Yielding: Exploring II Chronicles 7:14

The principle of yielding, as seen in the Old Testament, is deeply rooted in the practice of covenants and sacrificial offerings. Through worship, the people of Israel invited the Lord into their lives and circumstances, choosing to surrender to His will by engaging in sacrificial worship and genuine repentance. This act of yielding provided a means for God's presence to dwell among them and for His guidance to shape their lives. As we reflect on this, it becomes essential to consider the message found in II Chronicles 7:14.

II Chronicles 7:14 stands as a timeless promise from God, originally directed to ancient Israel but frequently referenced in contemporary faith communities. The verse highlights the importance of collective repentance, an intentional pursuit of God's presence, and a commitment to turn away from sin—steps that lead to both national and personal restoration. While interpretations of this verse may differ today, its foundational message remains significant.

Breakdown of the Verse

- "If my people, who are called by my name..."

This phrase identifies God's chosen people—Israel in its original context—who are set apart and known by their relationship with Him. In modern applications, this often refers to followers of Christ who embrace this identity.

- "...shall humble themselves..."

Humility is essential. It involves acknowledging personal and collective sin, recognizing God's authority, and setting aside pride to submit to Him fully.

- "...and pray..."

Prayer is the means of communication with God. Through prayer, believers seek His guidance and bring their needs and concerns before Him.

- "...and seek my face..."

Seeking God's face expresses a desire for a close, personal relationship with Him. It goes beyond requesting blessings, focusing instead on pursuing His presence and direction.

- "...and turn from their wicked ways..."

Genuine repentance is required—this means actively abandoning sinful behaviors and making a conscious decision to pursue righteousness.

- "...then I will hear from heaven..."

God responds to these actions by attentively listening to the prayers of His people.

- "...and will forgive their sin..."

Forgiveness is a key aspect of restoration, as God removes both the guilt and shame and the penalty of sin.

- "...and will heal their land."

In its original setting, this promise involved the restoration of tangible blessings—such as rain, fruitful harvests, and protection from calamity. For many today, it represents a broader hope for moral, spiritual, or even national renewal and healing.

Embracing Kingdom Concepts in Evangelism & Discipleship

When engaging in spiritual warfare, one must stay focused and steadfast on the opportunities that God puts before us to reach His harvest.

As we move forward in this work, and particularly as we approach the *Conclusion,* our focus centers on the integration of "Kingdom Concepts: Evangelism & Discipleship." At the heart of this journey lies the understanding that a believer's lifestyle is best described as a daily walk of faith.

Living Each Day by Faith; Matthew 6:34 offers profound guidance for the believer's daily life. In paraphrased form, Jesus encourages us, "Take no thought for tomorrow, for tomorrow shall take thought of the things of itself." This teaching draws attention to the inevitable difficulties and troubles that arise in everyday life. The practical interpretation of these words is an invitation to live intentionally in the present, trusting God each day, since the future remains unknown to us. By doing so, we acknowledge that every day is filled with both new opportunities and unique challenges.

Perseverance Amidst Challenges: As we continue to develop this work, our motivation is to press forward, regardless of the obstacles we encounter. It is essential to remember this foundational principle: when God opens a door, no one can shut it; conversely, when God shuts a door, no one can open it.

If our well-considered and prayerful plans seem unfulfilled, it should not be taken as a sign that God has ignored our prayers. Instead, it becomes our responsibility to discern the meaning behind God's answers or His apparent silence. God also answers in silence, which means a resounding NO. But a silent answer isn't always no. Sometimes it means waiting. If that's the case, we should take the first steps to go through the door. When faced with such challenges, it is advisable to examine where the door leads. If it is closed, develop plans A, B, and C and continue pressing toward the opportunity before you.

CHAPTER 10.

Spiritual Prayer Warriors: Authorization Phase II

When we are engaged in battle, the term "wage" signifies an ongoing struggle—a conflict that unfolds over time and requires persistent fighting. In the context of spiritual warfare, it is crucial to remember that the "battle (fight) is the Lord's," yet we are not passive bystanders; we have a part to play in the process.

The Lord's Stance and Our Role: The dynamic between God's intervention and our responsibility is clearly illustrated in Exodus 14:13-14: *"Moses told the people, Fear not; stand still (firm, confident, undismayed) and see the salvation of the Lord which He will work for you today. For the Egyptians you have seen today, you shall never see again. The Lord will fight for you, and you shall hold your peace and remain at rest."*

Application for Today: Practically speaking, this passage is relevant in modern times when God's people, following God's promise, encounter an impasse—a place where there appears to be no way forward. For the Hebrews, it came in the form of the raging Red Sea, a tangible obstacle that stood between them and the Promised Land. This sea represented an overwhelming challenge that defied human reasoning.

Today, such obstacles can manifest as closed doors—situations that naturally resist our efforts to progress. Under God's guidance, a closed door is not the end; it signifies that God is opening another way. Our responsibility is to follow the "cloud," which refers to being led by God's Spirit within us.

Our first recourse is to "rest in the Lord"—to hold our peace, stop complaining, and trust the Lord to create a path forward.

This means allowing God to authorize His angels to overcome the spiritual forces blocking our way and to fight our battles on our behalf. When spiritual battle is conducted on your behalf, God can open the closed door or lead you to another door.

Concerning the first option, God's opening closed doors requires persistence from us, meaning examining why the door was closed and making our case for it to reopen. If that fails, the latter is necessary: finding the new door by embracing a new opportunity that you may not have considered before.

Standing Still with Purpose: Therefore, to hold our peace and stand still in a crisis does not mean we do nothing. The battle is not in vain; it is fought for our deliverance and for the deliverance of God's people who are impacted by the outcome. When we yield ourselves to the Lord, we are pledging our allegiance to His cause, trusting that He will bring us through the challenge.

Prayer: In the Spirit, Private, and Collective

Prayer in the Spirit refers to a directive for heartfelt prayer, emphasizing the need for communication with God from the human spirit (God-consciousness), rather than from the self-consciousness or soul expressed through our five senses, focused on superficial, materialistic concerns.

This approach centers on seeking God first and practicing effectual, fervent prayer. However, we should not be dismayed by the words "effectual" and "fervent" in prayer as if we should be proficient, articulate, and ardent in prayer. In simplicity, all prayer is talking to God, as if talking to another person, from the heart in plain language. Such prayer is considered a prescription for divine intervention in life's affairs, as highlighted in II Chronicles 7:14, and is essential for overcoming evil.

God's intervention, as with Abraham, occurs in at least three ways: when humanity self-destructs (Genesis 6), when humanity perverts itself (Romans 1), or when God's Covenant People invite and yield to His will (II Chronicles 7:14).

The battle between good and evil is ultimately the Lord's fight, and spiritual warfare in the heavenly realms has a profound impact on governments, politics, religion, and society, as described in Ephesians 6:10-12. The Church must awaken to this reality, recognizing that prophetic times have arrived unexpectedly. Like Elijah, believers are called to pray consistently and persistently each day until God's intervention is evident. As James 5:16 states, *"Confess your faults one to another, and pray one for another, that ye may be healed. The effectual fervent prayer of a righteous man availeth much."*

Private Personal Prayer—Guidelines for Sincere Prayer

The Model Perfect Prayer Prescription from the Lord: Private personal prayer involves seeking details and guidance from the Lord in a secluded or quiet space, away from distractions. If it is not possible to find such a place or pray at designated times, one should pray whenever and wherever possible, even if only uttering a prayer in one's mind and spirit. An example for an opening prayer might be, "Lord, I join my faith with those who are praying, and trust Your word associated with the prayer petitions."

The posture or location of prayer is less important than its essential nature—communion with God. Matthew 6:6-15 provides instructions for private prayer:

- When you pray, do not imitate the behavior of hypocrites. They enjoy praying while standing in synagogues and on street corners, hoping to be noticed by others. Such people have already received their reward through the attention they seek. Instead, when you pray, seek out your most private room. Close the door and speak to your unseen Father. Your Father, who observes what happens in secret, will reward you openly.

- Avoid repeating phrases or multiplying words, as some Gentiles do. They believe they will be heard because of their many words, but you should not be like them. Your Father knows what you need before you even ask.

- Pray in this manner: Our Father Who is in heaven, hallowed be Your name. Worship and praise God for His goodness and salvation as you enter into prayer.

- Father, your will be done on earth, in my life, and in the lives of others for the salvation of the soul, as it is in heaven. Bring your kingdom to pass according to your divine sovereign will.

- We ask for our daily bread, trusting in God's provision for our everyday needs. Along with our request for sustenance, we seek forgiveness for our debts, just as we have forgiven those indebted to us. This act of forgiveness involves leaving behind resentment, forgiving what others owe us, and letting go of any bitterness toward those who have wronged us.

- The Prayer of Forgiveness and Deliverance. If we forgive others for their trespasses—their reckless and willful sins, letting them go and giving up resentment—our heavenly Father will also forgive us. However, if we do not forgive others, neither will our Father forgive our own trespasses. This highlights the necessity of forgiveness in our relationship with God and with others.

- Guidance and Protection: We pray not to be led into temptation, but to be delivered from the evil one. In this, we acknowledge God's authority and power to protect us from harm. The prayer concludes by affirming that the kingdom, power, and glory belong to God forever. Amen.

Collective Group Prayer

The Power of United Prayer: United prayer is significant because it draws strength from the collective unity of believers. When many people come together to pray, the combined faith and agreement amplify the impact of their petitions. This unity is not just about gathering in numbers, but also about being in agreement and tying our prayers to faith in the cause of Christ.

Agreement and Intent in Prayer: For united prayer to be truly effective, those participating must pray about the same things.

It is important to pray both in the spirit and with understanding, often through petitions that have been thoughtfully prepared in advance. This intentional approach ensures that the group remains focused and aligned in purpose.

Biblical Mandate for Group Prayer: Scripture provides clear guidance for collective group prayer. The passage from James 5:13-18 highlights several key mandates:

- If anyone is suffering or afflicted, they should pray.

- If someone is joyful, they should sing praises to God.

- If anyone is sick, they should call upon the church elders to pray over them and anoint them with oil in the Lord's name.

- The prayer offered in faith will save the sick, and the Lord will restore them. Any sins committed will be forgiven.

- Believers are encouraged to confess their faults to one another and pray for each other, leading to healing and restoration of mind and heart.

- Heartfelt and persistent prayer from a righteous person has great power and is effective.

The Example of Elijah: James cites Elijah as an example of the effectiveness of earnest prayer. Although Elijah was a human being with emotions and weaknesses like everyone else, his fervent prayers led to remarkable outcomes. He prayed that it would not rain, and it did not rain for three and a half years. Later, he prayed again, and rain returned, resulting in the land producing crops as usual.

Understanding What It Means to "Pray in the Spirit"

Engaging in spiritual warfare requires a particular kind of prayer—prayer in the Spirit. The Scriptures, specifically Ephesians 6:10-17, describe the armor a spiritual soldier must wear to stand strong against spiritual adversaries. However, this description does not end with the armor itself; it culminates in a call to prayer.

In verse 18, the apostle Paul instructs believers to *"pray at all times (on every occasion, in every season) in the Spirit, with all [manner of] prayer and entreaty."* This exhortation highlights the necessity of continual, Spirit-led prayer as an essential part of spiritual readiness and defense.

The Call to Vigilance and Intercession: Paul further emphasizes that believers must remain alert and persistent, watching with strong purpose and perseverance. This vigilance is not just for oneself but includes interceding on behalf of all the saints—God's consecrated people. Such prayer is both a discipline and a weapon in the spiritual realm, ensuring that the spiritual community is covered and supported through every season and circumstance.

Whether one believes it or not, the events unfolding in our world are the results of "Spiritual Warfare" occurring in the heavenly realms. The encouraging truth, however, is that this battle belongs to the Lord; it is not ours to fight alone. Victory is not determined by the strength of numbers on our side, but by the presence and power of God. Even if we are few, there are more in the heavenlies for us than against us. I John 4:4, *"Little children, you are of God [you belong to Him] and have [already] defeated and overcome them [the agents of the antichrist], because He Who lives in you is greater (mightier) than he who is in the world."*

An example of this reality can be found in II Kings 6:16-17: *"[Elisha] answered, Fear not; for those with us are more than those with them. Then Elisha prayed, Lord, I pray You, open his eyes that he may see. And the Lord opened the young man's eyes, and he saw, and behold, the mountain was full of horses and chariots of fire round about Elisha."* This passage highlights that although we may appear outnumbered in the physical world, in the spiritual realm—where true battles take place—God's forces outnumber the opposition.

The Power of a Few in Prayer: This principle demonstrates that vast numbers of believers are not required to overcome seemingly overwhelming odds. The strength and victory come from God's presence and intervention, not the size of the praying group. One example is found in Judges 7:2-3:

The Lord spoke to Gideon, warning him that the number of people with him was too great for Him to deliver the Midianites into their hands. The concern was that Israel might claim credit for their victory, boasting, "My own hand has delivered me," instead of acknowledging God's intervention. In verse 3, Gideon was instructed to proclaim to the men, "Whoever is fearful and trembling, let him turn back and depart from Mount Gilead." As a result, 22,000 men returned home, leaving only 10,000 who remained with Gideon. Ultimately, Gideon's army was reduced to just 300 men, facing an overwhelming multitude of Midianites.

The phrase "one shall put to flight many" or "one man putting a thousand to flight" appears in several scripture passages, such as Joshua 23:10, Leviticus 26:8, and Deuteronomy 32:30. These verses recount the Israelites' remarkable military victories, made possible because God fought for them. Through His power, a small number of faithful individuals could overcome much larger enemy forces. These examples underscore that with God on our side, even a minority can prevail against overwhelming opposition.

Prayer in the Spirit: Exploring "Unknown Tongues"

Understanding Prayer in the Spirit: Prayer in the spirit is a vital element of God's armor, but one of the most misunderstood and neglected prayer components in Scripture.

The apostle Paul, in I Corinthians 14:15, encourages believers to pray both in "unknown tongues" and with their natural language: *"Then what am I to do? I will pray with my spirit [by the Holy Spirit that is within me], but I will also pray [intelligently] with my mind and understanding; I will sing with my spirit [by the*

Holy Spirit that is within me], but I will sing [intelligently] with my mind and understanding also."

This dual approach to prayer and worship has sparked considerable debate, particularly in light of cessationist theology, which questions the legitimacy of "unknown tongues."

Paul wrote I Corinthians around 55–57 AD while in Ephesus during his third missionary journey, approximately 24 years after Pentecost. To assess the legitimacy of unknown tongues, it is valuable to connect the relevant passages of Scripture.

Glossolalia—The Phenomenon of Tongues: The term "tongues," derived from the Greek word glossolalia, is a compound of glōssais/glossa (tongues) and lalien (languages), meaning "to speak." From Scripture, tongues can be categorized into three forms: the phenomenon of tongues at Pentecost, unknown tongues at Corinth, and personal individuals with tongues.

The Phenomenon of Tongues at Pentecost

The saying, "If Scripture sense makes common sense, seek no other sense," provides a straightforward approach to understanding the purpose of tongues at Pentecost. This principle suggests that the events described should be interpreted in the depth of the original meaning, where it tells the story behind the story of Scripture in plain language, the place where we will explore "unknown tongues."

The event of Pentecost, as described in Acts 2:1-4, marks a significant moment in Christian history. The passage recounts how, when the day of Pentecost arrived, all the believers were gathered together in one place. Suddenly, a sound from heaven, like the rushing of a violent tempest, filled the entire room where they sat.

The Manifestation of Tongues: A spiritual phenomenon appeared unseen by the natural eye during this remarkable event; tongues resembling fire appeared, separated, and settled on each of those present. The believers were all filled with the Holy Spirit, which diffused throughout their souls. This infilling led them to speak in different languages, foreign tongues—as the Spirit enabled them to do so. The Spirit provided them with clear and loud expressions in each tongue, using appropriate words for each language.

The Nature of Glossolalia: An important consideration in understanding this phenomenon is the nature of glossolalia or speaking in tongues. The question arises: were these tongues legitimate, recognizable languages spoken in the world, or were they unknown, unidentifiable languages? This distinction is crucial, especially when examining the transliteration of tongues from a Creation Science perspective.

The Role of the Holy Spirit in Communication: It is noted that the Holy Spirit not only enabled the speakers to communicate in different languages but also adjusted the hearing of the audience. This suggests that the miracle of Pentecost involved both the articulation of language by the speakers and the comprehension by the listeners. The combined effects ensured that the message was clearly understood by all present, regardless of their native language.

The Miracle of Tongues at Pentecost

Divine Intervention in Language: The event of Pentecost showcases a profound miracle involving the human brain and divine intervention. The Holy Spirit specifically anointed the frontal lobe—responsible for speech and writing, notably Broca's area—enabling the 120 disciples to speak languages they had never learned. Simultaneously, the Holy Spirit influenced the parietal lobe, which interprets language and words, in the minds of over 3,000 listeners. This allowed the vast crowd, composed of pilgrims from diverse nations gathered in Jerusalem, to hear and understand the message in their native languages.

Under normal human circumstances, it would be utterly impossible for such a large and diverse audience to decipher messages spoken in their own tongues, given the chaos and multitude present during the celebration of Pentecost. Moreover, it would be equally impossible for the 120 disciples to simultaneously speak every language and dialect represented in the crowd. It would be confusing and chaotic.

The variety of nations and dialects present—including both specifically enumerated groups and more general categories like Proselytes—created an environment where human communication alone could not produce such clarity and understanding. Therefore, only a miracle of divine intervention could make this possible. This event stands as evidence that spiritual gifts, including speaking in tongues, are themselves acts of divine intervention.

Biblical Foundation of Tongues at Pentecost: Scriptural evidence leaves no doubt that the tongues spoken at Pentecost were legitimate and diverse languages, described elsewhere as "another tongue." Isaiah 28:11 states, *"Indeed, He will speak to this people through stammering lips and a foreign tongue."* In this context, tongues serve as a prophetic sign fulfilling the Covenant Promise, spoken through the Assyrian language. The reference to "stammering lips" points to ecstatic speech, while "another tongue" refers specifically to the language of the Assyrians, who were historically Israel's enemies.

This prophecy signified that, due to Israel's disobedience to the covenant, God would get their attention through communication from a people outside the covenant. The passage further emphasizes God's intent to provoke His people to jealousy and to demonstrate, through startling proof, that He kept His promise to the patriarchs. Ellicott's Commentary explains that the "stammering lips" belonged to Assyrian conquerors, whose speech sounded barbarous and foreign to the people of Judah. These conquerors, with their abrupt commands, were the next voice of Jehovah for those who ignored the prophets. This description reappears in Isaiah 33:19 and is later referenced in I Corinthians 14:21, where the gift of tongues is considered unintelligible to listeners, much like the speech of foreign conquerors.

In summary, the miracle of tongues at Pentecost can be understood in two primary ways. First, the assembled Jews at Pentecost heard the 120 disciples from the Upper Room speak in the ancient Assyrian language—the tongue of their traditional enemies. This served as a mockery, signaling that because Israel had not obeyed the covenant, God would communicate with them through a despised people who were not covenant recipients. Today, the historical homeland of the Assyrians encompasses areas in northern Iraq, southeastern Turkey, northwestern Iran, and northeastern Syria, but the language is extinct.

Second, the outpouring of God's presence in the Upper Room spilled out into the streets, resulting in the anointing of the 120 disciples. This miracle enabled the multitude of Jews and Proselytes from every nation to hear the message in their native dialects, all concerning the wonderful works of God. Thus, the phenomenon of tongues at Pentecost, as well as during three other outpourings in the Book of Acts, served as a sign that the recipients had been received into the Body of Christ—the Covenant Community.

Learning to Pray in the Spirit

The Church at Corinth demonstrated a passionate desire for spiritual gifts, seeking the experience of speaking in tongues as described in the Book of Acts. This longing for spiritual manifestation continued into the early 20th Century, particularly in 1905, when believers earnestly sought to speak in tongues that were honored by God. This collective yearning led to the birth of the Pentecostal movement. Today, believers have the opportunity to experience the same spiritual phenomena based on their personal desire.

The Edifying Power of Prayer in the Spirit: Regardless of personal beliefs about the legitimacy of speaking in tongues in the present day, the practice of praying in the spirit remains a source of spiritual edification. According to John 14:26 in the King James Version, the Holy Spirit is identified as the Comforter:

"But the Comforter, which is the Holy Ghost, whom the Father will send in my name, he shall teach you all things, and bring all things to your remembrance, whatsoever I have said unto you." The Greek term "Paraklétos," translated as Comforter, encompasses meanings such as advocate, intercessor, helper, consoler, and counselor. The influence of the Holy Spirit on the human spirit during prayer—especially when speaking in tongues—acts as a counselor, encouraging and strengthening believers mentally and emotionally by emboldening their faith.

Biblical Perspective on Speaking in Tongues: The passage from I Corinthians 14:2, 4 provides a foundational understanding of the phenomenon of speaking in tongues within the Christian context. The Apostle Paul's discussion offers valuable insights into the purpose and effects of this spiritual practice.

Speaking in Tongues: Communication with God

Understanding "Mystery" in the Greek Context: In the Greek language, the term "mystery" refers to something unknowable or concealed, accessible only through revelation from God. This concept underscores the profound nature of spiritual truths that are hidden and can only be understood when God chooses to reveal them.

The Meaning of "Edifies" in I Corinthians 14:4: The word "edifies" found in verse 4 is a transliteration of the Greek word oikodomeó. This term is derived from the word "edifice," which means to erect a building. In the spiritual context, it refers to the building up of character in Christ and the act of encouraging others. Thus, the act of speaking in tongues is seen as a mysterious way to build up one's character in Christ and to provide encouragement, resulting in mental and emotional upliftment.

Paul's Exposition on Tongues: Paul's detailed explanation of speaking in tongues in I Corinthians 14 provides a deeper understanding of this phenomenon, as initially described in the Book of Acts. His exposition helps clarify the role and significance of tongues within the Christian experience.

The Emphasis on the Human Spirit: Paul's writings place particular emphasis on the "spirit"—not with a capital "S" referring to the Holy Spirit, but with a lowercase "s," indicating the human spirit. This is seen in conjunction with the concept of praying "in the spirit." Speaking in tongues is thus described as the prayer language of the human spirit, which is inspired by the Holy Spirit.

Understanding Speaking in Tongues: Biblical Context and Interpretation

Speaking in tongues, often described as an ecstatic and unintelligible utterance, has long been considered an "unknown" phenomenon as noted in I Corinthians 14. There is an ongoing debate about whether these utterances were ever identified as Assyrian language. For the Jewish community at Pentecost, tongues served as a prophetic sign that the Covenant Promise made to Abraham and the other patriarchs was being fulfilled.

The Promise of the Father: During Pentecost, Jesus instructed his followers not to leave Jerusalem but to wait for the promise from the Father. He said, *"Of which you have heard Me speak. For John baptized with water, but you will be baptized and empowered and united with the Holy Spirit, not long from now."* (Acts 1:4-5). This promise, referred to as the indwelling of the Holy Spirit, was foretold in Jeremiah 31:31-33 and reiterated by Peter in Acts 2:38-39. The significance of this indwelling was the transformation of God's Moral Law from being engraved on stone to being written on the hearts of believers, making the human body God's temple rather than a physical structure.

Tongues in Corinth: Paul's letter to the Corinthian Church was written approximately 24 years after Pentecost, placing the meaning of "unknown tongues" in a different context from the glossolalia experienced at Pentecost. By this time, the sign of tongues was no longer necessary, as the Church had been established throughout the known world.

Some commentators contend that the translators of the King James Version of the Bible added "unknown" in *italics* to the margins of the text as a side note because it was not in the original text, or they did not understand the meaning and conformed it to standard English. Other translations, like the New American Standard Bible (NASB), left out the italicized word "unknown" because it was not in the original manuscript. It simply reads in the NASB, *"For one who speaks in a tongue does not speak to men but to God; for no one understands, but in his spirit he speaks mysteries."*

The Phenomenon of Glossolalia—Biblical Foundations and Practice: The concept of "glossolalia," commonly referred to as speaking in tongues, is rooted in the biblical passages of Acts 2:4, I Corinthians 12:7, and I Corinthians 14:2. This etymology underlines the unity of meaning in each passage where the phenomenon is mentioned, suggesting that the languages spoken were consistent and unknown to the speakers.

Biblical Evidence of Unknown Tongues: An examination of the relevant biblical texts reveals that the crucial aspect of unknown tongues is not the specific language being spoken, but rather the interpretation of that language.

In Acts 2, where the event of speaking in tongues first occurs, the phenomenon may have appeared as unintelligible speech or gibberish to those outside the Covenant Community. However, through the work of the Holy Spirit, these tongues became intelligible to individuals entering the Covenant Community through interpretation. Historically, tongues served as a sign for unbelievers, not believers. The legitimacy of the phenomenon was established through interpretation, rather than the use of a well-known language.

The Prophetic Foundation: The original mention of speaking in tongues is found in Isaiah 28:11: *"No, but [the Lord will teach the rebels in a more humiliating way] by men with stammering lips and another tongue will He speak to this people [says Isaiah and teach them His lessons]."* This prophecy is further referenced by Paul in I Corinthians 14:21: *"It is written in the Law, By men of strange languages and by the lips of foreigners will I speak to this people, and not even then will they listen to Me, says the Lord."* These passages establish the axiom that God would communicate to His Covenant Community, Israel, in an unknown language, made understandable through interpretation.

It is important to distinguish between translation and interpretation. Translation involves converting one language into another, whereas interpretation of tongues refers to understanding an unknown language without prior knowledge of it. Interpretation may involve conveying a long message in a short phrase, or vice versa.

Individualized Speaking in Tongues: Speaking in tongues is unlike legitimate languages that are unique to the person. Speaking in tongues, like spirituality, is unique to each believer and is expressed through the human spirit; it may sound similar to others or different, and it changes for individuals speaking in tongues.

It is undeniable that glossolalia exists today; otherwise, we cast aside genuine believers as just as illegitimate as the tongues they speak in. Tongues today, as experienced then, continue as unknown languages expressed by the human spirit under the anointing of the Holy Spirit as a result of the ecstatic groanings, or language of the human spirit. Romans 8:26-27:

So too the [Holy] Spirit comes to our aid and bears us up in our weakness; for we do not know what prayer to offer nor how to offer it worthily as we ought, but the Spirit Himself goes to meet our supplication and pleads in our behalf with unspeakable yearnings and groanings too deep for utterance.

And He Who searches the hearts of men knows what is in the mind of the [Holy] Spirit [what His intent is], because the Spirit intercedes and pleads [before God] in behalf of the saints according to and in harmony with God's will.

The conclusion drawn from these observations is that anyone "In Christ" can speak in tongues if they desire to do so. Believers are encouraged to desire spiritual gifts.

Practical Application—Speaking in Tongues: For any believer, speaking in tongues begins with a desire. But first, one must make sure that they are in Christ by reaffirming their faith. The process involves uttering words that originate in the mind and speaking to them aloud. Once the first words are spoken, a fluent flow of language follows under the anointing of the Holy Spirit. From that point onward, the believer can speak in tongues at will, much like turning on a faucet. Paul referenced his consistent dependence on praying in tongues in I Corinthians 14:18, "I thank God that I speak in [strange] tongues (languages) more than any of you *or* all of you put together." Some interpret this as legitimate languages because the apostle, out of scholarship, spoke several languages, but the prefix is on "unknown." Regularly praying in the spirit is encouraged, as it serves as a personal prayer language.

CHAPTER 11.

Mobilizing Spiritual Warfare: Authorization Phase III

The Body of Christ, commonly referred to as the Church, is God's mobile agency of reconciliation on earth—bringing people into a relationship with God through Christ, and reconciling differences between them—encompassing cross-cultural reconciliation, a mandate of the Great Commission (Matthew 28:18-20).

The Church isn't a static, stagnant institution. She, the Bride of Christ, is a mobile network of believers connecting through prayer and strategizing outreach to reach those in need of Christ and humanitarian services (Matthew 25).

The Hebrews were mobilized in the sense of proactive involvement in the world through "Shema" to love their neighbors and strangers and to assimilate them into the nation of Israel. But they failed God's divine providence out of pre-ordination to bring salvation to the Gentiles. The Early Church engaged and won by establishing God's Church. In each case, God's call is to reconcile the world to Him, "the" mandate of the gospel.

The parable of the Good Samaritan, recorded in Luke 10:25-37, is a symbolic portrayal of the Church, Jew, and Gentile reconciled in one body, traveling the roads least traveled and stopping by those less loved, lifting, carrying, caring, healing, and reviving. It is a true-to-life story of what it means to evangelize and disciple the world.

Prelude

There is ample evidence in history and the sciences of anthropology and archeology that verifies the authenticity of the historic Christ and the Early Church. However, aside from any physical evidence, a believer's faith in God's Word is their evidence. Hebrews 11:1, *"Now faith is the assurance (the confirmation, the title deed) of the things [we] hope for, being the proof of things [we] do not see and the conviction of their reality [faith perceiving as real fact what is not revealed to the senses]."* Spiritual believers' life journey becomes the experience that substantiates their faith with assurance. Consequently, they live and walk by faith. Authorizing and mobilizing for *Spiritual Warfare* begins with FAITH.

Scripturally and historically, the Hebrews were called to proactive involvement in the world but failed. In contrast, the Early Church actively engaged the world and succeeded by establishing God's Church. In every era, God's call has remained consistent: to reconcile the world to Himself.

—*Faith as the Foundation*—

The journey of spiritual believers becomes the "live" experience that reinforces and validates their faith. As a result, they are called to live and walk by faith. It is from this foundation of faith that the authorization and mobilization for spiritual warfare truly begins.

Faith Step One: *Lifestyle and Friendship Evangelism*

Evangelism begins with a lifestyle shaped by love—this love forms the foundation for fulfilling all ten commandments sincerely, from the heart.

This foundational principle, discussed in previous chapters, highlights that Christian living is not about following a strict set of rules or outward religious acts, but about embodying love in everyday life.

Friendship evangelism, as demonstrated by Jesus in John 15:15, involves walking alongside others, sharing our lives and experiences openly as we journey together. This includes expressing emotions and being genuine in our interactions. However, wisdom is required in sharing personal matters;

premature or indiscriminate sharing can lead to misunderstanding or even harm.

Jesus himself said, *"I do not call you servants (slaves) any longer, for the servant does not know what his master is doing (working out). But I have called you My friends, because I have made known to you everything that I have heard from My Father. [I have revealed to you everything that I have learned from Him.]"* This demonstrates the depth of the relationship Jesus offers, moving from servanthood to friendship through transparency and shared understanding by openly sharing His emotions. Similarly, Paul models this lifestyle in Acts 24:16: *"Therefore I always exercise and discipline myself [mortifying my body, deadening my carnal affections, bodily appetites, and worldly desires, endeavoring in all respects] to have a clear (unshaken, blameless) conscience, void of offense toward God and toward men."*

In summary, the Christian lifestyle is marked by integrity and honesty—a transparent life that reflects genuine faith. It stands in contrast to approaches that rely solely on outward religious activities such as public preaching of "doom and gloom," door-to-door programs, or distributing tracts. Instead, the essence of Christian living is found in loving God, loving ourselves, and loving our neighbors and others.

Lifestyle and friendship evangelism can naturally lead to community events that make the name of Christ visible and enduring, much like a billboard on a busy highway.

Ultimately, lifestyle and friendship evangelism is about being Christ's witness in the midst of daily routines—whether at home, work, or in recreation—always prepared to share the reason for our hope.

Faith Step Two: *The Inside/Out Method*

The inside-out approach to ministry, also known as indigenous ministry, focuses intentionally on people living in low to marginal-income communities. This approach stems from missional studies that examine the demographic realities of mission work, especially in Third World environments and among those living in similar conditions within developed nations.

The perspective is not political or philosophical, but biblical: Scripture declares that there should be no poverty among plenty. When Jesus stated, "The poor you always have with you..." (Matthew 26:11; Mark 14:7; John 12:8), He was not excusing poverty or blaming the poor for their state in life. Rather, he was responding to criticism that the expensive perfume used on Him could have been sold to help the poor. Instead, Jesus's words highlight the ongoing opportunity to serve the needy, especially after His physical departure by stating, "the poor you always have with you." This reflects Deuteronomy 15:11, which teaches that poverty results from societal disobedience to God's commands for justice and generosity. Caring for the poor is thus a perpetual, not occasional, duty; the poor are to be seen as representing Christ Himself.

Historically, in advanced nations, the gospel has been widely communicated through powerful media and technology. However, there is a need to clarify the true nature of the gospel—the mandate is the proclamation of the "Gospel of the Kingdom of God" (Matthew 24:14), not just a denominational or doctrinal message, but the essentials of faith.

Prophetic Scripture underscores the urgency of reaching disadvantaged and downtrodden people, as their inclusion is linked to the fulfillment of God's redemptive plan, including the salvation of Israel and Christ's return. Romans 11:25-26 explains that when the full number of Gentiles comes in, Israel will be saved, and the Deliverer will come from Zion.

Bottom-Up Versus Top-Down Approaches: Lifestyle and friendship evangelism can lead to community events, but top-down ministries must integrate with bottom-up, relational approaches.

The outside-in (top-down) method is project-oriented, which brings people alongside them to meet them on the grounds of the server and offer temporary assistance that often creates dependency, referred to as "spiritual welfare." This approach doesn't empower those served to God-reliant dependence. In contrast, the inside-out (bottom-up) approach is relational and ongoing: helpers come alongside people, meet them in their context, provide ongoing resources to foster independence, and aim for conformity to Christ rather than themselves.

The Effects—Multiplication: Indigenous or "Inside/Out Ministry" reflects the model outlined in Ephesians 4:11-13 for evangelism and discipleship. This approach enables those being discipled to reproduce ministry in others, embodying a kingdom principle in which servant/leaders set aside selfishness (Philippians 2:5-9) and dedicate themselves to empowering potential indigenous leaders. Through this empowerment, new leaders are raised up and equipped to do the work of ministry in the communities of service.

This method is highly effective and timely for serving at-risk communities, though it can be challenging for those used to holding power and control. The inside-out model shifts power to indigenous leaders, as instructed in Matthew 20:25-28, and enables servant/leaders to become supervisors and coaches (Matthew 23:11-12). Indigenous leaders, in turn, submit to the guidance of servant/leaders, becoming teachable and receptive to instruction.

In this process of spiritual mobilization, the servant/leader's main role is to encourage and motivate indigenous leaders to succeed in living for Christ. As a result, the ministry and outreach of these leaders will flow naturally from their transformed lives and authentic Christian living.

Faith Step Three: *Discovering Your Spiritual Gifts*

Identifying one's spiritual gifts is distinct from technological or systematic processes such as matchmaking or personality assessments.

Matchmaking typically relies on algorithms, data, and expert analysis to pair compatible individuals, using methods like assorted mating, stable matching, and DNA testing. Similarly, personality assessments seek to determine compatibility based on psychological profiles. Both approaches are organized, data-driven, and rooted in theories of attraction and compatibility, commonly found in artificial intelligence applications and sociological studies.

However, from a biblical perspective, love cannot be quantified or evaluated by an app or a simple test. Love is not a theory but a lived reality. In Scripture, the common Greek word for love is "agape," which refers to a spiritual attraction originating from a heart filled with God's unconditional and sacrificial love. This divine love, which flows from Christ, forms the foundation of our relationships—whether in marriage, friendships, or ministry—and is essential for effective ministry work. Spiritual gifts assessments are grounded in this love, as the nature of each gift is reflected in its name and purpose.

Categories of Spiritual Gifts

The Greek word "Charisma" is the most common term for "gifts" in the New Testament. It refers to "a specific endowment or enablement of spiritual ability" provided to believers for service. Spiritual gifts are generally grouped into three categories:

- **Enabling Gifts** (Ephesians 4:11-13): These gifts descended from the throne of grace upon the 120 disciples in the upper room, forming the foundation of the Early Church. Their divine purpose is threefold: to plant, grow, and establish the church.

- **Functional Gifts** (Romans 12:6-8): These gifts help the church function smoothly, much like the organs and systems of the human body work together under the direction of the head. They support the internal operation of the church by interfacing, interacting, and interchanging with each other.

- **Sign Gifts** (I Corinthians 12:4-11): These gifts are outward-facing, designed to capture the world's attention and draw interest to the gospel. As believers engage in outreach, these gifts are manifested as a testimony to God's power.

Scripture further emphasizes the order and importance of Enabling Gifts, as seen in Ephesians 4:11 and I Corinthians 12:28: *"So God has appointed some in the church for His own use: first apostles (special messengers); second prophets (inspired preachers and expounders); third teachers; then wonder-workers; then those with ability to heal the sick; helpers; administrators; [speakers in] different (unknown) tongues."* In this list, "helpers" and "administrators" are highlighted, along with gifts such as "hospitality" and other abilities that support the practical administration and upkeep of the church. These gifts often operate behind the scenes, faithfully supporting the ministry's day-to-day needs.

The Purpose of Spiritual Gifts: Spiritual gifts connect us to the purpose of our calling, as described in Ephesians 4:1: *"I therefore, the prisoner for the Lord, appeal to and beg you to walk (lead a life) worthy of the [divine] calling to which you have been called [with behavior that is a credit to the summons to God's service]."*

The Greek word for "calling" here, "klēsis," has a legal root, meaning "summons" or a divine invitation to a vocation—an assigned task.

The Holy Spirit equips each believer for their specific assignment, which is discovered through the process of identifying the gift and the assignment itself. Salvation is not merely for personal benefit; rather, God saves us so that we may bring others along with us. Every member of the Body of Christ is given a gift by grace, meant to be used in service. If there is no active service, the gift and its purpose remain dormant, as noted in Ephesians 4:7.

How to Identify Spiritual Gifts: There is no mystical formula or technological process for discovering spiritual gifts. God does not announce our gifts through dramatic signs or audible declarations. Instead, spiritual gifts are revealed through an exploratory process rooted in service and faith.

1. **By a Burden of Concern:** Often, God leads us to our gift and calling by placing a burden on our hearts for an unmet need within the church or in the wider community.

2. **By Engaging in Voluntary Service:** Participating in church outreach or charitable activities can help clarify where your passions and concerns align with God's purposes. As Romans 12:1-2 encourages, dedicating ourselves to God's service and being transformed by the renewal of our minds allows us to discern His will more clearly. The more we serve, the more we understand what God is calling us to do.

3. **By the Joy That Comes from Service:** God often confirms our gifts by giving us a sense of excitement, enthusiasm, and pleasure in the work. While we may feel a burden for a need, serving in our spiritual gift brings joy rather than weariness.

Staying Connected and Edified: To remain effective and joyful in using spiritual gifts, it is important to maintain regular fellowship with other believers. This community provides encouragement and spiritual vitality, helping each person stay edified and invigorated in their ministry.

Faith Step Four: *Covenant Commitment*

The concept of covenant first appears in Scripture in Genesis 9:8-9, where God declares to Noah and his sons, *"Behold, I establish My covenant or pledge with you and with your descendants after you."*

The Hebrew term for covenant, "berith" (ber-eeth'), translates as "a cutting," which essentially refers to drawing blood. In biblical practice, God's covenant promises were perpetually sealed with blood, as blood functioned as the means of atonement and forgiveness for the sin of the human party. The blood of a sacrifice symbolically substituted for the person offering it, so that God would accept the blood as representative of the individual. In this way, the penalty for sin was paid, God remained just, and forgiveness was extended to the one making the sacrifice. This concept ultimately points forward to Jesus Christ's sacrifice on Calvary. Covenants also took place between real estate owners as a vow or pledge to consecrate the land to God.

God's New Covenant Promise for the Willing: The New Covenant of Grace, which fulfills all previous covenants through the lineage of Christ, stands apart from human covenants or secular business contracts. Although humanity receives the blessings of the covenant, God's covenant is a mutual agreement between the Sovereign God and the Messiah—the Father and Son—which makes the covenant immutable because it's not based on human imperfection, rather divine perfection. Hebrews 10 outlines the fulfillment of all the covenants' promises made to the patriarchs, being fulfilled in Christ.

While God communicated an oral law to Israel with such conditions for the building of their theocratic nation, it was not the foundation of His covenant promise, the New Covenant is. This covenant was made and confirmed with Christ's own blood (Testator), acting on behalf of the Chosen people of God (Beneficiaries)—the broad faith community known as the Body of Christ, which includes both Jews and Gentiles. It is not based on a conditional exchange. Rather, it is unconditional, based on the Word of the Testator, Christ, meaning that as believers follow the directives of the Lord's Word, they inherit the benefits in time. It is a sure promise.

When Scriptures refer to the "Chosen" or "Elect" of God, these terms are traditionally associated with the doctrine of Predestination, which contrasts with the position regarding falling from grace and losing salvation. However, the biblical meaning of salvation strikes a balance between the two distinctives by affirming eternal security and including the human will. The translated terms "Chosen" or "Elect" are understood from the original languages as "called out for salvation." While affirming God's sovereignty, God's eternal plan of salvation, established through His omniscient foreknowledge, was ordained before the foundation of the earth. In time, God calls individuals who are willing after the Gospel was revealed to their hearts by the Spirit of God. Thus, under the New Covenant of Grace, Jews and Gentiles are united as one people in the Lord, with neither considered more special to God, who "shows no partiality" (Acts 10:34).

The Seed of Abraham and the Immutability of God's Covenant: References in Scripture to the "Seed" of Abraham directly point to the Messiah, who would be born through Abraham's lineage. This connection underscores the unchangeable nature of God's covenant, for the Godhead cannot lie (see Numbers 23:19; Titus 1:2).

Believers, as they follow the Lord's directives, inherit these promises in due time. While God gave oral laws to Israel with specific conditions for establishing their theocratic nation, these were not the foundation of His covenant promise.

An Example of a Covenant Commitment

A covenant commitment among believers serves as a model for what such a covenant can look like when at least three disciples join together, preparing to engage in spiritual warfare. The example provided here may be modified, or groups may choose to write their own version.

As devoted followers of Jesus Christ and under God's New Covenant provisions of Grace procured by the Blood of Christ on Calvary, we commit ourselves to the mandate of the Great Commission to make Disciples for Christ as opportunity arises. We joyfully accept the challenge, anticipating the fruit of our work, the salvation of souls.

We humbly submit to Christ's authority, charged with this ministry, and resolve to be accountable to maintain the integrity of the relationship. We submit to the cause of Christ for this ministry in loving fellowship and peaceful partnership with one another. We acknowledge the hard work before us and resolve to strengthen and encourage each other for renewal. We renounce any form of discord that would hurt anyone's character and willingly abstain from gossip and rumors. We will hold each other up in edification of the truth and accountability to error. If we find ourselves out of character with this ministry, we resolve to remove ourselves without clamor. We willingly give ourselves to 100% agreement on the action we take for outreach evangelistic ministry. We understand that this commitment does not mean that we will be perfect, but that God's grace will give us the ability not to give up on each other and the people we are seeking to reach until the work is done. Therefore, under the Blood of the New Covenant of Grace that redeems us from all our sin and differences, we enjoin ourselves to each other as Blood Brothers and Blood Sisters in Christ Jesus our Lord. AMEN.

CHAPTER 12.

Responsible Disciples: Authorizing by Faith

Here, we lead into authorizing spiritual warfare with the roles and responsibilities of the followers of Christ.

We have reflected on the process in the previous chapters with three foundational steps: engaging, waging, and mobilizing spiritual warfare. These steps should culminate in a decisive, mutual agreement among at least three disciples who are prepared and committed to action as spiritual warriors. This transition marks a shift from individual efforts to a collective, purposeful approach to spiritual warfare.

Agree to Come Together for Consistent Prayer: The first step in authorizing spiritual warfare is for at least three disciples to agree to consistently participate in "prayer in the Spirit." This principle is rooted in the Kingdom of God's legislative framework, as depicted in Matthew 28:18-20.

Jesus declared that all authority in heaven and on earth has been given to Him, commissioning His followers to make disciples, baptize, and teach everything He commanded, with the promise of His perpetual presence.

Binding the Devil with Spiritual Legislation: Christ's words were not about individuals randomly "binding" the devil or "loosing" people from spiritual bondage. Instead, He described the governance of God's Kingdom on earth through spiritual legislation. This legislation enacts divine power to overcome the devil's strongholds.

While Western Christianity acknowledges the role of spiritual warfare in mission, it often fails to recognize the full extent of the authority granted to the Church through Christ's redemption and the Gospel's power under the Holy Spirit's anointing.

The principle of legislative binding finds its foundation in Matthew 18:18-20, which references the elders of Israel who met at city gates, serving as aldermen, to decide what would be allowed to influence city life. In that context, to "bind" means to disallow, and to "loose" means to allow. When anointed servant-leaders agree in unity to bind a strongman, Christ's anointing from heaven manifests spiritually on earth, driving out evil spirit influences and transforming the atmosphere to advance the Gospel as natural obstacles are overcome.

Many mainline churches overlook the authority described in Ephesians and the prophetic books, as well as Christ's commissioning in Matthew 28. The Church possesses greater spiritual authority than earthly governments, enabling it to dismantle spiritual strongholds beyond the government's reach. Regional meetings of anointed leaders with pure hearts can reconcile, agree, and bind strongmen, as outlined in Ephesians 6:10-18.

Once a covenant commitment is made, a prayer schedule should be established, drawing from "Prayer—In the Spirit, Private and Collective." This involves both private and group prayer, each serving a distinct but complementary role.

Private Prayer

Please refer to the previous section on "private and group prayer." This is a refresher course.

Private prayer involves seeking divine guidance in a quiet, distraction-free space. When such a space or time is unavailable, believers are encouraged to pray wherever and whenever possible, even silently in their hearts and spirits. A suggested opening prayer is: "Lord, I join my faith with those who are praying, and trust Your word associated with the prayer petitions."

Group Prayer

Group prayer requires agreement among at least three committed participants, with a goal to expand the group up to eight and then multiply by forming new groups.

The timing and format—often through conference calls or video meetings—should be convenient and agreeable for all. For united prayer to be effective, participants must pray about the same topics, both in spirit and with understanding, using thoughtfully prepared petitions to maintain focus and unity.

—*Using the Internet for Spiritual Battle*—

The internet has become a significant arena for spiritual activity, as discussed in my article "The Shift." This section builds on that teaching, offering practical guidance for those involved in human rights and social justice within a spiritual warfare framework.

Daniel 12:4 prophesies about the last days, predicting increased travel and a surge in knowledge—reflected in technological advancements like computerized algorithms and artificial intelligence.

These technologies operate along the "information highway," making the internet a focal point for both enlightenment and deception. The prophecy in Daniel 10 describes the sealing of the book, which suggests that its true meaning will be revealed in a time marked by widespread delusion and deception so that the truth stands out like light contrasted with darkness.

Information Overload: During my time as a seminary professor, my article "The Shift" was shared with staff and students, addressing new marching orders from prophecy about how God operates today.

The internet is a battleground for both positive and negative spiritual activity. The concern was for new church plants and faith-based groups to establish an online presence to counter toxic conspiracy theories with the Word of God. While some dismissed the idea, others saw its necessity, especially as the year 2000 marked a shift toward social media, podcasts, and influencers spreading unfounded theories to millions. The approach to address these is detailed in subsequent sections.

Daniel 12:4's prophecy about "running to and fro" and increased knowledge is interpreted as rapid travel and knowledge growth through technological advances. The internet embodies this, and the sealing of prophetic books hints at the meaning that the "Truth" will be revealed only in times of great deception. Each sign serves as a preview of God's next revelation, encouraging faith over reason.

Vulnerable Characteristics to Watch For: Scripture provides insight into how people are influenced by demonic forces in the last days. II Timothy 3:1-7 lists traits shaped by false doctrines, conspiracy theories, and lies—often spread through the internet and social media, attributed to the "prince and power of the air." Influencers and online personalities attract millions, amplifying these ideas.

The Role of the Body of Christ

The Body of Christ, also referred to as the Bride of Christ, is a powerful representation of the Church throughout all ages, places, and among all people. This identity emphasizes that the Church is not limited to specific facilities or buildings, but instead, encompasses the global community of believers. The Body of Christ stands as a living, active organism, unified in purpose and mission.

Spiritual Warfare and the Church's Mission: Spiritual warfare is deeply intertwined with the mission of the Church. The unified effort of believers—who collectively form the Body of Christ—is to fulfill the Great Commission, which is the call to spread the gospel throughout the world. This mission sets the Church directly against the agenda of Satan, resulting in spiritual attacks aimed at hindering God's work. The purpose of this mission is to rescue individuals from the "kingdom of darkness" and bring them into the "kingdom of Light." Thus, spiritual warfare refers to the ongoing struggle against spiritual powers and demons that seek to oppose this divine mission.

Engaging in spiritual warfare is not a separate or optional activity for believers; it is an essential part of fulfilling the

Church's mission. This involvement requires both resisting the forces of evil and boldly proclaiming the gospel, even in the face of spiritual opposition.

Mission Meeting Spiritual Opposition: From a biblical perspective, the mission of the Church is to convert people and build the Body of Christ within local communities and churches. This process becomes a form of spiritual warfare, described as "plundering the enemy's kingdom," where individuals are held as spiritual hostages. The mission includes confronting the spiritual powers that keep people in "disobedience" or "wrong thinking."

In Matthew 16:13-19, Jesus's words to Peter serve as a prophetic prediction of the birth of the New Testament Church, practically embodied in the Body of Christ. By referring to Peter as Petros (a large piece of rock) and Petra (a strong, massive rock like Gibraltar), Christ establishes the foundation of the Church. The Apostles and Prophets are built upon Christ as the Chief Cornerstone, as stated in Ephesians 2:20. This foundation demonstrates Christ's power through the Church: *"I will build My church, and the gates of Hades (the powers of the infernal region) shall not overpower it [or be strong to its detriment or hold out against it]."*

This declaration does not imply that the Church will be passive or fearful in the face of Satan's attacks. On the contrary, it means the Church will actively pursue its mission, working to destroy Satan's strongholds and rescue those destined for God's harvest. The Early Church, as described in the Book of Acts, exemplifies this active approach. Jesus's statement is a Providential Promise that the Church will assault the gates of Hades, positioning believers as aggressors in the spiritual battle against evil.

Covenant Promise of Victory: Prevailing against spiritual resistance is a Covenant Promise ensuring the Church's ultimate and enduring victory over all adversity, including spiritual forces.

The phrase about the gates of Hades is a powerful image of spiritual warfare, depicting the Church as the aggressor attacking the gates of hell and prevailing. Since city gates were defensive structures, Jesus's statement is understood as a military metaphor: the forces of death and the underworld will not conquer the Church. More broadly, it is a promise of the Church's enduring nature—no matter what opposition or persecution arises, the Church will not be destroyed.

Spiritual Warfare and Opposition to the Gospel

Spiritual warfare refers to the ongoing struggle against evil spiritual forces that actively seek to hinder the church and its mission. These forces attempt to obstruct the spread of the gospel, positioning the church as the frontline in this spiritual conflict.

The Battleground: The spiritual battleground begins with a descent, drawing a parallel to Lucifer's fall and transformation into Satan, the chief fallen angel. Now occupying the heavens as the "prince and power of the air," Satan's attacks originate from above.

Scriptural references such as Daniel 10 and Ephesians 6:1-12 illustrate how Satan's influence descends—first affecting governments, then churches, and ultimately society at large. Historical examples include the persecution faced by the Early Church from governing bodies like the Sanhedrin and the Roman Empire. The attacks are towards the thoughts about God and humanity as a whole. Ultimately, these spiritual attacks are directed toward the most threatening individuals within the Body of Christ, who fight to free the minds of people from untruth about God in Christ. (They are defenders of the faith)

The true conflict is fought within the minds of individuals, causing religious, ethnic, cultural, political, and social dissonance, requiring the church to be spiritually equipped to counter these influences.

Scripture clarifies that the weapons used in this warfare are not physical, but spiritual and powerful before God for destroying strongholds. Believers are called to refute arguments, theories, and every proud thought that sets itself against the true knowledge of God, leading every thought into obedience to Christ, as stated in II Corinthians 10:4-5:

"For the weapons of our warfare are not physical [weapons of flesh and blood], but they are mighty before God for the overthrow and destruction of strongholds, [Inasmuch as we] refute arguments and theories and reasonings and every proud and lofty thing that sets itself up against the [true] knowledge of God; and we lead every thought and purpose away captive into the obedience of Christ (the Messiah, the Anointed One)."

Defensive Stance: Many theological perspectives emphasize that Christ has already won the decisive victory in spiritual warfare. The church's role is therefore to "stand" in this victory, resist the devil, and maintain Christ's triumph rather than strive to win it anew. This approach can become the norm—status quo Christianity—where a dormant faith, lacking active works, allows existing conditions to persist.

Equipping the Church: To understand and engage in spiritual warfare, believers must be equipped with the "armor of God." This spiritual equipment enables them to resist the devil and fulfill their mission to proclaim the gospel. Essential to this equipping is personal spiritual discipline, especially the practice of taking every thought captive in obedience to Christ.

Impact on Relationships: Spiritual opposition also targets relationships within the church and families. The church's mission includes building a community that exemplifies Christ's love, grace, and hope, countering the enemy's efforts to sow discord and division.

—Historical Lessons and the Church's Challenge—

Experience has shown through trial and error that spiritual warfare is directed at stopping the church's mission—a battle that began with the Old Testament Hebrew people and even at creation, when Satan opposed God's original plan for humanity.

The Book of Revelation's account of the Seven Churches of Asia serves as a warning, each church reflecting a spiritual condition in need of repentance. When the church conforms to secular society—adopting governmental policies or cultural values—it dilutes its effectiveness. The church then risks shifting its focus to a cultural gospel, weakened in its power to combat evil.

Paul's warning to the Galatians underscores the danger of embracing a distorted gospel. He writes:

"I am surprised and astonished that you are so quickly turning renegade and deserting Him Who invited and called you by the grace (unmerited favor) of Christ (the Messiah) [and that you are transferring your allegiance] to a different [even an opposition] gospel. Not that there is [or could be] any other [genuine Gospel], but there are [obviously] some who are troubling and disturbing and bewildering you with a different kind of teaching which they offer as a gospel and want to pervert and distort the Gospel of Christ (the Messiah) [into something which it absolutely is not]. But even if we or an angel from heaven should preach to you a gospel contrary to and different from that which we preached to you, let him be accursed (anathema, devoted to destruction, doomed to eternal punishment)! As we said before, so I now say again: If anyone is preaching to you a gospel different from or contrary to that which you received [from us], let him be accursed (anathema, devoted to destruction, doomed to eternal punishment)!" (Galatians 1:6-9)

Historical Lessons and the Mission of the Church

Throughout history, both experience and observation reveal that spiritual warfare is fundamentally aimed at halting the mission of the church. When the church begins to conform to secular influences—whether through government policies, cultural trends, or prevailing social values—it risks being diluted by worldly philosophies. Such conformity ultimately weakens the church's effectiveness in combating evil and shifts its message from the gospel of Christ to a "cultural gospel."

Exposing Spiritual Blindness: A significant issue facing many today, including those who claim to be Christians, is spiritual blindness. This condition is reminiscent of Saul's experience before his transformation into the Apostle Paul, as described in Acts 9. Saul remained physically and spiritually blind until his encounter with the Lord on the road to Damascus. The purpose of this analysis is to expose the underlying spiritual activity that influences decisions and actions, whether these influences benefit or harm society. The goal is to raise awareness—both within the Christian community and among the broader public—of the higher truths revealed in Scripture.

Biblical Example— The Book of Job: The Book of Job stands as a profound biblical example of uncovering spiritual forces at work behind real-life events. Likely written around the time of Abraham's calling, Job offers invaluable insight into the ways of God, the involvement of Satan, and the complexities of human nature. Through this narrative, readers can gain a deeper understanding of the spiritual dynamics that shape both humanity and the Church, helping to prepare God's people for the pivotal events that each generation faces before Christ's return.

The Influence of Events on Leadership: This analysis emphasizes that it is the times we live in—the progression and escalation of significant events from one generation to another—that shape history, rather than the actions of prominent leaders alone. The character and outcome of an era are determined more by unfolding events than by any individual leader. When we look at world conditions and society as a whole, the conditions we see today are not much different than events in the past, which means the methods employed by God's people to overcome opposition are the same today.

Providence in the Rise and Fall of Leaders: The emergence and removal of leaders is understood as a matter of divine providence. In His sovereignty, God orchestrates the rise and fall of leaders, using both the righteous and the wicked to fulfill His purposes. While some self-proclaimed prophets may identify specific individuals as being central to the times—either for good or for evil—the broader prophetic truth is that God can use anyone to achieve His will. If certain leaders were absent, others would emerge, for the times themselves call for specific types of leadership.

Leadership as a Reflection of the Times: Prominent leaders in any era serve as representations of either good or evil. Through their actions and character, they chart paths for others to follow or avoid. Good leadership serves to guide people toward higher truths, fostering the development of righteous and just character. On the other hand, evil leadership leads to decline, demoralization, and the corruption of human nature.

Discerning and Following Good Leadership: It is essential to recognize the signs of the times and to seek out and follow good leadership, regardless of the promises made by those in power. The character and direction of leaders have far-reaching consequences, shaping not only individual lives but society as a whole.

CHAPTER 13.

Strategically Approaching Spiritual Conflict

Here, we come to full authorization of spiritual warfare, engaging, waging battle against spiritual enemies.

The Community of Faith is essential in establishing spiritual walls of protection for individuals pursuing human rights and social justice, regardless of their backgrounds or affiliations. This protective role is enacted through six primary practices, referred to as faith steps, which are detailed below.

Practical Application—Countering Oppression: In the natural world, the concept of "fighting fire with fire" is practiced by firefighters through methods such as backburning or counter-firing—setting controlled fires to halt the progress of a wildfire. Drawing parallels, advocates for human rights and social justice must employ strategic foresight, using data and statistics to anticipate the direction of injustice and implement preemptive countermeasures. This approach is comparable to a strategic game of chess, where success depends on staying ahead of the opponent's moves.

My approach to interpreting Scripture emphasizes practical methods over theological doctrine, engaging in spiritual conversations through pragmatic means. As an educator, I leveraged demographic studies to identify geographical spiritual strongholds by correlating observable patterns with Scriptural principles.

—The Spiritual Strategy—

The Apostle Paul provides insight into overcoming spiritual opposition, stating, *"To keep Satan from getting the advantage over us; for we are not ignorant of his wiles and intentions"* (II Corinthians 2:11). The context of this statement is the restoration of a young man convicted of adultery, as detailed in I Corinthians 5:6-7. Paul warns that unchecked wrongdoing can spread throughout the community, creating strongholds rooted in concealed sin and compromising truth.

Rather than listing the numerous Scriptures that mandate outreach and support for the poor, a kingdom concept-neutral perspective was revealed to me, emphasizing how to address oppression beyond human allegiances.

Drawing from Joshua 5:13-14, the narrative illustrates that God's stance transcends human divisions—He sides with His own purpose to reach all people with the Gospel of the Kingdom, rather than aligning with any particular group. An example of this is Joshua 5:13-14. Joshua encountered a man with a drawn sword and asked if he was for Israel or their enemies. The man, identified as the "Commander of the army of the Lord," answered, "Neither," clarifying that he came to lead God's purpose and plan, not take sides.

The strategy derived from Scripture encompasses several faith steps inspired by II Chronicles 7:14:

1. Mobilize small discipleship teams within a central location or in a group member's home, targeting areas identified as spiritual strongholds.

2. Establish a covenant relationship built on integrity and confidentiality, ensuring that disclosures within the group remain private.

3. Confess and pray for personal indiscretions and weaknesses.

4. Equip each member for spiritual combat, focusing on the armor of God (Ephesians 6:10-18), the fruit of the Spirit (Galatians 5:22-23), and prayer in the Spirit (Ephesians 6:18, Jude 1:20, I Corinthians 14:15).

5. Yield and invite the presence of the Lord into circumstances through intercessory prayer.

6. Meet regularly and consistently, praying together for results.

The essence of this approach is to pray not for one side to triumph over another, but for the salvation and redemption of all involved. This is supported by I Timothy 2:1-4, which calls for prayers, intercessions, and thanksgivings on behalf of all people, especially those in positions of authority, to foster peace and godliness. God's desire is for all to be saved and to come to a knowledge of the truth.

Discerning the Opposition: Effectively countering oppression requires discernment similar to a chess match, where each move is thoughtfully planned. Believers utilize the "gift of discerning of spirits" to identify and address strategies of opposition. By anticipating and preparing for the opposition's next move, two outcomes result: the public is informed about impending developments, and, when these events occur, the accuracy of the predictions garners greater support and alignment with the cause. This strategy strengthens the collective voice for truth without resorting to protest or interference with law enforcement, instead inviting divine intervention against spiritual forces of hate and violence.

The prayer initiatives are followed by a demographic diagram for identifying spiritual strongholds within various communities that will be available for request via the website at www.jarvisjimmyrossauthor.com.

A Non-Judgmental Approach: Jesus taught that righteousness must exceed that of the scribes and Pharisees (Matthew 5:20), warning against the bondage of manmade religious laws.

Religious judgmentalism often leads to punitive measures and condemnation, whereas divine judgment is characterized by justice and righteousness. Christians are called to respond to injustice and hatred without vengeance. Oppression and suppression of rights signal the presence of a dictatorial spirit, likened to the "spirit of antichrist." In these circumstances, the adversary is not the individual but the evil spiritual influences at work. Guided by Romans 13, believers are instructed to adhere to the law and moral conscience, seeking to avoid confrontation even when threatened. Scripture urges caution and wisdom, as in Ephesians 5:15-16, emphasizing purposeful and sensible living amid evil times.

Jesus' Teaching on Non-Resistance: In Matthew 5:39-41, Jesus presents principles that encourage resolving conflict peacefully rather than through altercation. His teachings do not advocate total non-resistance to evil but highlight alternative approaches rooted in righteousness. The Beatitudes and parables emphasize heart character—meekness as strength, not weakness. Christlike character calls for justice from a higher ground, relying on intercessory prayer and truth-telling rather than political attacks or retaliation.

The term "Beatitudes," taken from Matthew 5, is derived from the Latin word *beatus*, which means "blessed" or "happy." These statements describe the blessed state that comes from embracing Christlike attitudes. Beatitudes are commonly known as part of "The Sermon on the Mount." Christ's Kingdom Concepts introduce a significant shift from the traditional approach of seeking legal remedies for resolving conflicts in relationships. Rather than focusing on external solutions or rigid legal jurisdiction, Christ emphasizes developing inner virtuous character. This inner transformation becomes the key to addressing and dismissing relational problems.

According to Christ's teaching, the resolution of conflict and the path to true blessedness begin with obedience to God's word, applying it directly to life's situations. Cultivating a pure heart and a love that extends even to one's enemies are central. By modeling Christ's example, believers are called to look beyond animosity and respond with love, allowing their character to reflect the depth of Christ's teaching. The results of Christlike behavior towards those who persecute are "heaping coals of fire" on their heads (Romans 12:20), causing them to burn in their conscience with guilt and shame that may soften their hearts and move them to repentance, the opposite of getting vengeance.

Differences Between Religious Judgment and Divine Judgment: Religious judgmentalism involves human assessment of perceived sin, often resulting in punitive consequences. In contrast, divine judgment is inherently just, reflecting God's nature.

God holds humanity accountable through His will and the conscience, which acts as a moral compass, calling people to repentance. Christ's sacrifice on the cross means God does not judge sin as people do; instead, Christ bore humanity's judgment, offering righteousness to those who accept Him (II Corinthians 5:21, Romans 8:1-3).

The Role and Corruption of the Conscience: In secular contexts, judgment is often self-inflicted by ignoring conscience. Genesis 6 illustrates this with humanity's corruption leading to judgment—Noah's warnings offered safety, symbolizing the Gospel message. Romans 2:14-15 demonstrates that even without divine law, conscience serves as an internal witness to moral truth. However, Scripture warns that conscience can become corrupted, resistant to God's voice, and unrepentant—a condition ultimately exposed at the final judgment.

The unrepentant conscience will condemn itself, resulting in eternal separation from God with a burning conscience out of hatred for God. But hope is always alive. As we proceed towards the conclusion of this work, I will share an often overlooked Kingdom Concept of a second chance at the white Throne Judgement.

Spiritual Protection for Advocates: The Community of Faith is instrumental in forming spiritual barriers of protection for those advocating for human rights and social justice. This approach to countering oppression relies on discerning opposition strategies and preparing responses in advance. This collective advocacy strengthens the voice for truth and justice.

Maintaining Spiritual Health in Ministry Teams: Drawing from agricultural principles, climate and atmosphere affect the ground's conditions. Spiritually, attitude is akin to climate and mood to atmosphere. The Bible acknowledges that believers experience different seasons of trials and testing (II Corinthians 7:8; Galatians 6:9; II Timothy 4:2; I Peter 1:6). Ministry teams must remain steadfast through fluctuating moods and attitudes, trusting in their calling regardless of circumstances. Just as weather varies regionally, ministry workers must "elevate" their minds above what is seen and felt, maintaining consistency and faith in their mission.

Growth in strategic ministry is influenced not only by agricultural principles but also by seasonal readiness for change. Participants must commit to steady involvement, neither rushing nor lagging, and persevere until the process is complete. Strategic ministry requires a covenant commitment from all participants, ensuring stability and sustained progress.

Recognizing Spiritual Attack on the Church from Within

Our objective is to move toward Revelation chapters 20-22 for the real eutopia on earth—the mission and journey of the church that the church should be enthusiastic to bring others along on that journey.

Biblical Prophecy Real Talk approaches the Book of Revelation by focusing on its narrative structure. This perspective visually traces events at the micro level, following their progression through generations. Ultimately, these generational events build up to a macro scale, which is recorded in the final chapters, Revelation 20-22. Here we highlight the methods of understanding the unfolding story as it moves from individual experiences to broader, cosmic fulfillment.

Methods of Spiritual Attack: Spiritual attacks on the church manifest in several distinct ways, each targeting unity, purpose, and leadership. One prominent strategy is "Divide and Conquer." Here, Satan manipulates conflicts, presenting them as unsolvable. This creates misunderstandings and the sin of betrayal, hostility, and unfounded accusations among church leaders, which in turn result in disunity and fallout within the congregation. Such division ultimately damages the church's witness and reputation to the world (John 13:35; Matthew 12:25; Ephesians 4:3). If you have ears to hear, somewhere along the line, you will hear church members gossiping and spreading rumors about the leadership.

Another method of spiritual attack involves false teachings and erroneous doctrine. Misleading or incomplete doctrinal information shifts focus away from God's higher purpose and the plan of salvation, with the idea of being popular coupled with a celebrity aspiration. Sermons tend to focus on "feel-good" cliches to "tickle the fancy" of the congregants rather than the conviction of the gospel (II Timothy 4:2). Then, attention is diverted to the maintenance and housekeeping of church facilities to make the facilities more aesthetic and raise funds for that purpose, which fails to help people and sows confusion. This confusion can lead individuals to leave the church (I Timothy 4:1) and, in some cases, walk away from living for Christ out of frustration.

A loss of purpose also threatens the church. By concentrating on minor disagreements, personal frustrations, or worldly concerns, the enemy diverts energy from the church's mission. Logistical matters such as budgets, bills, and membership giving become the main focus rather than outreach and missions (Matthew 28:19-20).

Personal attacks are a further tactic. Key leaders are targeted, which results in attacks on those who support them. These internal assaults breed feelings of uselessness, making leaders vulnerable to temptation, depression, fear, spiritual fatigue, loss of joy, and ultimately weakening the church from within.

Spiritual Principles for Defense: To counter spiritual attacks, the church must rely on several core principles. The "Armor of God," as outlined in Ephesians 6:10-18, provides spiritual defense. This includes the offensive weapon, the "Sword of the Spirit," which is the living word of God that also counters offense by cutting to the truth. Hebrews 4:12, *"For the Word that God speaks is alive and full of power [making it active, operative, energizing, and effective]; it is sharper than any two-edged* *sword, penetrating to the dividing line of the breath of life (soul) and [the immortal] spirit, and of joints and marrow [of the deepest parts of our nature], exposing and sifting and analyzing and judging the very thoughts and purposes of the heart."* The rest of the armor involves practicing truth, righteousness, faith, peace, salvation, and perseverance in prayer.

Unity and love are essential for resilience. Maintaining edifying love and collective prayer strengthens the church against spiritual attacks.

Spiritual disciplines such as continual prayer, worship, fellowship, fasting, and study of God's word insulate and fortify believers. These practices invite the presence of the Lord, filling believers with the Holy Spirit.

Discernment is also vital. Recognizing demonic presence, deceitful behavior, sinful tendencies, and manipulative cliques within the church guards against harmful teachings and practices.

Why the Church is Specifically Targeted

The church is a primary target for spiritual attack because it embodies God's kingdom on earth. As His agency of reconciliation, the church unites believers across all cultures, ethnicities, and socio-economic backgrounds. This unity becomes a threat to the dismantling and disbanding of Satan's kingdom and spiritual opposition.

Leadership is especially impactful. Key leaders and influential members directly affect the lives of others, either weakening or strengthening them.

The church also serves as a channel for God's work. Disruptions to the smooth flow of church life cause regression and hinder spiritual growth. This lessens the church's impact on the broader community and serves as a counteraction from within.

—*Conclusion*—

The church faces spiritual attack because it represents Christ on earth—God's presence, purpose, and plan for humanity that will be manifest in the New Jerusalem. The enemy aims to fracture the church into smaller groups, disseminate contradictory information, distort the truth, and obscure individual callings and gifts, financial integrity, community support, and dependence on God's power. Instead, this attack reinforces dependence on men in exalted positions, intellect, and emotional discourse disguised as spiritual communication and preaching as motivational speaking.

Believers are called to embrace the gospel, advocate constant unity and community engagement, exercise discernment, persist in prayer and fasting, and relentlessly study Scripture, including the original languages, using modern tools.

Ultimately, these understandings frame spiritual attacks not as signs of failure but as indications that God is at work. Spiritual opposition means you have gained the devil's attention and are on the right track, echoing heavenly affirmation. Stay the course!

CHAPTER 14.

Signs of the Last Days

Just as road signs are placed along highways to guide travelers safely to their destinations, spiritual signs described in Scripture serve to guide and direct followers of Christ in the real world toward their ultimate destiny. However, Scripture and life distinguish between human fate and divine destiny. Human fate is in humanity's hands, but divine destiny is in God's Hands. So, when we see chaos and destruction in the world, it stems from human fate and when good prevails, it's divine destiny. The good news is that human fate ends where divine destiny begins—the last days point to the end times when divine destiny will be fulfilled through Christ and His Gospel.

These prophetic indicators are intended to keep believers alert and prepared, providing direction in uncertain times and applying to sincere believers.

The Initial Signs: *The Beginning of Sorrows*

The phrase "beginning of sorrows," as described in Matthew 24:8, refers to a period marked by intensifying "birth pains."

The Greek word "odínōn" (sorrow) means birth pains preceding the birth of a child, or travail pains through struggle and suffering—a metaphor for the intense pain that precedes monumental changes and the birth of mass revival.

As labor pains increase in frequency and intensity before childbirth, likewise, global tribulations will escalate as the end approaches, culminating in Armageddon (Revelation 16:16). Armageddon is symbolically described as the gathering place, "Mount Megiddo," where the rulers of the world unite to battle against the glorified Lord on the "great day of God Almighty."

This catastrophic war will ultimately spare the remnant of true believers and will be the last war in world history, which should generate good news.

These birth pangs, associated with fear and deception, increase in both frequency and severity as the world approaches the Tribulation period and the Second Coming. These events are not the end in themselves but serve as a prelude, signaling a time of escalating global turmoil and moral decline. Believers are called to remain vigilant, faithful, and enduring through hardship, recognizing these events as precursors rather than reasons for panic. Thus, the words of Christ in Matthew 24:13, *"But he who endures to the end will be saved."* The word "saved" generally means to rescue, deliver, protect, or keep alive, coming from the Greek word "sozo." In this prophetic context, it is a reference to physical survival and deliverance through the *beginning of sorrows*, rather than strictly eternal salvation, emphasizing staying faithful amid tribulation and trouble.

The concept of "birth pangs" symbolizes the growing fear, stress, anxiety, and frustration that will permeate society in the future. These pains are a call for believers to recognize the unfolding of God's plan, which includes exposing the spirit of antichrist and heralding the "latter rain"—an outpouring of God's Spirit akin to the experience at Pentecost, leading to renewed faith and spiritual revival.

Jesus, in John 16:20-22, assures His disciples that sorrow will ultimately turn to joy, just as a mother's anguish in labor gives way to happiness at the birth of her child. Although the last days are characterized by suffering and struggle as we get closer to the end times, they are ultimately a sign of impending joy.

Bridging the Last Days and End Times: Scripture highlights a central prophecy that connects both Old and New Testament teachings: the Olivet Discourse, recorded in Matthew 24. This discourse is pivotal because it bridges the "last days" and the "end times," outlining the events that will occur at the transition from one period to the next.

I can't say it enough, but the last days, according to biblical chronology, began at Pentecost. This was when Peter, referencing the prophecy of Joel (Joel 2:28-32), declared in Acts 2:17a, *"And it shall come to pass in the last days, God declares, that I will pour out of My Spirit upon all mankind."* The end times, however, commence only after the last days conclude. The present focus is on the last days, with the end times to be addressed in subsequent reading.

—*Timeline of the Last Days*—

In Matthew 24:34, Jesus summarizes the span of the last days and the events of the end times: *"Truly I tell you, this generation (the whole multitude of people living at the same time, in a definite, given period) will not pass away till all these things taken together take place."* By connecting prophecies from both Testaments, a sequential timeline emerges that illuminates the conditions defining the "last days" and "end times" across generations. The events specifically associated with the last days are detailed from verses 4 through 8.

The Greek term for "generation," "Genea," can, when repeated or coupled with additional time-related words, signify an unbounded duration. Thus, the signs identified in Matthew 24:4-8 are not confined to a single era but recur in successive generations. This repetition is not intended as a guaranteed timeframe for Christ's return, but as a call for Christians to remain prepared in every era. When these signs are viewed alongside other prophetic Scriptures, it becomes clear that their presence will increase from generation to generation. These escalating signs include wars and rumors of wars, famines (interpreted as economic hardship), pestilences (such as widespread diseases and sickness), earthquakes in various locations, extreme weather events (like tornadoes, hurricanes, and floods), the rise of false prophets, apostles, and messiahs, the proliferation of new age doctrines and policies, and the emergence of dictators. These are indicators that the end times are near, but not yet present.

There is no fixed timeline for the fulfillment of these scriptural events. Jesus states in Matthew 24:22, *"And if those days had not been shortened, no human being would endure and survive, but for the sake of the elect (God's chosen ones) those days will be shortened."* This means that the intensity of suffering and persecution could reach a point of destruction, but for the sake of the elect—the faithful remnant—these days will be mercifully shortened. This demonstrates God's patience and compassion, ensuring that the period of intense suffering preceding the end times will be brief. Although history has yet to repeat the full magnitude of the events experienced during Christ's ministry and the early Church, it is evident that today's era is marked by increasingly prominent signs of the last days.

Prelude to the End Times

Each passing generation, measured across millennia, witnesses an escalation in the signs associated with the rise of a religious-political messiah. With the dawn of the new millennium in 2000, prophetic indicators have become more pronounced. The proliferation of social media platforms in the 21st century has greatly increased the dissemination of information, but also of conspiracy theories and misinformation. These platforms can propagate unfounded opinions and false narratives about Christianity and the faith, reaching millions around the world through the internet.

Information Overload in the Last Days: I've shared this previously, but it is worth noting here. Daniel 12:4 contains a key prophecy regarding the last days: *"many shall run to and fro, and knowledge shall increase."* This is understood as a prediction of a time marked by rapid travel and a surge in knowledge, facilitated by technological advancements such as computers and artificial intelligence. The internet, or "information highway," is an embodiment of this prophecy.

Daniel is instructed to seal the book until the end of time, suggesting that the true meaning would be revealed only at the appointed time when deception and delusion are widespread. A guiding principle for discerning future events is that when one sign appears, it serves as an indication of the next. God reveals His plans step by step, prompting faith over reason, and each revelation serves as a preview of what is to come. It's like staying one step ahead of an opponent in chess.

The Vital Signs Leading to the End Times

Vital Sign One: Greed for Wealth

An important indicator frequently cited in discussions regarding the approach of the end times is the growing prevalence of material greed.

Wealth, by itself, is a neutral element—it can serve good or evil purposes. The real issue arises not from money itself, but from an unhealthy and excessive desire for wealth that turns money into an idol, something to be worshipped. As Jesus states in Matthew 6:24: *"No one can serve two masters; for either he will hate the one and love the other, or he will stand by and be devoted to the one and despise and be against the other. You cannot serve God and mammon (deceitful riches, money, possessions, or whatever is trusted in)."* Here, the Aramaic word "mammon" is used to personify materialism and the love of money as an idol, contrasting it with devotion to God. In early translations, such as the Latin Vulgate and the King James Version (KJV), "mammon" was left untranslated, which led medieval writers to interpret Mammon as a proper name for a devil or evil deity.

The temptation of material wealth is further highlighted during the onset of Jesus' public ministry. In the wilderness, the devil took Jesus to a high mountain, showing Him a vision of all the wealth and splendor of the world in an instant. The devil promised to give all this to Jesus if He would bow down and worship him as God (Matthew 4:8-11; Luke 4:5-8). Jesus refused, rebuking the devil with the word of God. This encounter serves as a reminder for believers that God's word is the answer to fear and deceptive lies that come from the devil. Jude 1:9 also offers insight: *"[But when even] the archangel Michael, contending with the devil, judicially argued (disputed) about the body of Moses, he dared not [presume to] bring an abusive condemnation against him, but [simply] said, The Lord rebuke you!"*

When greed for wealth prevails, it is often for evil purposes. First Timothy 6:10 is clear about the effects of such greed: *"For the love of money is a root of all evils; it is through this craving that some have been led astray and have wandered from the faith and pierced themselves through with many acute [mental] pangs."*

The "love of money" is described as the root of all evil. The Greek word "Rhiza" for "root" likens this desire to the roots of a plant, which can grow into various other sinful activities, ultimately corrupting the human spirit and dulling God-consciousness. This means that one's moral compass is numbed, leading to destructive behaviors.

The initial consequence of this greed is a departure from the basic, saving faith. This does not necessarily appear as an overt abandonment of faith; instead, individuals may be drawn to a version of Christianity that justifies and supports their pursuit of wealth and pleasure. Ultimately, this path leads to widespread disappointment and self-inflicted suffering. However, turning away from this error can become difficult, as the conscience and human will are corrupted and rendered incapable of repentance. Those who become covetous—always seeking more than enough—will engage in evil and corrupt activities in their relentless quest for more than enough.

The Apostle James, in James 5:1-3, issues a warning to the rich who have "hoarded wealth in the last days." He explains that they face impending judgment, and their wealth will ultimately be redistributed to the poor who have suffered under their oppression.

The Bible does not condemn wealth itself. In Ecclesiastes 10:19, it states that money is used to address the issues of life—money runs the world—but can also ruin the world. Scripture cautions against covetousness and greed, which lead to moral decline and social decay—conditions that foreshadow the end of the age.

Vital Sign Two: The Spread of a Politicized New Age Gospel

An obsession with wealth leads people to prioritize material gain over devotion to God. As a result, many embrace a politicized version of Christianity that promises wealth within an economy supported by New Age philosophies. The combination of politics with esoteric (mystical, secretive, philosophical) teachings forms a false theocratic government. An example of these philosophies is found in II Timothy 4:3-4. After encouraging his son in the ministry, Timothy, to consistently preach God's word, he explains why: *"For the time is coming when [people] will not tolerate (endure) sound and wholesome instruction, but, having ears itching [for something pleasing and gratifying], they will gather to themselves one teacher after another to a considerable number, chosen to satisfy their own liking and to foster the errors they hold. And will turn aside from hearing the truth and wander off into myths and man-made fictions."*

Preaching will be more like motivational speaking, minus the conviction of the gospel, focusing on the eloquence of "tickling the fancy" (Preaching what they want to hear that gives them pleasure and gratification) of the hearers.

Throughout his epistles, Paul warns believers about "another gospel." This is echoed in Revelation chapters 17 and 18, where the figure of the "Whore of Babylon" represents an alternative form of Christianity intertwined with political power and promises of increased wealth to those who align their faith with the movement.

Revelation 18 describes an end-time economic and religious system—referred to as "Babylon"—built on luxury and greed. The chapter predicts that merchants who profited from her "extravagant luxury" will mourn when this system suddenly collapses.

In His central prophecy in Matthew 24:12, Christ warns, *"And the love of the great body of people will grow cold because of the multiplied lawlessness and iniquity."* Jesus prophesies that as lawlessness abounds, the love of many will grow cold. Commentators often interpret this coldness as a lack of concern for the needs of others, fueled by selfish desire. Thus, the pursuit of wealth and the spread of lawlessness lead to a decline in love, compassion, and empathy among people.

Vital Sign Three: The "Great Falling Away"

A surge in the pursuit of wealth, combined with the rise of a politicized faith, sets the stage for what Scripture refers to as "the great falling away." This is recorded in II Thessalonians 2:3-4: *"Let no one deceive or beguile you in any way, for that day will not come except the apostasy comes first [unless the predicted great falling away of those who have professed to be Christians has come], and the man of lawlessness (sin) is revealed, who is the son of doom (of perdition), Who opposes and exalts himself so proudly and insolently against and over all that is called God or that is worshiped, [even to his actually] taking his seat in the temple of God, proclaiming that he himself is God."*

Two key thoughts emerge from this passage. First, the "day of the Lord" will become imminent—not merely apparent—when a great departure from the Christian faith occurs. Many who once professed Christianity will turn to a different version of the faith, deviating from what is recorded in Scripture. This is known as the apostasy, and false prophets and false apostles will drive it. The Great Whore of Babylon, as depicted in the Book of Revelation, will serve as the headquarters and launch pad for this false religion, which, according to biblical numerology, will seduce one-third of humanity.

Second, when this falling away occurs, it signals the imminent emergence of the actual antichrist—called the "lawless one." This figure, embodying the spirit of iniquity and anarchy, will violate every law through lies and deception, ultimately claiming that he is God.

CHAPTER 15.

Signs of the End Times: First Half Tribulation

The purpose of biblical prophecy is to foster preparation and readiness. As outlined, it is essential to recognize that the period known as the "last days" will eventually come to a close, marking the beginning of the "end times." The focus of this section is to clarify the transition between these two periods and to present a scenario that sequentially organizes the end-time events. This approach aims to provide a clear, chronological visualization of what will unfold according to the prophetic sequence.

To truly grasp the meaning behind the end-time signs described in Scripture, we need to look beyond the surface of mysteries, metaphors, and symbolic language that fill predictive prophecy. The Book of Revelation emphasizes this approach by highlighting the importance of "wisdom" as a necessary tool for interpretation. Importantly, deciphering these prophecies does not require expert linguistic training or special knowledge reserved for a select few. Instead, Revelation 1:3 makes it clear: *"Blessed (happy, to be envied) is the man who reads aloud [in the assemblies] the word of this prophecy; and blessed (happy, to be envied) are those who hear [it read] and who keep themselves true to the things which are written in it [heeding them and laying them to heart], for the time [for them to be fulfilled] is near."*

The Universal Call to Listen and Heed: The words of predictive prophecy apply to anyone willing to listen to what the Spirit is saying to the churches. As Revelation 2:7 states, *"He who is able to hear, let him listen to and give heed to what the Spirit says to the assemblies (churches). To him who overcomes (is victorious), I will grant to eat [of the fruit] of the tree of life, which is in the paradise of God."* Therefore, the prophecies in the Book are intended for everyone who has a spiritual ear to listen and take them to heart. Predictive prophecy is not meant to be a mystery; it is written practically, using common sense.

When the Antichrist appears after the Great Falling Away, two significant events will take place: Christianity and the Bible, as we know them, will be banned and censored in the nations under his control. In their place, a new version of Scripture will be established that exalts the Antichrist as Lord.

If you believe we are already living in the "end times" and that the Antichrist and the conditions described are already present in the world, then, based on Scripture and the points made so far, this suggests that the Antichrist has approximately seven years (give or take) to reign before being destroyed. His destruction is then followed by the return of Christ, according to dispensationalist theology.

The Antichrist's time of chaos and destruction is relatively short, so there is reason for encouragement: this period will pass, and righteousness will eventually prevail. Furthermore, if you hold to the dispensationalist view and believe in the "rapture," it's important to note that we are still here. However, Scripture indicates that there are additional events that must occur before the final fulfillment, which will be examined in the following sections.

Sequential Signs of the End Times
The First Half Tribulation

According to prophetic Scripture, the Antichrist will remain anonymous for a period leading up to the Great Tribulation. Biblical, theological, and eschatological interpretations suggest that the Antichrist will not be revealed immediately; rather, his initial anonymity will conceal his true identity until he is unveiled during the second half of the tribulation, known as the Great Tribulation.

He will be hidden in plain sight. This concept forms the foundation for the mystery surrounding the Antichrist and the prevailing views regarding the transition from the last days into the end times.

The First Sign: *The Great Falling Away (Apostasy)*

I have addressed this sign concerning the last days. However, this sign runs from the end of the last days to the beginning of the end times. The apostasy will initiate the end times, as recorded in II Thessalonians 2:3. This falling away will impact both professed Christians and non-Christians across various nations.

According to biblical numerology and the symbolism found in Revelation, the nations involved are represented by seven heads and ten crowns, signifying the countries the Antichrist will occupy. According to the nations mentioned in prophecy, these nations are considered some of the most powerful in the world, while most other countries will not be part of their regime. The judgment upon those who follow the Antichrist's ways is described as affecting one-quarter to one-third of humanity.

The metaphor of the Great Whore of Babylon is often interpreted to represent a false Christian religion and the rise of a One World Government-New Age Order. This movement will seduce one-third of humanity, enticing them with promises of wealth and pleasure and leading them away from true faith.

Whether the "Whore of Babylon" is a literal figure or a metaphor, either way, it symbolizes the new age one-world government. Acceptance into this system requires the renunciation of Christ and the acknowledgment of the Antichrist as Lord. The widespread acceptance of this system will require years of propaganda and deception, so we are many, incalculable years from this event.

At the beginning of his reign, the Antichrist will remain anonymous, possibly projected as a hologram image or some AI projection on the internet. The Great Whore will "ride the Beast" as described in Revelation 17:3, signifying a government run by the beast—a vast, powerful computer system with artificial intelligence on behalf of the Dragon, literally Satan. As Christ, the Son, was to the Father, so the Antichrist (false messiah) will be to the Dragon, Satan. The personalities behind these symbols and metaphors will be explored further.

The Second Sign: *The Rebuilding of the Temple*

The Antichrist is anticipated to emerge as a handsome, charismatic political and religious leader, presenting himself as a man of peace and a problem-solver for global issues. This statement is represented by the first horse of the apocalypse in Revelation 6. When the Lamb of God, Christ, breaks the first seal (initiating the beginning of the tribulation), a man riding a white horse appears holding a bow without arrows, indicating overcoming war by the diplomacy of peace, which will be more like forceful business deals.

The rebuilding of the temple in Jerusalem, often referred to as the third temple, is expected to begin during the first three and a half years of the tribulation, coinciding with the Antichrist brokering peace from an undisclosed location, possibly in Turkey. Daniel 9:27 supports the prophecy that the temple will be rebuilt, and the Antichrist will demand worship at the midpoint of the tribulation, breaking the covenant of peace by making his appearance in Jerusalem.

In Matthew 24:1-2, Jesus utters a stunning prophecy regarding Jerusalem's magnificent temple: *"Do you see all these things? Truly I tell you, not one stone here will be left on another; every one will be thrown down."* This declaration prompts His disciples to inquire privately, in verse 3, about the timing of these events and the signs of His coming and the end of the age: *"While He was seated on the Mount of Olives, the disciples came to Him privately and said, Tell us, when will this take place, and what will be the sign of Your coming and of the end (the completion, the consummation) of the age?"* Jesus' statement initiates the Olivet Discourse and subsequent revelations about future events.

The prophecy regarding the temple's destruction was fulfilled in 70 AD, when Titus of Rome led the Roman legions to demolish the Second Temple in Jerusalem during the Jewish-Roman Revolt. This event marked a devastating moment in Jewish history and culture. The city and temple fell after prolonged conflict, resulting in the holy site being looted and besieged. Today, only the Western Wall, also known as the Wailing Wall, remains—a place where Jews and pilgrims continue to pray, placing written prayers in its crevices. The temple's destruction, however, also foreshadows the construction of a third and final temple—a subject that will be explored in subsequent reading as it is linked to the onset of the end times.

Revelation 11:1-2 describes the act of measuring the temple, the reasons for which are not explicitly stated but are part of end-times events. Ezekiel chapters 40 through 48 provide detailed accounts of a future millennial temple, aligning with the restoration of all things mentioned in Acts 3:21. Zechariah 6:12-15 also references "the branch" as a symbol of future restoration, further emphasizing the temple's significance in the fulfillment of biblical prophecy.

The Third Sign: *The 144,000 Evangelists*

The Great Falling Away will trigger an unprecedented wave of evangelism, leading to the emergence of the 144,000 described in Revelation 7:4-8. These individuals will serve as the reapers of the Jewish harvest, representing the restoration of the ten lost tribes, as they unite with Judah and Benjamin, the southern tribes. Their appearance is a sign that the end is approaching. This prophecy fulfills Isaiah 66:8 and Romans 11:26, which states that a nation will be born in a day.

The vision in Revelation 12 is interpreted as the period when the 144,000 are revealed through the outpouring of the "latter rain" prophesied in Joel 2:23. This prophecy is threefold: literal rain for abundant harvest as Israel returns to the Lord; the outpouring at Pentecost considered the former rain; and the "latter rain," a spiritual outpouring akin to Pentecost, which is believed to apply to the 144,000.

The latter rain and the 144,000 will coincide with the Great Falling Away. 144,000 are part of the "remnant" who remain faithful, distinguishing themselves from those who have abandoned the faith and initiating a network of evangelism and discipleship. The birth of the remnant is also associated with the scene depicted in Revelation 12.

—*The 144,000*—

The 144,000, consisting of twelve thousand from each of Israel's twelve tribes, will be instrumental in the salvation of the Jews during the Great Tribulation. The sequence of God's redemption plan hinges on the salvation of the "last Gentiles."

Recent writings have highlighted the focus on missions among indigenous peoples and impoverished minorities in both developing and developed nations. Both evangelistic movements will signify the "Latter Rain," the final outpouring of God's Spirit, reminiscent of Pentecost.

Before the coming judgments, as described in Revelation 7:3, the "bond servants" (144,000) of God are sealed on their foreheads, likely representing the sealing of the Holy Spirit. These servants, drawn from each of the twelve tribes (Revelation 7:4–8), are later depicted ruling with Christ, the Lamb, on Mount Zion (Revelation 14:1–5).

By tracing the chronological order of prophecy, the child symbolizes the 144,000 who will evangelize the scattered lost tribes of Israel during severe persecution and oppression.

As the truth becomes apparent, humanity will turn to God's people for answers. This scenario connects with other prophetic passages: Isaiah 43:19 ("making a way in the wilderness"), Isaiah 35:6 ("running to God's House for knowledge" and "healing" due to streams in the desert), Isaiah 2:2-3 and Micah 4:1-2 ("many nations shall come" and "stream" to the mountain of the Lord's house), and Zechariah 8:21-23 (people running to God's House to seek Him). These passages paint a picture of a future gathering of nations, unified in worship and eager to experience God's presence during times of trouble.

The Fourth Sign: *The Second Casting Down & Persecution*

The construction of the newly built third temple is identified as the "second sign" marking the onset of the Tribulation, specifically the first three and a half years. During this period, the second sign will be visibly displayed across the internet and on billboards worldwide in the image of the Dragon. This image will become the brand of the Antichrist, associated with the infamous number of the beast. As previously detailed, this number consists of six random digits in three increments, serving as a mark of loyalty to the Antichrist.

Those who bear this mark will be identified and permitted to operate within the Antichrist's economy and government, which is overseen by an AI system known as the Beast. This system will establish a false religion that encompasses both conforming Jews and Gentiles, forming a new age order that will further divide Christianity.

According to biblical numerology, one-third of the world's population will seek refuge from impending disasters under this new world order, as they run from the judgments that were self-induced. Two-thirds of humanity will be preserved from this judgment and will stand before the White Throne Judgment, where they will be given a second chance to acknowledge Jesus as Lord and Savior. Although this is a non-traditional view, I will connect the dots of Scripture to substantiate the point.

Revelation 12 describes the aftermath of the woman's childbirth, where she escapes into the wilderness. Verse 12 proclaims, *"Therefore be glad (exult), O heavens and you that dwell in them! But woe to you, O earth and sea, for the devil has come down to you in fierce anger (fury), because he knows that he has [only] a short time [left]!"* With only three and a half years remaining, Satan is released on earth to cause unprecedented destruction.

In this context, the Dragon uses his tail to bring down one-third of the stars, casting them to earth. This act symbolizes spiritual warfare in the stellar heavens, as seen in earlier chapters. The first heavenly conflict, which occurred in eternity past, resulted in Lucifer and a third of the Sons of God being cast to the pre-Adamic earth, which was then submerged in the waters of judgment. Jesus, in His divine authority, referenced this event in Luke 10:18: *"And He said to them, I saw Satan falling like a lightning [flash] from heaven."*

Lucifer's fall was part of God's preordained plan of salvation, designed to establish His kingdom with humanity, created in harmony with His image. Not that God caused it, but God saw it coming through free will and made a plan in advance (eternity) through His foreknowledge to continue building His kingdom through the gospel.

As we connect the dots of Scripture, free will is the basis of loving God that solidifies His enduring kingdom because of collective, undeniable, perennial agreement with God. If human nature is selected by God without the willingness of free will, God's kingdom is vulnerable and fragile to voluntary rebellion. Therefore, God does not force His will upon anyone because it would violate His loving nature. Love must be freely given both ways for love to be complete. The ultimate end of this statement is I Corinthians 15:26-28:

The last enemy to be subdued and abolished is death. For He [the Father] has put all things in subjection under His [Christ's] feet. But when it says, All things are put in subjection [under Him], it is evident that He [Himself] is excepted Who does the subjecting of all things to Him. However, when everything is subjected to Him, then the Son Himself will also subject Himself to [the Father] Who put all things under Him, so that God may be all in all [be everything to everyone, supreme, the indwelling and controlling factor of life].

Nothing surprises God; in His foreknowledge, He orchestrates events in harmony with human free will. He preordains and decrees what will happen by His Word, ensuring His purposes never fail—hence, believers are encouraged to rejoice. Peter refers to this mystery in God's Master Plan of Salvation, noting that even angels are eager to understand it. As stated in 1 Peter 1:12, *"It was then disclosed to them that the services they were rendering were not meant for themselves and their period of time, but for you... Into these things [the very] angels long to look!"* The fall of Lucifer marked a new phase in creation, including the creation of humans in God's image.

Despite his fall, Satan retained access to the stellar heavens, as seen in the Book of Job. The stellar heavens are the arena for ongoing spiritual warfare, but the earth will be the final battleground between God and Satan, culminating in Armageddon (Revelation 16:16). Armageddon, derived from the Hebrew "Har Megiddo," refers to a strategic hilltop in Israel overlooking the Jezreel Valley—historically a major battlefield and the prophesied site of the final cosmic conflict between good and evil.

In Revelation 12, Satan and his fallen angels are ultimately cast out of the stellar heavens to earth, setting the stage for the final battle of all time—Armageddon. Enraged by the knowledge that his time is ending, Satan unleashes his fiercest assault on humanity.

The Fifth Sign: *The Image of the Beast*

The Dragon & Satan's Appearance: In Revelation 12, the Great Dragon—who is identified as Satan—makes an extraordinary appearance described as a "Wonder." This passage is understood to reveal not just a symbolic figure, but Satan's actual presence as depicted in Scripture. Additional clarity about his presence is found in Isaiah 14 and Ezekiel 28:11-19, which provide detailed descriptions of his role in the Paradise of God.

Satan, originally an archangel, is described as a Cherubim adorned with precious jewels and gold. The King James Version refers to him as the "anointed cherub that covers," signifying his responsibility in God's creation: overseeing the "sons of God" on earth within paradise, before the creation of the first man and woman. This period is sometimes called the "Pre-Adamic Creation," believed by some to have occurred between Genesis

1:1 and Genesis 1:2, and may be prehistoric in nature. During this time, it is thought that the creation of the earth existed in eternity rather than within the bounds of time, and time began with the new creation in Genesis 1:2 when the evening and morning are signified. This belief also explains why the earth is seen as eternal and as the future dwelling place of God's New Jerusalem.

Just as each category of angels is described as having faces, it is reasonable to believe that Satan possessed a human-like face and a body adorned with jewels and gold.

After falling into narcissistic pride and rebelling against God, Satan deceived one-third of the sons of God and attempted to overthrow God's throne. However, he was defeated by Michael and cast back to earth, which was then submerged in the waters of judgment. This led to Genesis 1:2: the re-creation of the earth and the subsequent creation of man and woman in God's image to inhabit this renewed world.

Satan's subsequent appearance in the Garden of Eden was in the form of a serpent. Ezekiel 28:13 specifically notes that Lucifer was present in the Garden of God before the first man and woman were created. His appearance, as a radiant angel adorned in glowing ornaments with a beautiful human-like face, gave him a god-like presence. This interpretation suggests that Satan's appearance was not metaphorical but literal. The logical conclusion is that Satan manifested as the most magnificent creature in the garden—a dragon—perhaps as an embodiment of the species in the garden. The serpent that tempted Eve is traditionally understood to have been cursed to crawl on its belly, leading to the assumption that it became a snake. However, it is possible that this species as a whole was cursed, thus coming to symbolize evil, and became extinct.

The Vision of Revelation 12

The remainder of the vision in Revelation 12 describes the dragon as fiery red, with seven heads, ten horns, and seven crowns. This dragon symbolizes the coming New Age Order and One World Government, which will be established to worship

Satan through the Antichrist. This worship will be facilitated by electronic communications, specifically, the image of the dragon disseminated across the internet.

The Woman and the Child

In the vision, a woman appears, pregnant and clothed with the sun—a symbol of life and energy—and is about to give birth. The woman is interpreted as the Body of Christ, distinct from the institutional church. She, as the Bride of Christ, is on the verge of bringing forth the 144,000, who will form a global network of fellowship.

The dragon stands ready to prevent the birth, but the child—representing the 144,000—is caught up to God. The term "caught up" is understood to mean ecstatic joy, as when Paul was caught up and saw a vision of heaven. Similarly, those represented by the child's birth experienced a vision of God's soon-coming kingdom that generates great joy. The woman (The Body of Christ), representing those who remain on earth, receives the "latter rain" outpouring. Her journey into the wilderness symbolizes the Body of Christ being protected during the coming Great Tribulation. This period of protection will last for three and a half years until the Second Coming of Christ to deliver the world from evil.

According to this perspective, the Body of Christ will not be raptured before the Tribulation but will remain on earth, preserved by God's providence and protection—much like the Hebrews were safeguarded in the wilderness following their exodus from Egyptian bondage. However, we will look at the most popular sources for interpreting the "last days" and "end times" by comparing Covenantalism and Dispensationalism concerning the order of culminating events.

The rise of the 144,000 will trigger a worldwide revival of faith that the world has ever seen, which will bring down the Antichrist's empire through "Spiritual Warfare."

—Flash Back—

In the context of "that which was," the scene in Revelation 12 flashes back to the spiritual warfare surrounding the birth of Christ. Foreshadowing, it prefigures the final spiritual conflict—Armageddon—between God and the devil, good and evil, that will be fought on the earth as the last war.

—The Dragon and the Godhead—

The Dragon is identified as Satan, the Beast as the Antichrist, and the False Prophet as the Antichrist's spokesperson. Collectively, they are often called the "Unholy Trinity," reflecting a counterfeit of the divine Godhead. These figures are highlighted throughout Revelation chapters 12, 13, 16, and 19-20.

The Dragon is explicitly named as Satan in Revelation 12:9 and 20:2. The first beast, symbolizing the Antichrist, rises from the sea (Revelation 13:1-10), while the second beast, or False Prophet, appears in Revelation 13:11-18. All three are seen together in Revelation 16:13 and 19:20. While these are figurative descriptions, the Dragon refers to a literal being—Satan.

—The Casting Down—

During the Great Tribulation, the Dragon, Satan, and his fallen angels are cast back to earth after being expelled by Michael. The positive aspect of this vision is that the woman—the Body of Christ—gives birth to a son, identified as the 144,000. When we place the chronology of events in place along a timeline, these 144,000 are destined to rule with Christ on earth. Twelve is the number of divine governments that correlates with the twelve tribes and twelve Apostles forming the Church of Jews and Gentiles.

This prophecy has a dual fulfillment: first, at Christ's birth, illustrated by Mary and Joseph's flight into Egypt to protect Jesus from Herod, paralleling the child's escape into the wilderness in Revelation 12; and second, in the end times, where the woman (a type of the Bride of Christ) brings forth the 144,000 evangelists mentioned in Revelation chapters 7 and

174

14. This group is closely connected to the restoration of Israel as described in Romans 11:25-26—when the last Gentile is saved, all Israel will be saved.

Preceding the 144,000, the reference to the last Gentile being saved is a direct correlation to the "latter rain" outpouring among Gentiles from Third World Countries, and those living in third world conditions—the poor and oppressed—that will experience an unprecedented revival and come to the Lord's house in record numbers as recorded in Isaiah 2:2. *"It shall come to pass in the latter days that the mountain of the Lord's house shall be [firmly] established as the highest of the mountains and shall be exalted above the hills, and all nations shall flow to it."* Micah 4:1-2: *"But in the latter days it shall come to pass that the mountain of the house of the Lord shall be established as the highest of the mountains; and it shall be exalted above the hills, and peoples shall flow to it. And many nations shall come and say, Come, let us go up to the mountain of the Lord, to the house of the God of Jacob, that He may teach us His ways, and we may walk in His paths. For the law shall go forth out of Zion and the word of the Lord from Jerusalem."*

The "latter rain" also correlates with Christ's predictive prophecy in Matthew 24:14, where reference is made to the "Gospel of the Kingdom of God" being preached in all the world as a witness to all who hear. Here, it presents the last opportunity in time to receive Christ as Lord and Savior.

One must remember that only one-third of humanity will follow the Antichrist. Two-thirds of people will see the Antichrist for what he is and turn to and seek the Lord amid persecution and chaos.

CHAPTER 16.

Signs of the End Times: Second Half Tribulation

The events outlined in Revelation chapters 4 through 19 occur during a prophetic era called the Great Tribulation. This period is described as lasting seven years and is distinctly divided into two halves.

As the Tribulation enters its second half—lasting another 3 ½ years—a dramatic shift unfolds. The antichrist, who initially brokered peace, will turn against Jews and Christians, targeting disciples of Christ. This era is marked by severe and widespread persecution of these groups.

It is important to interpret these passages within the broader narrative of end-time events, rather than in isolation. Their significance is rooted in the culmination of history as depicted in the final chapters of Revelation. Thus, these references point to future events that may not be far off.

Christ's Instruction to John: In Revelation 1:19, Christ gives clear instructions to the apostle John regarding the structure of his writings: *"Therefore write the things which you have seen [John's Vision], and the things which are [The Condition of the Seven Churches], and the things which will take place after these things [The Future not the Past]."* This guidance highlights the need to distinguish between past, present, and future events within the book of Revelation.

Revelation 1–3: The Sign for Repentance in Churches

The commendations to the seven churches emphasize ongoing good works, while admonitions urge avoidance of false teachers and doctrine, and a renewal of their first love and good deeds. To accurately interpret the prophecies in Revelation 1–3, it is necessary to consider them within the context of last-time events. Taking these passages out of context can lead to misunderstanding their true meaning and application.

The Seven Churches of Asia: The seven churches addressed in Revelation were real Christian communities located in Asia Minor, now the broad region of modern-day Turkey: Ephesus, Smyrna (Izmir), Pergamum (Bergama), Thyatira (Akhisar), Sardis, Philadelphia (Alaşehir), and Laodicea. Each church represents a unique spiritual condition relevant to churches worldwide and is called to repentance to avoid end-time judgment.

Experience, observation, and extensive research show that spiritual warfare aims to hinder the church's mission—a struggle that began with the Old Testament and the Hebrew people. This conflict can be traced to creation, where Satan first opposed God's plans for humanity.

Revelation describes the Seven Churches of Asia, each needing repentance for spiritual shortcomings. When the church conforms to secular influences—such as government policies, cultural trends, or social values—it risks dilution by worldly philosophies. This conformity weakens the church's effectiveness in combating evil and shifts its focus to a "cultural gospel."

The Call to Repentance and Judgment: Each church in Asia is urged to recognize its spiritual state and repent. This call echoes Peter's warning in I Peter 4:17–19: _"For the time [has arrived] for judgment to begin with the household of God; and if it begins with us, what will [be] the end of those who do not respect or believe or obey the good news (the Gospel) of God? And if the righteous are barely saved, what will become of the godless and wicked? Therefore, those who are ill-treated and suffer in accordance with God's will must do right and commit their souls [in charge as a deposit] to the One Who created [them] and will never fail [them]."_

The Exposure of Sin in the Churches: One of the initial signs of the "end times" is the exposure of corruption within prominent churches and among well-known pastors. This exposure serves as a warning, underscoring the urgent need for repentance among God's people as the final events of judgment approach, especially for pastors, which is why the messages are directed to the seven "stars." These stars are described as angels of the seven churches, which are mostly interpreted as the seven pastors, and the candlesticks (lampstands) as the churches reflective of their lamps trimmed and burning or going out. Pastors hold a key influential role in churches that can affect the congregation with sin or righteousness. The reference is "a little leaven" that spreads sin in the church. It can be linked to the church failing to be "Salt" and "Light" to hold back God's judgment, as seen when Abraham pleaded for the residents of Sodom and Gomorrah.

Revelation 4–6: The Sign of the Seven Judgments

John's Vision of God's Throne Room: In Revelation 4–6, John is given a vision of God's eternal throne room, where God directs history through His providence, perfecting His kingdom. This vision demonstrates the grandeur of God's reign and His authority over time and creation.

John sees a door opening in heaven, revealing God's throne surrounded by twenty-four elders representing divine government and the complete church—twelve for the tribes of Israel and twelve for the apostles. Around the throne are seven angels and four living creatures: a lion, a calf, a man, and an eagle, symbolizing God's care over all geographical directions, including wild and domesticated animals, human beings, fowls of the air, and fish of the sea.

God's throne acts as the universe's control center, initiating the Tribulation's events. Angels and symbolic messages are dispatched through the breaking of the first six seals, which are called the "Last Judgments."

—*Three Progressive Judgments*—

There are three sequential series of end-times judgments: **Seals** (scrolls holding the world's destiny), **Trumpets** (announcing war and God's wrath), and **Bowls** (prayers of the saints, representing God's response to calls for justice). Each series signals the approach to the Final White Throne Judgment. The Judgment Seat of Christ precedes the White Throne Judgment and will be addressed in chapter seventeen. The White Throne Judgment is correlated with the second resurrection, where the goats will be separated from the sheep. All believers and those who endured the Tribulation receive rewards at the second coming of Christ after the tribulation.

The Nature of the Judgments: These judgments, initiated by Christ, render humanity powerless without God's help. Human ingenuity cannot solve the disasters, echoing the warnings given in Noah's day. The judgments intensify with each judgment during the Tribulation, and with each series of judgments, God's mercy and longsuffering are displayed, giving humanity a chance to repent. Compared to Genesis six, humanity, like in Noah's day, will see life through their imagination that has been corrupted.

The Seven Seals

The Seven Seals are integral to the vision of a scroll, viewed as the earth's title deed, which only Jesus is worthy to open. This act signifies His authority to reclaim the earth from the dominion of man and the power of Satan. The opening of the seals marks a progression of divine judgments that ultimately lead to Christ's Second Coming and the culmination of human rule. Many interpret the Seven Seals as depicting a chronological sequence of events during the final Tribulation period, impacting a third of the earth, sea, freshwater, and sky. These events expose humanity's tendency toward self-destruction, as God purges the chaos resulting from evil and unbelief—the ultimate rejection of forgiveness, known as the "unpardonable sin." This rejection is attributed to a conscience corrupted by evil and rendered unredeemable.

First Four Seals: The Four Horsemen of the Apocalypse

The judgments begin with the opening of the first four seals, as described in Revelation 6 and 8. These are symbolized by the appearance of the Four Horsemen of the Apocalypse, each representing a stage in the rise of the Antichrist: False Peace, Cataclysmic War, Famines leading to Economic Collapse and Scarcity, and Mass Deaths.

First Seal: The White Horse

The first seal reveals a white horse, whose rider is given a crown and carries a bow without arrows. This figure symbolizes conquest achieved through diplomacy and wealth, signifying the rise of the Antichrist and marking the commencement of the Tribulation.

Second Seal: The Red Horse

The second seal brings forth a red horse. Its rider wields a large sword and represents the outbreak of war and the onset of Armageddon. This reveals the true nature of the Antichrist and brings an end to global peace.

Third Seal: The Black Horse

The third seal unveils a black horse, whose rider holds a pair of scales. This image signifies severe financial depression and widespread scarcity, comparable to the famine experienced in Egypt during Joseph's time.

Fourth Seal: The Pale Horse

The fourth seal is marked by a rider named Death upon a pale horse. This figure brings widespread sickness, disease, and death, ultimately resulting in the loss of a quarter of the world's population, primarily due to war and famine.

Fifth Seal: The Cry of the Martyrs

The fifth seal reveals the souls of martyrs reflected from beneath the altar, symbolizing their worship of the Lord—those who refused to worship the Antichrist. They are depicted crying out for justice and are assured that their fellow believers will soon join them. Each receives a white robe and is told to rest until the full number of martyrs is complete.

Sixth Seal: Cosmic Disturbances

The sixth seal introduces cosmic catastrophes and displays of divine wrath. These manifest as natural disasters and phenomena resembling climate change, setting the stage for the subsequent trumpet judgments.

Seventh Seal: Silence and Transition

Upon the opening of the seventh seal, a profound silence falls in heaven for about half an hour. This pause is filled with awe and marks the transition to the next series of judgments—the seven trumpets. During this interval, the golden censor symbolizes praise and prayer, and the silence is followed by thunder as angels prepare to sound their trumpets.

The Seven Trumpets

The Seven Trumpets, detailed in Revelation 8–11, are sounded thirty minutes after the seventh seal is broken. Seven angels sound the trumpets, each bringing a specific judgment:

- **The First Trumpet:** Many scholars interpret this as a cataclysmic, volcanic event or an asteroid impact affecting the Mediterranean region. Hail, storms of fire, rain down mingled with blood, and blood burn one-third of the trees and all the grass.

- **The Second Trumpet:** A massive burning mountain is "cast" into the seas, which could erupt from a massive earthquake, causing celestial darkness.

- **The Third Trumpet:** A star named Wormwood falls from the sky, possibly an asteroid poisoning a third of the rivers and fresh water, causing many people to die from the bitter water.

- **The Fourth Trumpet:** One-third of the sun, moon, and stars are darkened (Revelation 8:12) struck possibly with an eclipse, causing a third of the day and night to become dark—cosmic darkness.

- **The Fifth Trumpet:** (First Woe) Demonic locusts torment unsealed humans for five months (Revelation

9:1-12): A "star" (angel) falls from heaven and opens the bottomless pit, releasing demonic "locusts" with scorpion-like tails. They torture those without God's seal for five months, causing immense pain from a possibly incurable disease, but no death, just demonic torment that has been evoked by the Whore of Babylon.

- **The Sixth Trumpet:** (Second Woe) A demonic army influences Satan's forces of humans to kill a third of humanity (Revelation 9:13-21). Four angels, bound at the Euphrates River, are released, leading a massive, supernatural army that kills a third of mankind.

- **The Seventh Trumpet:** (Third Woe) Announces the kingdom of God and final judgment. The final kingdom is heralded, and the bowl judgments (Revelation 11:15-19) are announced, "The kingdom of the world has become the kingdom of our Lord and of his Christ." It initiates the final judgment and opens God's temple in heaven.

The first four trumpets affect nature, while the last three are "woes" involving intensified demonic activity and final divine rule.

These judgments are catastrophic plagues associated with demons from the abyss, including ecological destruction, demonic locusts, cosmic disturbances, and possibly small-scale nuclear war. They intensify God's wrath during the Tribulation.

Revelation 7–11: The Sign of Natural Disasters

The Final Judgments and the Two Witnesses: In Revelation chapters 9–11, an angel appears with a small book containing the final judgments. During this period, international prophets are raised in the spirit of Moses and Elijah to proclaim their message globally, using the World Wide Web. An envoy from the beast opposes them and kills them, but after three and a half days, they are resurrected and seen worldwide via satellite TV.

The seventh trumpet then sounds, marking Christ's imminent return. John's eating the book echoes Ezekiel 2:9–3:3, symbolizing receiving and internalizing God's word, which is sweet to receive but bitter to deliver due to its judgment.

Inductively, these two witnesses, symbolizing the law and prophets, along with the 144,000, represent reaching Israel worldwide among the Jewish community along with the 144,000.

The Sealing of God's Servants and the Role of the Angels: John observes four angels at the earth's corners—north, south, east, and west—restraining the winds. Another angel from the east, carrying the "Seal of God," instructs the others to pause judgment until the 144,000 witnesses are sealed and protected. These witnesses play a critical role in the vision. The angels are ultimately tasked with unleashing natural disasters, interpreted as climate change disturbances from the human perspective.

Revelation 12: The Sign of the Restoration of Israel & Global Revival

In the vision described in Revelation 12, a remarkable sign appears in heaven. This sign is not a literal image, but a symbolic celestial phenomenon intended to convey profound spiritual truths to those who witness it. The image depicts a woman, radiant and clothed in the sun, with the moon beneath her feet. This woman represents the Body of Christ reigning with Christ in the promised restitution of all things. She is about to give birth to a man-child—one who wears twelve crowns, symbolizing divine authority and government of the 144,000. As she undergoes the pains of childbirth, the drama of spiritual conflict intensifies.

The woman herself symbolizes the Body of Christ, while the dragon is an image of Satan, who holds sway over the nations and seeks to dominate them. The man-child she delivers is interpreted as the nation of Israel, reborn and represented by the 144,000 from every tribe of Israel, who are taken up to God's throne, meaning protected. This fulfills longstanding biblical promises about Israel's restoration. The narrative draws a parallel to the birth of Christ: just as Satan attempted to destroy the Christ-Child, he now turns his wrath against the newly restored nation of Israel.

Despite Satan's persecution, God intervenes to protect Israel. The woman is shielded in the wilderness from the flood unleashed by the dragon, which symbolizes the persecution and opposition stirred up by people under Satan's influence. This echoes the divine protection granted to Israel during the Exodus and to Jesus in His early years. This dramatic event is announced from heaven, marking the arrival of complete salvation for the world.

The Beginning of Satan's End: The story intensifies as a cosmic battle erupts in heaven. Michael the Archangel leads the heavenly armies in a decisive war, ultimately casting Satan and his followers down to earth. This defeat marks the beginning of Satan's final phase, as he launches a desperate assault on humanity. The world enters a period marked by heightened demonic activity and turmoil.

The Rise of the Beast and World Domination: With Satan cast down to earth, he empowers a new ruler—the Beast, also known as the Anti-Christ, who governs the huge, monstrous computer called the Beast. The Beast is granted authority to rule the world for three and a half years. Through deception, particularly by feigning a resurrection, possibly projected through AI technology, the Beast draws global admiration and worship. He emerges from the sea with ten horns, ten crowns, and seven heads. The heads are marked by blasphemous statements designed to degrade God, pointing to the abomination that causes desolation described in prophecy.

The Beast's Appearance and Power: The beast is depicted as a leopard, with the feet of a bear and the mouth of a lion—three of the most formidable wild animals. This combination suggests strength, agility, and ferocity. The beast possesses ten horns crowned with ten crowns, symbolizing authority and power.

The Source of the Beast's Power: The dragon, identified as Satan, bestows his power upon the beast. One of the beast's seven heads receives a mortal wound that results in death, but the beast appears to be resurrected. This resurrection is described as likely being an AI projection across the internet, which causes those whose names were not written in the Lamb's Book of Life to worship and serve the beast.

Interpretation of the Seven Heads: The seven heads of the beast in the Book of Revelation are more commonly interpreted as seven consecutive, dominant world empires or kings—governments that have opposed God's people throughout history. Specifically, these represent Egypt, Assyria, Babylon, Medo-Persia, Greece, Rome, and a final, future power that will be "Babylon the Great," the kingdom of the Antichrist, which will turn against the great whore of Babylon. "A Kingdom Divided Against Itself Cannot Stand." Together, these nations throughout history symbolize political power that will culminate and fall with the Antichrist's kingdom. The angel announces self-destruction.

Another beast appears with two horns, doing great wonders, like a lamb who advocated from the platform of the "Whore of Babylon" (a form of new age religion) worship of the first Beast. The Anti-Christ uses the second beast, a leader from the earth, to assist in consolidating control. The second beast causes the first beast to talk and transmits the image of the first beast across billboards and the internet for worship. This leader is the false prophet whose role is to carry out a census and mark all people. This mark becomes essential for participating in economic life—no one can buy or sell without it. Furthermore, those who refuse to acknowledge the first Beast as Lord face the threat of death, underscoring the severe and all-encompassing nature of the Beast's global regime.

Revelation 13–14: The Final Contrast and the Ultimate Victory

Revelation chapters 13 and 14 mark a turning point in the narrative, presenting a stark contrast between the followers of the Lamb, Jesus, and those who align themselves with the beast, Satan. This section not only emphasizes the differences between these two groups but also introduces a pivotal moment when three angels deliver crucial messages to all humanity.

The Messages of the Three Angels (Revelation 14:6–13): The first angel proclaims the "everlasting gospel," urging every nation, tribe, language, and people to fear, glorify, and worship God because the "hour of his judgment has come." The second angel announces the fall of "Babylon the Great," which symbolizes empires or systems that oppose God. The third angel issues a severe warning: those who worship the beast and receive his mark will face the full and undiluted wrath of God, resulting in warranted eternal torment.

Key Messengers and Symbols: The 144,000 witnesses will proclaim the "Gospel of the Kingdom of God" across the world. Under the influence of the "latter rain," their mission will be to reach and restore Israel. In addition, the two witnesses—representing Moses and Elijah, who symbolize the law and the prophets—will also declare God's judgments, reminiscent of the days of Noah.

The introduction of Revelation presents seven stars and seven candlesticks. Scholars interpret the seven candlesticks as guardian angels assigned to each church, and the seven stars as the pastors of the seven churches in Asia. The messages of Revelation are directed to these leaders first, offering them the opportunity to repent and to share the message of Christ's return and the impending judgments. In this way, people will be forewarned about what is to come.

Encouragement and Warning for Believers: Within these chapters, a vision of ultimate victory is presented, but it is coupled with warnings of impending judgment. The everlasting gospel is proclaimed, offering every individual—including the unrepentant—a chance to turn to the Lord. Believers are called to persevere during the tribulation, as those who die in Christ are described as blessed; they find rest from their labor. This is also the moment when the "gospel of the kingdom of God" is preached throughout the entire world.

The Vision of the 144,000 on Mount Zion: The chapter opens with the three angels sequentially announcing the events to come, reminiscent of the structure found in the opening chapters of the Book of Job. The scene shifts to a vision of Jesus, the Lamb, standing on Mount Zion with the 144,000 who were previously sealed in Revelation 7. These individuals are identified as the "first fruits" of the resurrection, as described in I Corinthians 15:20-23. They are depicted as faithful, "undefiled," and unwavering in their commitment to the Lamb, following Him wherever He goes. Their unique connection to Christ is celebrated as they sing a "new song" of redemption, a song only they can learn.

Eternity Perspective and the Fall of Babylon: Revelation 14 offers believers an "eternity perspective," assuring them that even amid severe persecution, God will ultimately triumph, and the kingdom of darkness will be fully defeated. The downfall of Babylon the Great is foretold. The vision continues with the appearance of a white cloud, upon which the Son of Man sits with a drawn sword and a sharp sickle, prepared for the harvest. This period will witness the greatest gathering of believers, even as it coincides with the most troubled time in history. The vineyard symbolizes Israel's restoration and being grafted back into the Church (Romans 11:11–24), while the winepress serves as a metaphor for the sacrifices of believers—the martyrs—who give their lives for their faith in the Lord.

Revelation 14:14-20: The Final Harvest and Vintage

The chapter concludes with two distinct and symbolic scenes of reaping. In the Grain Harvest (14:14–16), one like the "Son of Man" (Jesus) sits on a white cloud and reaps the harvest of the earth with a sickle, gathering the righteous. In the Grape Harvest (14:17–20), another angel collects the "grapes"—the wicked—and casts them into the "great winepress of God's wrath." The devastation is so overwhelming that blood flows as high as a horse's bridle for approximately two hundred miles, illustrating the completeness of God's judgment. This scene is correlated to Christ's parables of the wheat and tares.

The Parable of the Wheat and the Tares

The Parable of the Wheat and the Tares is a story found in Matthew 13:24-30. The parable is also known as the story of the weeds that look like wheat. In this parable, the wheat represents the "children of the kingdom" or the remnant, while the tares symbolize the "children of the wicked one"—those who masqueraded as Christians. The narrative describes the kingdom of heaven as a field where an enemy secretly sows weeds among the wheat. Both the wheat and the tares are allowed to grow together until the final harvest.

Elements of the Story

- The Field: Represents the world.

- Wheat: Symbolizes the children of the kingdom.

- The Tares: Symbolize the children of the wicked one.

- The Harvest: Represents the end of the age.

The Landowner's Instruction: To protect the wheat, the landowner instructs his servants to let both the wheat and the tares grow together until the harvest. This is to avoid uprooting the wheat (judging true believers) while pulling out the weeds. At the time of the harvest, the tares are gathered and burned.

Relevance: The parable is relevant to the end-time harvest, illustrating the coexistence of good and evil until the final judgment, when a clear separation will occur.

[*Eternal Life and the Millennial Reign*

In Revelation chapters 20 through 22, we are given a profound vision of the bliss associated with eternal, immortal life. This vision is explored from the perspective of human existence, aiming to make sense of a life that experiences the most significant joys even before the resurrection. The passages invite us to consider what it means to participate in the fullness of life as described in these closing chapters of Revelation.

Millennial Views and the Separation of the Sheep and Goats

As we examine the differing Millennialist viewpoints regarding the thousand-year reign of Christ, a central question emerges: When does the separation of the sheep and the goats occur? Is it before the thousand-year reign or after? While interpretations vary, a careful comparison of the relevant Scriptures suggests that, regardless of the timing, the goats—those who are separated—will be allowed to repent. However, the narrative indicates they will ultimately reject this chance, a decision rooted in the deep corruption of evil within them. Consequently, after a thousand years or before, the wicked will once again unite with the Antichrist for the final battle and ultimately be cast out from the presence of God.]

The Seven Bowls Final Judgments

Revelation 15 serves as a brief, dramatic introduction to the final seven bowl judgments (God's wrath) that conclude the tribulation. It portrays victorious saints in heaven singing the song of Moses and the Lamb, praising God's righteousness before seven angels emerge from the heavenly temple to pour out the final plagues.

The bowls, described in Revelation 16, represent God's final, severe wrath, as humanity's rejection intensifies with each judgment. The seventh seal introduces the seven trumpets, and the seventh trumpet introduces the seven bowls. While Revelation 15:7 describes the bowls as full of God's wrath, they are connected to the "golden bowls full of incense" in Revelation 5:8, symbolizing the prayers of the saints. The prayers of the faithful, mingled with praise, are represented by a golden censor, emphasizing the importance of prayer during spiritual warfare. After half an hour of silence, thunder resounds, and the angels prepare to sound their trumpets, signaling the coming judgments.

These are the final, rapid, and most severe judgments reminiscent of the plagues in Egypt during the Hebrew bondage, when you consider the cumulative effects: Sores appear on humanity, the sea turns to blood, and rivers turn to blood. A devastating earthquake and massive hail, concluding with "It is done." In summary, they are part of a cascading series of judgments, not the final act itself.

Revelation 15-16: The Seven Bowl Final Judgments

The seven bowls judgments of Revelation (Revelation 16) are the final, immediate, complete judgments of God's wrath poured out on the earth during the end-times Tribulation targeting the antichrist, the Beast, and those that follow them. These plagues are reminiscent of the plagues in Egypt during the Hebrew bondage that cause immense destruction, including physical sores on the body, the death of marine life, water turning to blood, scorching heat, darkness, the drying of the Euphrates, and a catastrophic earthquake.

John sees seven angels with seven plagues, which are the final stage of God's wrath (or judgments) before the end of the age. The saints who overcame the beast and its mark stand on a "sea of glass mixed with fire." This represents their victory, while the fire signifies God's holiness and purification. These victorious believers sing a song praising God as "Lord God Almighty," "King of the nations," and recognizing His works as "just and true"—God is exonerated of any unjust acts concerning His judgments in the eyes of humanity.

The "temple of the tabernacle of the testimony" opens, and seven angels emerge dressed in pure, bright linen with golden sashes. One of the four living creatures gives the seven angels seven golden bowls full of the wrath of God. The temple is filled with smoke from God's power and glory, preventing anyone from entering until the plagues are completed. This signifies that the final judgment is absolute, imminent, and cannot be stopped.

Revelation 16 details the seven bowl judgments. These swift, destructive plagues target the Antichrist's kingdom and those who took his mark, culminating in the battle of Armageddon and the collapse of human rebellion. Unlike previous, partial judgments, these seven bowls are total, targeting the center of the Beast's power. These judgments conclude the series of end-times, following the seven seals and seven trumpets, serving as the final, absolute manifestation of divine justice against wickedness. We see from the final judgments that the battle is truly the Lord's.

- **First Bowl:** Harmful, painful, and ugly sores that fester and break out on those who have the mark of the Beast and worship its image.

- **Second Bowl:** The sea turns into blood like that of a dead person, killing every living thing in it. The sea and freshwater sources destroy marine life and water supplies.

- **Third Bowl:** Rivers and springs turn into blood, a righteous retribution for those who shed the blood of saints and prophets.

- **Fourth Bowl:** The sun is allowed to scorch humanity with intense fire, yet people curse God and refuse to repent.

- **Fifth Bowl:** Total darkness falls upon the kingdom of the Beast, causing intense anguish, but people still refuse to repent.

- **Sixth Bowl:** The Euphrates River dries up, preparing the way for kings from the East to assemble the battle of Armageddon.

- **Seventh Bowl:** A voice from the Temple declares "It is done," followed by the largest earthquake in human history, the fall of Babylon, and massive, 100-pound hailstones.

Revelation 17-19: From Judgment to Rejoicing

After the pouring out of the seventh bowl of wrath upon the earth, a voice from the Temple proclaims, "It is done." This moment is accompanied by the largest earthquake in human history, signaling the fall of Babylon—the dwelling place of demons. The heavens announce Babylon's downfall, and a voice urges God's people to "come out of her," echoing the warning given to Sodom and Gomorrah. This call is to avoid sharing Babylon's sins and the plagues she will receive, which will come suddenly in a single day.

"Babylon the Great" is depicted as a prostitute riding a seven-headed, ten-horned scarlet beast. She represents a corrupt, apostate religious system that allies with political powers—dictators of the earth—to persecute Jews, believers, and the downtrodden. Ultimately, she is destroyed by the same powers she manipulated, fulfilling the warning found in scripture: *"Do not be deceived and deluded and misled; God will not allow Himself to be sneered at (scorned, disdained, or mocked by mere pretensions or professions, or by His precepts being set aside.) [He inevitably deludes himself who attempts to delude God.] For whatever a man sows, that and that only is what he will reap."* It can mean an eternity of the same pain inflicted on others that those guilty were warned about.

Her intoxication comes from the genocide and annihilation of Christ's followers, who are exalted in heaven as martyrs. The beast's seven hills are interpreted as the seven hills of Rome, the seat of power in John's Day, expected to rise again in the end times, or represent a sequence of historical empires. The ten horns symbolize ten kings or rulers who align with the beast to make war against the Lamb (Jesus), but will eventually turn against the harlot and destroy her. This causes widespread mourning, as her destruction means the loss of wealth, luxuries, and illicit trade—including the "bodies and souls of men."

Believers should be encouraged, not at death, but rather at the truth that God's enemies from every generation will ultimately fail and fall.

—*The Question of Hades and Hell*—

The judgment of hell is not for humanity to decide. God, in His sovereignty, acts according to His will—what He wants, when He wants, where He wants, and to whom He wants, and how He wants His world to be governed in righteousness. His judgments are beyond humanity's authority. Romans 9:20-21 asks, *"But who are you, a mere man, to criticize and contradict and answer back to God? Will what is formed say to him that formed it, why have you made me thus? Has the potter no right over the clay, to make out of the same mass (lump) one vessel for beauty and distinction and honorable use, and another for menial or ignoble and dishonorable use?"* This passage suggests that while human fate rests in human hands, divine destiny is determined by God, who chooses our destiny based on human will, which may sound like a contradiction to human reasoning. I Corinthians 2:16, *"For who has known or understood the mind (the counsels and purposes) of the Lord to guide and instruct Him and give Him knowledge? But we have the mind of Christ (the Messiah) and do hold the thoughts (feelings and purposes) of His heart."*

The question arises: How can God be good while casting people into hell and causing destruction? God's goodness in judgment is measured by His mercy, extended through time by purging the world of evil corruption caused by the devil. The blame for death and destruction lies with the devil, who seeks to lead as many as possible to hell with him. Hell was originally made for the devil and his demons, but humans are swayed to follow him. The goodness of God is evident in His cleansing the world from evil and corrupt influences.

Those who are judged prefer an eternity without God because they hate Him. Their death is an eternity apart from God's presence, with burning memories of their wickedness, as illustrated by the story of the rich man in Luke 16:19-31. He is tormented with memories, a glimpse into the nature of hell as the consciousness of darkness, the abyss, separated by a gulf. Christ's parables use metaphoric language like "weeping and gnashing of teeth" and "where the worm never dies," describing the eternal effects of death.

The rich man's torment leads him to ask Abraham to cool his tongue with water and warn his family, but an unbridgeable gulf separates heaven and hell. This parable warns against spiritual adultery—aligning with worldly systems instead of God—and underscores the inevitable fall of deceptive worldly systems at the end of time.

Hell is not the annihilation of the soul or an experience limited to this life, followed by ceasing to exist after death. This idea would excuse corrupt behavior and avoid God's justice, making it seem as if one could get away with anything in this life. Think of it this way: if heaven and hell are real, why take a chance? Life insurance is one thing for this life, but eternal security is for life after death. It is an unknown reality that can only be known when we trust the promise of God.

The Final Downfall of Babylon: In Revelation 18, a mighty angel throws a large millstone into the sea, symbolizing Babylon's violent destruction and its permanent disappearance. While some associate Babylon the Great with the Roman Empire, Babylon more broadly represents any worldly system founded on greed, idolatry, and persecution of believers. Revelation 18 marks the final downfall of this system, demonstrating God's justice over worldly corruption.

Celebration and the Marriage Supper of the Lamb: Revelation 19 is a joyful celebration of Babylon's fall, with no love lost, and the anticipation of the Marriage Supper of the Lamb. Drawing from the parable of the five wise and five foolish virgins, it emphasizes readiness for Christ's coming. Christ returns as a warrior-king on a white horse, defeating the Beast and the false prophet, and establishing a righteous reign as the hallelujah chorus erupts in praise.

Christ's Ultimate Victory: Christ is revealed not as a humble servant, but as "Faithful and True," coming to judge and make war for God's justice. He is named the "Word of God" and "King of Kings." This chapter is the climax where divine justice is fully executed, bringing an end to wickedness and ushering in Christ's final victory. The subsequent chapters (20-22) will explore the bliss of eternal life in the New Jerusalem and the relationships within the Body of Christ, beyond imagination.

CHAPTER 17.

Unraveling the End Times

Revelation 20:7-10 describes the concluding events of the 1,000-year millennial reign. At the end of this period, Satan is released from the Abyss, also referred to as the Bottomless Pit. Once free, Satan resumes his role as deceiver, leading the nations—collectively called Gog and Magog—into rebellion against Christ. **(Gog and Magog could very well be nations form the East and West, rather than two assumed nations, united with the Antichrist in battle against the Host of the Lord.)** This uprising results in swift judgment: fire descends from heaven, destroying the rebellious forces. Following this defeat, Satan is cast into the lake of fire, joining the beast (the Antichrist) and the false prophet, marking their eternal punishment.

We embarked on this journey by examining "Prophetic Interpretation" and the systematic-pragmatic approach to Scripture interpretation and "Biblical Prophecy's Inner Nature." As we progress towards the conclusion, please note that historically, it is a futile attempt to undermine Orthodox Christianity. However, it can be supported and made more accessible through a common language, which I've referred to as the "God-Talk" to inspire growth in the Christian faith among all people.

The God-Talk method in this work emphasizes that unorthodox theology should be built upon the foundation of orthodoxy by measuring doctrine in light of God's consistent word. The pragmatic approach aims to make the original language and meaning of Scripture accessible to everyone, regardless of their background or level of education. In conclusion, this section will offer a concise survey of the most prominent eschatological views and ultimately focus on a single biblical perspective. It is essential to acknowledge that the diversity of theological views can sometimes be confusing, potentially inspiring believers to live for Christ, or conversely, undermining their faith due to misunderstandings.

Purpose of Prophetic Warnings: Jesus counseled His disciples not to be alarmed or frightened by the unfolding events of the end times. Instead, these signs serve as a call to readiness, urging believers to remain watchful, prepared, and steadfast in their faith. The prophetic warnings signal the approaching culmination of history and stress the necessity for spiritual vigilance, accompanied by the joy that comes from knowing the Promise of Salvation is near fulfillment.

Key Terminology of the End Times

- **Eschatology:** Eschatology is the study of final events in history just before time ends, focusing on humanity's ultimate destiny and end-time occurrences. It highlights the concluding events that precede the transition from temporal existence to immortality.

- **Parousia:** This term denotes presence, arrival, or official visit, and is specifically linked to the Second Coming of Christ. At the culmination of the Ages, Christ's return inaugurates the New Jerusalem on Earth.

- **Time:** Though Hebrew lacks a specific term for "time," the concept emerges in various forms. In Greek, "Chronos" refers to chronological or sequential time, while "Kairos" describes an opportune or significant moment. Within God's plan for salvation, "Kairos" represents the opportune moment—God's perfect timing, with the return of Christ exemplifying this pivotal event.

To further clarify these views, we will compare and contrast them, ultimately identifying the perspective that aligns best with the systematic-pragmatic approach. An exegetical survey of the etymology of eschatological views reveals their roots in either Calvinism or Arminian theology.

Calvinism Focuses on Covenant Theology

Calvinist and Reformed faith traditions emphasize Covenants as defining God's relationship with humanity and revealing His will for the Church and human destiny throughout history. These covenants progress toward the seventh and final covenant—the "Everlasting Covenant," marking the New Jerusalem, or Heaven on Earth. The major covenants are Adamic, Noahic, Abrahamic, Mosaic, Davidic, and the New Covenant of Grace, concluding with God's Eternal Covenant recorded in Jeremiah 31:31-33.

While Calvinists may differ in their perspectives on the four views of Millennialism (Dispensational, Historical, Postmillennial, and Amillennial), most adhere closely to Amillennialism. This view interprets Revelation 20 symbolically, seeing the millennium as the period from Christ's ascension to His return, during which Christ reigns through the Church on Earth from heaven. As such, Calvinist traditions often support a theocracy of church doctrine and politics for governance. Others anticipate a golden church age where the gospel is spread globally before Christ's return. However, Reformed theology consistently asserts that Christ is already reigning over all things, exalted at God's right hand.

Arminianism Focuses on Dispensational Theology

Arminianism is characterized by Dispensational Theology, which views history as divided into periods, or dispensations, between covenants. Each dispensation highlights God's revelation for the Church and humanity. The seven dispensations—Innocence, Conscience, Promise, Law, Human Government, Grace, and the Millennial Kingdom—span from creation to Christ's rule.

Both Calvinism and Arminianism analyze salvation as a process involving personal participation, but counter their systems of faith. The primary distinction lies in Calvinism's doctrine of predestination, which holds that salvation is granted to the "elect" by God's will alone, without human effort, and is eternally secure (TULIP doctrine: Total Depravity, Unconditional Grace, Limited Atonement, Irresistible Grace, and Perseverance of the

Saints). In contrast, Arminianism affirms the role of human will, emphasizing that salvation is attained by faith and can be lost by renouncing that faith (Five Articles of Remonstrance: Conditional Election, Unlimited Atonement, Human Depravity & Grace, Resistible Grace, and Conditional Perseverance).

The Covenant Promise of Salvation transcends any system, process, or methodology. Pragmatically, salvation is a gift of grace and faith in Christ's finished work on the cross. From the moment of individual salvation to the New Jerusalem, God's Kingdom is built within believers through free will. Luke 17:20-21: *"Asked by the Pharisees when the kingdom of God would come, He replied to them by saying, The kingdom of God does not come with signs to be observed or with visible display, Nor will people say, Look! Here [it is]! or, See, [it is] there! For behold, the kingdom of God is within you [in your hearts] and among you [surrounding you]."* This perspective acknowledges one's body as the temple of God and God's rule through human conscience for eternity.

The Three Tribulations

The Tribulations viewpoint centers on three major perspectives regarding the timing of the rapture—the event in which believers are "caught up" with the Lord in the air. These views are:

- **Pre-Tribulation View:** This perspective holds that the rapture happens before the seven-year tribulation commences. Christians and the Holy Spirit are taken from the earth to heaven, escaping the period of wrath and the antichrist's reign. This view emphasizes the imminent return of Christ.

- **Mid-Tribulation View:** In this view, the rapture takes place in the middle of the seven years, around 3½ years in. Believers endure the first half of the tribulation (the "beginning of sorrows") but are taken before the great tribulation, the final 3½ years of God's wrath.

- **Post-Tribulation View:** Advocates of this view believe the rapture occurs after the entire seven-year tribulation.

The rapture and Second Coming of Christ are seen as a single event, with believers meeting Christ in the air upon His return.

These perspectives primarily differ in their timing and whether believers are taken to heaven before, during, or after the tribulation, ranging from escaping the tribulation entirely to enduring it until Christ's arrival.

The Great Tribulation Judgments

Transitioning from the end of the last days to the beginning of the end times, the "Gospel of the Kingdom of God" will have been preached in all the world as a witness against unrepentant humanity. These last judgments conclude the end of all judgments that will be finalized at the White Throne Judgment. Note that the Judgment Seat of Christ will precede the White Throne Judgment.

—The Judgment Seat of Christ—

The Judgment Seat of Christ, often referred to as the *"bema seat"*, is derived from the tradition of awarding Olympic athletes their medals on the highest platform. This platform symbolizes honor and recognition for achievement in service to humanity on behalf of the Lord as servant-leaders during Christ's second coming.

According to Zechariah 14:4, Scripture foretells that the Lord's feet will stand upon the Mount of Olives, which is situated east of Jerusalem. This event is described as taking place during the "Day of the Lord." The prophecy explains that the mountain will split in two, forming a very large valley when the Messiah returns to rule. This dramatic transformation is connected to the Second Coming of Jesus and marks the conclusion of the final battle for Jerusalem.

The Mount of Olives holds special significance as the location where Jesus ascended to heaven, as recorded in Acts 1:9–12. Because of this, there is a prevailing belief that Jesus will return to the same place. This moment is correlated with the "scepter" of rulership remaining in the lineage of David as God's "opportune

Moment" mentioned previously. **The Question Arises: Will Christ reign on earth for a literal thousand years from that moment on? Or will that moment bring in the final White Throne Judgment? The partial answer is, regardless of the time factor, the Judgment Seat of Christ must occur first.**

At the Judgment Seat of Christ, believers are rewarded for their faithfulness in service to the Lord. This is where the phrase "well done, good and faithful servant" finds its application, emphasizing commendation for devoted service. Importantly, this judgment does not concern sin or salvation; rather, it focuses solely on the believer's actions and their faithfulness towards eternal rewards.

The biblical basis is found in II Corinthians 5:10: *"For we must all appear and be revealed as we are before the judgment seat of Christ, so that each one may receive [his pay] according to what he has done in the body, whether good or evil [considering what his purpose and motive have been, and what he has achieved, been busy with, and given himself and his attention to accomplishing]."* This passage highlights the evaluation of the heart (conscience) concerning the quality, not quantity, of the works done in the name of the Lord. The motives and purpose behind the acts of service will be judged in a moment and flash into the awareness of the conscience. That is, the distribution of rewards at the Second Coming of Christ will not be like the secular experience of standing in line. Instead, just as we are "changed" from mortality to immortality in the "twinkling of an eye," our rewards will register in our consciousness. However, according to Scripture and the biblical basis for salvation as unmerited, undeserved, and unearned favor, all believers will not receive rewards but will still enter eternal glory.

Loss of Rewards for Believers

While believers retain their salvation, they can lose rewards for their service to God if their actions are characterized by unfaithfulness or works that are not motivated by genuine service to the Lord. The distinction between salvation and rewards is central; salvation is secure, but rewards are conditional upon the quality and motivation of one's works.

Key passages, such as I Corinthians 3:15, illustrate this concept by describing how certain works may be "burned up," resulting in the believer "suffering loss." Despite this loss, the individual will still be saved. This emphasizes that salvation is not at risk, but rewards can be forfeited through unworthy actions.

Additionally, Revelation 2:10 and I Corinthians 9:24-27 warn believers that the "crown of life" and the "imperishable crown" can be forfeited. These passages liken the Christian life to a race in which participants can be disqualified, leading to the loss of rewards.

The First Resurrection: Scripture explicitly defines "the first resurrection" in Revelation 20:4-6, describing it as a blessed event where believers, including martyrs, are raised to life to reign with Christ for a thousand years, and over whom the second death has no power. This resurrection refers to the resurrection of the just, or the resurrection to life of all believers from all ages, and those who endured the tribulation.

Then I saw thrones, and sitting on them were those to whom authority to act as judges and to pass sentence was entrusted. Also, I saw the souls of those who had been slain with axes [beheaded] for their witnessing to Jesus and [for preaching and testifying] for the Word of God, and who had refused to pay homage to the beast or his statue and had not accepted his mark or permitted it to be stamped on their foreheads or on their hands. And they lived again and ruled with Christ (the Messiah) a thousand years.

The remainder of the dead were not restored to life again until the thousand years were completed. This is the first resurrection.

Blessed (happy, to be envied) and holy (spiritually whole, of unimpaired innocence and proved virtue) is the person who takes part (shares) in the first resurrection! Over them the second death exerts no power or authority, but they shall be ministers of God and of Christ (the Messiah), and they shall rule along with Him a thousand years.

At the second coming of Christ, following the defeat of Satan, during the arrival of Christ, Romans 14:11 proclaims: "every knee shall bow, and every tongue confess that Jesus Christ is Lord." This signifies the universal recognition of Christ's authority and glory by all but applies to the Body of Christ that will occur at the first resurrection. According to I Thessalonians 4:15-17, the dead in Christ will be raised first at His second coming in the air, followed by those who are alive at the time.

I Corinthians 15:50-53: But I tell you this, brethren, flesh and blood cannot [become partakers of eternal salvation and] inherit or share in the kingdom of God; nor does the perishable (that which is decaying) inherit or share in the imperishable (the immortal).

Take notice! I tell you a mystery (a secret truth, an event decreed by the hidden purpose or counsel of God). We shall not all fall asleep [in death], but we shall all be changed (transformed)

In a moment, in the twinkling of an eye, at the [sound of the] last trumpet call. For a trumpet will sound, and the dead [in Christ] will be raised imperishable (free and immune from decay), and we shall be changed (transformed).

For this perishable [part of us] must put on the imperishable [nature], and this mortal [part of us, this nature that is capable of dying] must put on immortality (freedom from death).

The final chapter describes the glory and splendor of the first resurrection.

The Second Resurrection: The second resurrection, the resurrection of the unrighteous to judgment, is primarily described implicitly in John 5:28-29. *"Do not be surprised and wonder at this, for the time is coming when all those who are in the tombs shall hear His voice, And they shall come out—those who have practiced doing good [will come out] to the resurrection of [new] life, and those who have done evil will be raised for judgment [raised to meet their sentence]."* Note that the verse has a semblance of the sheep and goats—those who "practiced" good and those who have "done" evil. At the White Throne Judgment, there will be a continuation of the separation of the sheep and goats.

According to Matthew 25:31-46, the first separation of the sheep (righteous) from the goats (unrighteous) occurs at the second coming of Jesus during the first resurrection of those who are alive at His coming. The goats during that time are not resurrected but allowed to live mortal lives during the thousand-year reign of Christ and given opportunities to accept the Lord as Savior. During the second resurrection, after the thousand-year reign, He sits on his "glorious throne" and gathers all nations for judgment. The sheep are placed on his right hand and the goats on the left.

The sheep inherit eternal life and the kingdom, while the goats depart into eternal punishment. The distinction is based on actions of compassion, motivated by faith in Christ, specifically how people treated the "least of these" (the hungry, thirsty, strangers, naked, sick, or imprisoned—the poor oppressed). The goats going into eternal judgment will be "their" choice by failing again to accept and acknowledge Jesus as Lord and Savior because of a conscience corrupted with evil.

The second resurrection applies to every human being in world history who failed to acknowledge Jesus as Lord and Savior, given the opportunities that came before them. They will stand before the White Throne (Revelation 20:11-15). This is the final moment in time when goats stand without the presence of the sheep, as in the first resurrection. Revelation 20:31-46.

The "sheep" represent the righteous (those who followed God's commandments/mercy), while the "goats" represent the wicked. This is the final moment in time when God's grace extends the final opportunity to acknowledge Christ as Lord and Savior. Unfortunately for the wicked, their hatred for God did not wane because of the judgments. Instead, they will hate God the more and will choose eternal death over eternal life as the "secrets" of their hearts are exposed in their consciousness.

Self-Judgment of the Heart: The scriptures emphasize that God's judgment is not limited to visible outward actions alone.

In Romans 2:16, it is stated that God will judge the secrets of the heart through Jesus Christ. This passage highlights the comprehensive nature of divine judgment as conviction of the heart—declared guilt—extending beyond what is outwardly observable to include the hidden thoughts and intentions that reside within each individual.

Further reinforcing this idea, I Corinthians 4:5 declares that the Lord will bring hidden things to light and expose the motives of the heart. This underscores the reality that nothing remains concealed from God. Even the most secret motives and innermost thoughts are subject to His scrutiny, demonstrating the depth and thoroughness of divine judgment.

Together, these verses collectively affirm that divine judgment encompasses both external actions and internal motives.

—*God's Grace and Salvation: Hope Beyond the Grave*—

God's Grace will extend Salvation to the very end, even to the White Throne Judgment.

Please consider, with an open mind, the possibility that God's grace and mercy may extend salvation opportunities to the very end. Even individuals who appear not to have accepted Christ during their earthly lives—whether belonging to different faiths or Christianity—may have desired to believe in their hearts. According to a thorough comparison of Scripture, God's longsuffering and mercy provide these individuals with a chance at the White Throne Judgment to repent and confess that Jesus is Lord.

The Scriptures teach that salvation involves "believing" with the heart and "confessing" with the mouth in the present (Romans 10:9-10). However, the White Throne Judgment occurs at the conclusion of human history, after Christ's 1,000-year millennial reign, serving as the final transition into eternity. Since this event takes place in time, there remains an opportunity for those raised in the second resurrection to believe and confess Jesus Christ as Lord.

Hope for the Innocent: Reflect on the innocent victims of unjust wars called collateral damage, as if it's okay to kill a few to save the many, famines, leading to malnutrition and death, debilitating terminal diseases, natural catastrophic disasters, and even aborted babies. Concerning the latter, my faith and hope are anchored in the passage from II Samuel 12:16-23, where David, mourning his miscarried son, expresses, "I shall go to him, but he shall not return to me." This verse suggests a belief in an afterlife and the possibility of reunion with loved ones, even discarded unborn babies and children. It is often cited as a source of hope for encountering those lost in this life again in heaven, relegated to personal faith rather than any doctrinal or theological view.

The Compassion of God: Consider whether a magnanimous and compassionate God would condemn innocent people—those who have never heard the "Gospel of the Kingdom of God"—to eternal punishment. Ultimately, only God, the Judge of all the Earth, can answer this question. Hope remains the foundation for our conclusion.

The Corruption of the Human Heart: Jeremiah 17:9, *"The heart is deceitful above all things, and it is exceedingly perverse and corrupt and severely, mortally sick! Who can know it [perceive, understand, be acquainted with his own heart and mind]?"* According to Scripture, despite God's mercy, the corruption of the human heart in some individuals will be so profound that they will reject God's judgments. This pattern echoes the response of humanity in Genesis 6 during Noah's preaching and the impending judgment by water. Romans 1:28-30 describes the prevalence of evil and resistance to God:

And so, since they did not see fit to acknowledge God or approve of Him or consider Him worth the knowing, God gave them over to a base and condemned mind to do things not proper or decent but loathsome, Until they were filled (permeated and saturated) with every kind of unrighteousness, iniquity, grasping and covetous greed, and malice. [They were] full of envy and jealousy, murder, strife, deceit and treachery, ill will and cruel ways. [They were] secret backbiters and gossipers, Slanderers, hateful to and hating God, full of insolence, arrogance, [and] boasting; inventors of new forms of evil, disobedient and undutiful to parents.

Scripture puts these judgments in the context of the days of Noah and explains that people were consumed by the pleasures of daily life—eating, drinking, and marrying—ignorant of impending judgment until it was too late (Matthew 24:38-39; Luke 17:26-27). Matthew 24:37, *"As were the days of Noah, so will be the coming of the Son of Man. For just as in those days before the flood they were eating and drinking, [men] marrying and [women] being given in marriage, until the [very] day when Noah went into the ark, And they did not know or understand until the flood came and swept them."*

QUESTIONS ABOUT THE THOUSAND-YEAR REIGN

This section provides a succinct yet accurate overview of six main millennial views for analysis. While some are more prominent than others, here are the six prevalent views of the "last time" events that will take place on the earth:

Amillennialism: Amillennialism teaches that the Kingdom of God and reign of Christ began at Christ's resurrection ("inaugurated millennialism"); therefore, there is no thousand-year reign of Christ. When He claimed victory over Satan, and the Curse of the grave and death, Christ began to reign now and forevermore ("nunc-millennialism") at the right hand of the Father through His Church on the Earth. Upon the conclusion of this age, Christ will return and immediately bring the Church into their eternal state after judging the wicked. The term "amillennialism" can be misleading, as it suggests that Revelation 20:1-6 is ignored. In reality, Amillennialists interpret this passage—and much apocalyptic literature as non-literal.

Pre-Millennialism: Premillennialism is a literal interpretation of the 1,000-year reign of Christ with the Saints in the first resurrection—a reign of peace, justice, and righteousness. The proponents believe that Jesus will physically return to earth *before* (pre-) a literal thousand-year reign, commonly referred to as the millennium. The adherents of premillennialism view the millennial kingdom as the direct fulfillment of God's promises to Israel and as the climax of human history. According to this belief, Jesus will visibly return to earth in the clouds, and the saints will be "caught up" with Him in the clouds, and descend with Him to the Earth, Jerusalem. At His coming, He will defeat the Antichrist and bind Satan for 1,000 years. During this literal millennium, Christ will reign on earth, often in the company of resurrected saints. This period is characterized by peace, justice, and righteousness, that fulfills all Old Testament covenants. After the thousand-year reign, there will be a final battle, which is then followed by the final judgment. Ultimately, this leads to the creation of a new heaven and a new earth.

Dispensational Premillennialism: This view maintains that Christ will rapture the Church before the tribulation, so Christians will not experience the tribulation. After seven years, Christ will return to earth, Satan will be released for the final battle, which is followed by the White Throne Judgment and the establishment of the New Jerusalem.

NOTE: There is a technical distinction between "historic" and "historical" millennialism, though the terms are often used interchangeably in everyday conversation. "Historic Premillennialism" specifically refers to a well-defined, traditional theological system, while "historical premillennialism" acts as a descriptive phrase, emphasizing the continuity of this view with the same view held by the Early Church.

Historical Millennialism: Historical or Progressive Millennialists believe that prophecy unfolds over time through faith in God's Word, revealing the larger purpose of God's plan on a macro level. This revelation follows a continuum, recurring at a micro level throughout history and culminating in a broader fulfillment. The micro level suggests that similar prophetic events repeat across eras, progressing toward their ultimate completion. Personally, I lean more towards this view. Christ returns just before the millennium and after a period of apostasy and tribulation. Following the millennium, Satan is released, and Gog and Magog rise against God's kingdom, immediately followed by the final judgment. Although this view shares similarities with dispensational premillennialism (Christ's return precedes the millennium), it differs notably in its interpretation of Scripture.

Historic Premillennialism: Historic Premillennialism is a distinct theological "system" holding that the church will pass through the tribulation, experiencing a post-tribulation rapture/Second Coming. It differs from dispensational premillennialism by not requiring a strict, literal 7-year tribulation or a sharp distinction between Israel and the church. Sometimes people confuse "historic premillennialism" with "historicism," which is a method of interpreting Revelation (seeing it as a timeline of history), which is not the same thing. In summary, they usually describe the same eschatological position, but Historic Premillennialism is the formal title of the theological school, while historical emphasizes its age and origin. "Historic Premillennialism" is the recognized title for the formal theological system, while "historical" highlights the longstanding nature and origins of this interpretation.

Postmillennialism: Postmillennialism sees the millennium as an era—not necessarily a literal thousand years—in which Christ reigns over the earth through the growing influence of the Gospel. After this gradual Christianization, Christ will return, immediately judge the wicked, and usher in the Church's eternal state. Thus, Christ's return occurs after the millennium.

While these perspectives differ significantly, it is important to note that Christians who hold these views agree on most Christian doctrine and practice but disagree on views that are not their own. The concept of the Millennium Kingdom, the thousand-year reign of Christ, is based on interpretations from Revelation 20:1-10.

When forming one's own view, it is advisable to avoid arguments grounded solely in history or based on the actions of proponents of a particular doctrine. The eschatological views of the early church were largely undefined, and many early church fathers held beliefs that might now be considered unusual or unorthodox.

Example: Premillennialists are sometimes attacked because certain Christian cults adopt their ideas of apocalyptic cataclysm, and some adherents attempt to set dates for Christ's return. Postmillennialists have faced judgment because some rebels misused their principles in the Sixteenth and Seventeenth Centuries. Amillennialists have been criticized due to the misapplication of their beliefs by the Nazis. With these cautions in mind, the results of what the reader believes are a matter of their faith. The primary focus is salvation and the gift of eternal life.

The Tribulation Views and the Timing of the Rapture

There are three distinct perspectives on the timing of the rapture relative to the tribulation. These differing beliefs have shaped both theological discussions and popular media representations. Notably, the pre-tribulation theory gained widespread recognition through the *Left Behind* movie series, authored by Tim LaHaye, which portrays the Church as being "caught up" before the onset of the tribulation. Before this cinematic depiction, other eschatological films and writings by well-known evangelicals addressed these views as well.

- **Pre-tribulation:** This view holds that the rapture will occur before the tribulation begins. As a result, believers are assured that they will not endure the tribulation period. This is considered the most comforting perspective among the three.
- **Mid-tribulation:** According to this viewpoint, the rapture takes place after three and a half years of false peace, but before the onset of the "Great Tribulation." Believers are removed before the most severe period begins.
- **Post-tribulation:** This belief asserts that the rapture will happen after the seven-year tribulation period. However, believers are spared from experiencing the "wrath" of God and are raptured at the end, coinciding with the Second Coming of Christ.

Conclusion

When considering the diverse interpretations of Revelation 20:1-15, it is essential to acknowledge that even well-meaning and intelligent Christians hold a range of perspectives. The Book of Revelation is one of the most debated texts in the biblical canon, prompting us to approach each interpretation with caution and a sense of humility.

Within the Christian community, opinions about millennial views differ. Despite these differences, after examining the relevant Scriptures, whichever millennium approach one aligns themselves with (Hopefully the most consistent with a literal reading of the Bible) should not be debated but understood as not affecting their salvation. Interpretation of God's Word is best guided by the Bible's own testimony. If you remain uncertain after careful study, remember that salvation is not determined by your understanding of Revelation 20:1-15, but by faith in Jesus Christ.

The Final Battle

The culminating macro events recorded in Revelation 20 will happen on a micro level from generation to generation as signs and warnings for each generation to prepare for impending chaos and catastrophes by embracing the Person of Christ!

In this battle, the allies of the Antichrist will be crushed: Babylon the Great ...the Beast ...seven kings, five defeated, one unknown. From Revelation 17-19, we see the defeat...

Key details about Armageddon in Revelation:

- **Context:** It appears as part of the sixth bowl judgment, where demonic spirits gather nations for a final conflict.

- **Definition:** The term is derived from the Hebrew *Har-Magedon*, meaning "Mount Megiddo."

- **Significance:** It is often interpreted as the final, apocalyptic, and worldwide battle between the forces of good and evil.

- **Outcome:** Revelation 19:11-21 describes Jesus Christ leading a heavenly army to victory, with the beast and false prophet being defeated.

While some interpret this as a literal, geographical battle in the Middle East, others view it as a symbolic representation of the ultimate defeat of evil.

Final View: A Glimpse of Heaven on Earth

Christ's "Many Mansions" and the New Jerusalem: Scripture often relies on metaphors and symbolic language to make its meaning more accessible, but it remains truthful and trustworthy. When Christ declares that He is going to prepare a place for us, His words are genuine and not merely symbolic. In John 14:2–4, Jesus says: *"In My Father's house there are many dwelling places (homes). If it were not so, I would have told you; for I am going away to prepare a place for you. And when (if) I go and make ready a place for you, I will come back again and will take you to Myself, that where I am you may be also. And [to the place] where I am going, you know the way."* Christ is the Way, the Truth, and the Life.

The many mansions, referred to by Christ, were prepared before the foundation of the earth. Ephesians 1:4, *"Even as [in His love] He chose us [actually picked us out for Himself as His own] in Christ before the foundation of the world, that we should be holy (consecrated and set apart for Him) and blameless in His sight, even above reproach, before Him in love."* In this scriptural context, Christ was referring to His glorification after His ascension back to the right hand of the Father on high, when He received the promise of the Spirit that descended upon the 120 disciples in the upper room (Luke 24:49).

The Meaning of "Many Mansions": The original Greek term *monai* translates to "abodes," "rooms," or "dwelling places." This wording suggests that Christ's promise is not about individual, isolated estates, but rather about a shared dwelling in God's presence. The focus is not on the size of the space but on the availability and inclusivity. Heaven, according to this concept, has enough room for all those whose names are written in the "Lamb's Book of Life."

Space and Immortality in Heaven: The state of immortality that believers will experience is not limited by physical space. Instead, the nature of this space will be uniquely tied to each believer's reward for service during their earthly life. This means that the heavenly dwelling is both sufficient and uniquely suited to each person.

The New Jerusalem—Glory and Worship: Revelation 21:24 describes kings bringing their glory into the New Jerusalem, which symbolizes the submission of all earthly power and achievement in homage to Christ. This scene echoes Old Testament prophecies, particularly Isaiah 60:3–5 and 60:11, where nations and kings are depicted as bringing their wealth to the city of God. The implication is that everything honorable, valuable, and worthy in human culture—once purified—will be symbolically presented to God in worship, serving as a reminder of what was accomplished for the Lord during earthly life. Note here that God is not worshipped through the sacrifice of things. He is worshipped in the Person of Christ.

Revelation 20-22: The Final Promise

Revelation 22:20 heralds Jesus' final promise to humanity, affirming the "surety" of His physical return. *"He Who gives this warning and affirms and testifies to these things says, Yes (it is true). [Surely] I am coming quickly (swiftly, speedily). Amen (so let it be)! Yes, come, Lord Jesus!"* The verse signifies the absolute certainty of Christ's imminent return, which offers comfort to believers amid suffering in every generation and those despotically treated. It is also a final warning to the wicked and an urgent call for readiness and anticipation of His kingdom. The term "soon" or "quickly" (Greek *tachys*) signifies that when it happens, it will be sudden and without further delay. It emphasizes that no major prophesied events remain before His return. The response echoes the Early Churches' "Maranatha," come quickly, Lord Jesus, ending all suffering, pain, sickness, disease, death, and hell, signifying that all trials and temptations have come to an end. What a joyful proclamation that should be met with jubilation in this life! In essence, it is the final "sign-off" of the Bible, like the final sign-off of a popular broadcast that reinforces the "verity" of the story of redemption. Now let's take a look at **heaven on earth.**

Revelation 21:1-27

John sees a new sky, described as "heaven," and a new "earth" that had been renovated by fire, corresponding to Peter's vision of the new heaven and earth recorded in II Peter 3:10. *"But the day of the Lord will come like a thief, and then the heavens will vanish (pass away) with a thunderous crash, and the material] elements [of the universe] will be dissolved with fire, and the earth and the works that are upon it will be burned up."* But this is not a consuming fire. It is a purifying fire. In a physical sense, fire can severely injure or can kill. Scripture denotes God as a "consuming fire" and a "purifying fire." Here God removes all of the harmful elements from fire, and it appears as a bright light and puts out the sound of a supersonic boom—according to Peter a "thunderous crash"—in plain language, a nuclear cleansing without a toxic fallout. The appearance of God Himself removes all the toxins created by the exploitations of ecosystems for greed for wealth, and fire becomes a source of healing and renewal throughout the earth. Thus, a brilliant, pristine heaven and earth.

I have previously stated that the earth was created in eternity, therefore, eternal, as the final dwelling place of God, His angels, and humanity raised to immortality. There was no longer a sea, but the final chapters describe a "pure river of living water" coming out from the fountain head of God's omnipotent throne.

Revelation 22:1: *"Then he showed me the river whose waters give life, sparkling like crystal, flowing out from the throne of God and of the Lamb."* Verse 2 describes what is termed "Broadway," along which the river flowed, as clear as crystal, representing pure holiness, as it grows on either side of the river, implying rows of trees of life that bore twelve varieties of fruit corresponding to the number of divine governments that yielded their fruit each month. What a beautiful sight to the eyes! Oh, and the leaves were for the healing of the nations, which symbolizes eternal life, God's life-giving presence. Recall here, Adam clothing himself with fig leaves in the Genesis saga. It's an eternal reminder that all sin has been taken away and there is no longer a need to hide behind the works of our hands. Just as God clothed Adam with animal skins, symbolizing an innocent animal dying for the guilty person, Christ became the eternal offering for our sin.

But Scripture alludes to the possibility of plants and animals living outside of the walls of New Jerusalem in a fruitful garden of delights in peace and harmony with their environment, unspoiled by the dominion of mankind. Isaiah 11:6, *"And the wolf shall dwell with the lamb, and the leopard shall lie down with the kid, and the calf and the young lion and the fatted domestic animal together; and a little child shall lead them."* The latter reference is to the peace and harmony that will exist between animals and immortal humans.

—Editor's Note: Faith Perspective Considerations—

Although Scripture does not explicitly state that animals will live outside the walls of New Jerusalem, it does indicate that animals will exist in the renewed creation, referencing passages such as Isaiah 11:6-9 and Isaiah 65:17. The mention of "outside" in Revelation 22:15 is likely metaphorical, representing exclusion from salvation rather than describing a literal geographical location. Furthermore, the reference to "dogs" in this context is understood to symbolize evil people cast into outer darkness, rather than referring to animals themselves.

Biblical Imagery of Walls and Restoration: Zechariah 2:4 describes Jerusalem as having no walls in the New Jerusalem, suggesting that the walls mentioned in Revelation may be metaphors for reflecting God's glory and splendor, or that the city is "unwalled," allowing for the vast presence of people and animals. Isaiah 65:17 and Isaiah 11:6-9 depict a restored, peaceful, Eden-like state in New Heaven and the New Earth, where animals coexist harmoniously with humans.

However, the Bible does suggest that animals will be included in the restored creation, as indicated in Romans 8:20-22, which implies that the entire creation will be liberated from decay. This perspective reinforces the idea that animals will play a significant role in the peaceful and renewed environment envisioned in Scripture.

The Splendor of New Jerusalem: Revelation 22:1, indicates there is no longer a sea, and John sees the New Jerusalem descending from heaven like a bride adorned for her husband. This is the fulfillment of all prophecies concerning the "wedding supper" of the Lamb and His Bride, the Body of Christ. Therefore, the description of the architecture and arrayed ornamentation of the New Jerusalem could be a metaphoric reference to the beauty of Christ's Bride in the New Jerusalem. Remember, our bodies are the temple of the Lord (I Corinthians 6:19-20). Verse three quotes Jeremiah 31:31-33 as fulfilling the covenant promise, followed in verse four by God wiping away all pain, tears, anguish, sorrow, and mourning. What great news!

Immortality of the Body and Soul: Immortality wipes away the old conditions of human existence, and the former order of things has passed away. Here, let's take a peek at the nature of the resurrected body.

First of all, Christ was the prototype for the pattern and nature of our resurrected bodies when He rose from the dead (I Corinthians 15:20), which means our bodies will be fashioned after Christ's. When Christ appeared to His Disciples, they thought that they had seen a ghost, so He reassured them that a ghost does not have "flesh and bones" (Luke 24:39) and then dined with them as proof. Leviticus 17:11 says the life of the flesh is in the blood. Medically speaking, it is blood that sustains mortal life. Christ did not say "flesh and blood" because blood no longer sustains immortal life.

The Mystery of Transformation: I Corinthians 15:51-54

The Revelation of a Divine Mystery: The apostle Paul unveils a profound truth in I Corinthians 15:51-54. He urges his readers to pay close attention, declaring, "Take notice! I tell you a mystery (a secret truth, an event decreed by the hidden purpose or counsel of God). We shall not all fall asleep [in death], but we shall all be changed (transformed)." This statement reveals that not everyone will experience death, but all believers will undergo a dramatic transformation.

The Suddenness of Transformation: *In a moment, in the twinkling of an eye, at the [sound of the] last trumpet call. For a trumpet will sound, and the dead [in Christ] will be raised imperishable (free and immune from decay), and we shall be changed (transformed).*

This transformation occurs instantaneously—"in the twinkling of an eye"—and is marked by the last trumpet. At that sound, the dead in Christ will be raised in bodies that are imperishable, and all believers will be changed, experiencing this transformation together.

From Mortality to Immortality: *For this perishable [part of us] must put on the imperishable [nature], and this mortal [part of us, this nature that is capable of dying] must put on immortality (freedom from death).*

Paul explains that our current mortal bodies must change. The perishable must be clothed with the imperishable, and mortality must be replaced with immortality. This essential transformation enables entry into the kingdom of God.

Death's Defeat and Fulfillment of Scripture: *And when this perishable puts on the imperishable and this that was capable of dying puts on freedom from death, then shall be fulfilled the Scripture that says, Death is swallowed up (utterly vanquished forever) in and unto victory.*

Once this transformation is complete, the promise is fulfilled, and death is utterly defeated and swallowed up in victory. This passage affirms that the ultimate victory over death is realized when believers are changed from mortal to immortal.

The Meaning of Transformation: The phrase "this mortal must put on immortality," sometimes called the first resurrection, explains that to enter the kingdom of God, our bodies must be transformed from mortal and corruptible to immortal and incorruptible. This change is necessary for inheriting eternal life and participating fully in God's victory over death.

The question arises: How will we look and move about? The answer is like Christ.

The Nature of Identity, Movement, and Communication in New Jerusalem

Our Identity in New Jerusalem: Scripture teaches that in New Jerusalem, we shall know as we are known and will rejoice in fellowship with the Patriarchs. This implies a form of personal identification within the heavenly city. While our identity will be renewed—symbolized by receiving a new name—we will still retain "conscious" recognition of one another. According to Revelation 2:17, this new name will be written on a white stone, unique to each individual. Its meaning will be understood only by the recipient, likely as a result of the rewards earned in this life. This new name will bring us joy as we recognize its significance. Alongside this, we will partake of the new manna and drink from new wine referenced by Christ in Luke 22:15-16, *"And He said to them, I have earnestly and intensely desired to eat this Passover with you before I suffer; For I say to you, I shall eat it no more until it is fulfilled in the kingdom of God."* We will experience "purified" pleasure and taste as part of celebrating our transformed existence, even though physical food will no longer be necessary for sustenance. Our bodies will be glorified, reflecting the light of Christ.

Mobility and the Spiritual Body: In terms of movement, our experience will be modeled after Christ's actions following His resurrection. Contrary to popular depictions, we will not have wings and fly as angels are often shown. Instead, our mobility will transcend the laws of earthly physics, operating in ways comparable to teleportation or higher-dimensional movement— concepts known in science as quantum tunneling and instantaneous energy-to-matter conversion. Our spiritual bodies will no longer be bound by space and time. This process involves the ability to dematerialize at one location and rematerialize at another. While miraculous by earthly standards, these abilities will be a spiritual reality, accessible through faith in Jesus Christ rather than scientific means.

Communication and Fellowship: Although Scripture does not provide explicit descriptions of how communication will function in heaven, it does indicate that we will engage in "conscious" and intellectual interactions. As we worship and recognize one another, our fellowship will be enhanced. Communication will be perfected, free from the limitations we experience in this life, because God will be "all in all."

Revelation 22:4-21 – The Final Invitation and Promise

Christ's Identity Revealed—We Will See Him as He Is!

The greatest reward and glory of our journey of faith is that, at the end, we will see Christ as He truly is. This is the culmination of our walk of faith, echoing the hope described by Abraham in Hebrews 11:9-10: *"[Prompted] by faith he dwelt as a temporary resident in the land which was designated in the promise [of God, though he was like a stranger] in a strange country, living in tents with Isaac and Jacob, fellow heirs with him of the same promise. For he was [waiting expectantly and confidently] looking forward to the city which has fixed and firm foundations, whose Architect and Builder is God."*

This hope allows us to rejoice, knowing that the destination of our faith journey is to stand before God and see His face. The faithful will behold the face of God, which is the highest privilege, signifying true intimacy and acceptance in His presence. His name will be written on their foreheads, marking them as His own and guaranteeing His protection and their belonging to Him.

The Glory of the Eternal Season: In the presence of God, there will be one continuous season, shining forth from the rainbow that surrounds His throne. This symbolizes the faithfulness of God. Night and darkness will be no more; there is no need for any lamp or the light from the sun, because the Lord God Himself will be their light forever. The redeemed will reign with Him as kings for all eternity, their reign lasting throughout all ages.

Christ's Declaration & Promise: Jesus Himself announces, "Behold, I am coming quickly." Those who pay attention to, internalize, and obey the truths found in this prophetic book are called blessed. This includes not only the predictions, but also the comforts and warnings given throughout Revelation.

The State of Humanity Until the End: As mentioned previously, humanity that has been corrupted by evil will remain unchanged, even as the invitation to salvation extends to the very end. The book declares that the unjust, impure, righteous, and holy will continue in their respective states. This reality emphasizes the urgency and finality of the message. Jesus repeats His promise that He is coming soon, and states that He will bring rewards for everyone according to their works and deeds. Those who remain unrighteous—practicing sorcery, impurity, murder, idolatry, and deceit—will be excluded from the holy city. This division highlights the necessity of living righteously.

Jesus further declares Himself to be the Alpha and Omega, the First and the Last, covering all of history. Those who purify themselves are blessed, gaining the right to access the tree of life and to enter through the gates into the city.

The Final Universal Invitation: The Holy Spirit and the bride, representing the church, together extend a universal invitation: "Come!" Everyone who hears, everyone who thirsts for spiritual fulfillment, is invited to freely receive the water of life. Anyone who desires may come and take it without cost. Jesus then affirms His final promise to humanity: "I am coming quickly." The response to this promise is a heartfelt prayer: "Amen! Come, Lord Jesus!"

Benediction

The grace, blessing, and favor of the Lord Jesus Christ are invoked upon all the saints—those set apart for God. The concluding word is "Amen," expressing agreement and acceptance.

CONCLUSION

Noah's Perennial Prophecy: The Ethnological Destiny of Humanity

The Ethnological Heritage of Humanity from Adam through Noah's Sons to Christ

A Scientific and Biblical Perspective: Acts 17:26 states, *"And He made from one [common origin, one source, one blood] all nations of men to settle on the face of the earth, having definitely determined [their] allotted periods of time and the fixed boundaries of their habitation (their settlements, lands, and abodes)."* This passage implies that all nations originated from the bloodline of one man, Adam. As a result, humanity shares a common ancestry. This view contrasts with certain interpretations of prehistoric evidence, which suggest that modern humans (*Homo sapiens*) evolved from earlier hominids. Instead, biblical genealogical studies maintain that all nations descend from the creation of Adam. This common descent underscores that every human being is connected through a shared ancestry and possesses equal value. Such understanding is often cited to promote unity and to oppose racial division. All humans share a common origin from Adam to Christ.

The Role of Anthropology, Archaeology, and Genetics: The integration of anthropology, archaeology, and genetic science enriches our understanding of human history and supports the concept of a common human lineage found in biblical genealogy. **Archaeology** examines human history and prehistory through excavations and the analysis of artifacts and physical remains. **Anthropology** explores what makes us human, investigating various aspects of culture, behavior, and biology.

Genetic Science—notably in the fields of biological anthropology and archaeogenetics—applies DNA analysis to uncover details about human evolution, migration, and social structures that material artifacts alone cannot reveal.

Despite the insights provided by these scientific disciplines, they do not establish that Jesus Christ was "multiethnic" in the modern sense of having parents from distinctly different racial groups. Rather, the evidence indicates that Jesus was a 1st-century Judean Jew from Galilee, with physical features typical of a Levantine Semitic population. The Levantine Semitic people are the indigenous inhabitants of the Eastern Mediterranean Levant—modern-day Syria, Lebanon, Palestine, Jordan, and Israel—who historically spoke Northwestern Semitic languages. This group also includes ancient Canaanites, Phoenicians, Hebrews, and Arameans, and today encompasses Arab and Jewish populations who share deep, continuous genetic ancestry tracing back to the Bronze Age Levantines.

Christ's Ancestry—A Mosaic of Populations: These scientific findings support that Christ was not "white" or European, "black" or African, or any single ethnicity as defined today. Instead, his ancestral, cultural, and genetic context was a "mosaic" shaped by various populations that traversed the region over thousands of years. Matthew 1:1-17 outlines the genealogy of Christ, beginning with the words: *"The book of the ancestry (genealogy) of Jesus Christ (the Messiah, the Anointed), the son (descendant) of David, the son (descendant) of Abraham."*

Conclusion—Equality and Human Dignity: In summary, scientific evidence affirms that Jesus was a 1st-century Levantine Semite—biologically a blend of ancient populations, but not "multiethnic" in the sense of modern concepts of racial diversity. Furthermore, both biblical and scientific perspectives emphasize that all people are descendants of the first man and woman, Adam and Eve, highlighting the genetic relatedness of all humans. This principle asserts that, regardless of cultural, ethnic, or physical differences, every individual is equal before God. Consequently, the combined insights of biblical genealogy and science are frequently invoked to affirm the inherent dignity and equality of all humans and to reject notions of racial superiority.

The Humanity of Adam and Christ

The Scriptures, specifically I Corinthians 15:45-49 and Romans 5:12-21, present Adam and Christ as the "first" and "second" Adam, respectively. This direct comparison highlights the pivotal roles they play in the human story. Adam, as the original head of the human race, failed in his responsibility. In contrast, Christ, as the second Adam, succeeded in restoring humanity's relationship with God. Where Adam's failure brought separation, Christ's success brings reconciliation, hope, and unity of the races.

Theological Significance—The Hypostatic Union and Christ's Humanity: In theological discussions, especially those addressing the hypostatic union—the profound union of Christ's divinity and humanity in one Person with two distinct natures—it is easy to overlook the depth of Christ's human experience. His humanity is not incidental but essential, and His ethnic heritage connects Him to all people.

The significance of Christ's humanity is further emphasized through His blood atonement. Christ's blood does more than remove transgressions; it embodies the genetic makeup that, like Adam's, contains the DNA representative of all humanity. This unique aspect underscores a unity among believers, providing a scientific rationale for the spiritual truth that all are one in Christ.

Exploring Christ's Humanity—Genealogy and Genetics: This section delves deeply into the humanity of Christ by examining genealogical records found in Scripture and aligning them with insights from genetic science. Genetics, as the discipline focused on genes, genetic variations, and heredity, provides a framework for understanding how Christ, as a descendant of Adam in His humanity, is connected to all people. Through this lens, Christ's role as the second Adam is both a fulfillment of Scripture and an affirmation of the shared human identity He redeems.

—*Creation Science & Understanding Race*—

I believe that Creation Science and Biblical History disclose information that World/American History and Science gloss over. Therefore, I conclude that *creation science* and *biblical history* provide a *missing link* in the chain of world history and science. Here, we will explore the man-made concept of race compared to scriptural reality with scientific and historical evidence.

I do not oppose science, but believe that there are parallels between science and creation science in the chronology of historical findings. So, we correlate pertinent scientific information with Scripture. Creation Science is *"The belief that the universe and living organisms originate from specific acts of divine creation, as in the biblical account, rather than by natural processes such as evolution."* Christians and people who aspire to a creationist philosophy and theology about the origin of humans must begin their analysis of race from a Biblical frame of reference, and other considerations of science coming alongside to support a biblical view.

The Creation of the Races in Adam—The Genetic Problem: Adam was of no particular race. He was not White or Black, Asian, or Hispanic. He stood for all humanity. His name was indicative of his nature being without race. His name in the Hebrew language has a twofold meaning: "ruddy" and "humankind or species." Adam was a reddish-brown-complexioned man who represented all races of people. He was the federal head of the future human race. *"And just as we have borne the image [of the man] of dust, so shall we and so let us also bear the image [of the Man] of heaven"* (I Corinthians 15:49).

225

Understanding Biblical Theories for Race
—Adam's Phenotype and Genotype—

According to the Bell Curve and Eugenics, which laid the historical foundation for racial theories, the driving force behind institutionalized racism, there is a link between race and racism because of the belief of superior genetic heritage. One can include the infamous "one-drop rule," a legal and social doctrine in the United States that defined anyone with even a single ancestor of African descent ("one drop of black blood") as Black. This rule originated in the American South as a tool to uphold white supremacy and sustain the system of slavery. By defining racial identity in this way, the one-drop rule restricted rights and enforced racial segregation, relying on social constructs rather than biological evidence. The legacy of this rule persists in various forms to the present day, but has been debunked by modern science. Because of certain traits, our history has taught us to think that some people are superior to others because of genetic heritage. Racism goes as deep as genes!

Adam was a raceless man. The categorization and determination of races is a human development, not divine creation. God creates different ethnicities, not races.

Postulates of Scriptural Theories on Race: I have postulated three theories concerning the raceless nature of Adam and the subsequent families that came from him and Eve. I do not impose these views on others. Rather, it is up to believers to decide which aligns closest to what they think Scripture postulates.

There is no divine revelation on this subject; so, we must come to a logical conclusion through systematic study. *"And we are setting these truths forth in words not taught by human wisdom but taught by the [Holy] Spirit, combining and interpreting spiritual truths with spiritual language [to those who possess the Holy Spirit]"* (I Corinthians 2:13).

By process of deductive research and reasoning, we can safely say that when God commanded Adam *to replenish the earth* (Genesis 1:28), Adam's children would also have children. Note that Scripture chronicles genealogy through the male gender. Adam and Eve, to populate the earth, had more children than were recorded, including daughters. *"After he had Seth, Adam lived 800 years and had other sons and daughters."* (Genesis 5:4).

<u>The American Heritage Dictionary of the English Language</u> defines phenotype as *"the observable physical or biochemical characteristics of an organism, as determined by both genetic makeup and environmental influences."* I believe from a creationist standpoint that "environmental influences" are genetic traits for survival in various climatic and geographical conditions that are coded by the Creator and not by *natural selection.* Changes in the appearance of human beings are determined by miscegenation—crossbreeding through cohabitation. According to creation science, *environmental influences* apply to the lower order of creation, *plants*, and *animals*.

In simple terms, phenotypes are inherited traits that determine appearance. Genotype is *"the genetic construction of an organism or a group of organisms."* Genotype is the inner genetic code (DNA) containing all the information that will determine appearance. Did Adam look one way in his appearance (phenotype), and possessed the genetic codes for different ethnic family appearances (genotype)?

Adam's Phenotype

The color of Adam's skin had nothing to do with his race. Complexion is *"the natural color, texture, and appearance of the skin, especially the face."* Adam's complexion was ruddy or reddish-brown, which means to show blood in the face. Showing blood in the face, combined with the elements of soil around the creation basin, would indicate a reddish-brown complexion. Melanin in the skin for protection against the ultraviolet radiation of the sun in the torrid zone also plays into the creation equation.

Adam's body came from clay or mud. Consider for a moment the chemical compounds of the earth that composed his body (*Genesis 2:7*). Geographic studies point out that the soils in and around the region of creation were dark gray, red, and yellow in color. When we add up the biblical and scientific information, it becomes highly probable that Adam's complexion was olive-bronze, what we describe as reddish-brown. Once again, the color of Adam's skin had nothing to do with his race because he was a-racial. People become prejudiced when they base their judgment on physical characteristics, such as skin color.

[Note: The complexions of the ancient Hebrews, their etymological heritage derives from Shem and Ham's cohabitation. Therefore, they have a multiethnic heritage. Regardless of the debate over the complexion of the Egyptians, their biblical lineage comes from Ham, the youngest son of Noah, the Father of all African people.]

Scientists say if we were to combine all the possible colors, it would come out bronze. *"The law of color combination of pigments states the following: There are three primary colors from which all other colors can be made …Christ, suffering as a wicked man in the outer court, was represented as a bronze snake and as the sin offering on the bronze altar and as a bronze laver holding."*

Adam anatomically and physiologically represents all races of people, the human race. Based on scientific and creation science postulates, it is highly possible that Adam was of a bronze/olive-brown complexion. But, once again, his color had nothing to do with race.

Adam's Genotype

Genetically, Adam represented all human beings. Remember, Adam's name also means humankind or human species. When God said *"… Let us make man in our image, in our likeness …"* (*Genesis 1:26b*), He was referring to all humanity represented in Adam, the Federal Head of the Human Race.

All human beings descended from one man to become humanity. We do not believe that God created one man (Adam) and then created other races individually. Just as sin came from one man, Adam, God created all human beings from

Adam, and all human beings are members of one species, technically called Homo sapiens. All racial characteristics known to humankind today came from the loins of Adam and the womb of Eve. Adam and Eve gave birth to different families.

Three Theories on Race

Genetics can be a complicated science to understand. Each human being has twenty-three pairs of chromosomes. Twenty-three come from the male (father), and twenty-three come from the female (mother), for a total of 46 in each offspring. Each of these forty-six chromosomes carries information in DNA (deoxyribonucleic acid), which determines physical characteristics. (Example: complexion, eye color, hair texture, hair color, facial features, and body structure.) Additionally, the DNA transfers genetic codes to all offspring. How we look from genetic heritage depends on whether genes are dominant or recessive. I believe that genes are pre-determined by God based on His foreknowledge. Human traits are in fathers and mothers, sanctioned by the Creator, even before fertilization and conception occur. David describes our pre-determined genetic heritage beautifully in Psalms 139:13-16:

For You did form my inward parts; You did knit me together in my mother's womb.

I will confess and praise You for You are fearful and wonderful and for the awful wonder of my birth! Wonderful are Your works, and that my inner self knows right well.

My frame was not hidden from You when I was being formed in secret [and] intricately and curiously wrought [as if embroidered with various colors] in the depths of the earth [a region of darkness and mystery].

Your eyes saw my unformed substance, and in Your book all the days [of my life] were written before ever they took shape, when as yet there was none of them.

God foresees and oversees the creation of our genetic heritage. It was not by luck, coincidence, or happenstance that we became who we are. The distinctive qualities of our genetic heritage can come from two or three prior generations. I am a very light-skinned person of color. My wife is about the same complexion as I am, a shade darker. We have three children, and two of our children (the first and last) are much darker than us. Their complexion has to do with our genotypes. Both of our mothers are very dark-skinned, and our fathers were very light-skinned. The dark gene is the dominant gene in our genotype and family heritage.

Theory # 1 ~ Pure Genetics

Pure Genetics is an unproven scientific conjecture that a pure race is produced by self-fertilization or continual inbreeding; homozygous: a pure line. It stipulates that pure genetics is of unmixed blood or ancestry.

Adjective:
free from anything of a different, inferior, or contaminat ing kind …

"In Mendelian genetics, this means that an organism must be homozygous for every trait for which it is considered true breeding …"

No human being on planet earth is pure genetically. Science and the DNA research of the mediums of *Heritage* and *Ancestry* prove the point. All ethnicities today are descended from *Shem, Ham,* and *Japheth* through miscegenation.

Adam had no genetic heritage behind him. We have already postulated that Adam's complexion was possibly reddish-brown. That was his phenotype. Was Adam's genotype the same as his phenotype? If it were, scientifically it would mean that Adam was pure genetically, or one race. Eve was "made" from Adam, which would mean that she also was pure genetically, which would say that all their children were pure genetically and had the same complexion. Shem, Ham, and Japheth are direct descendants of Adam and generally accepted etymologically as olive, black, and light respectively (*Genesis 5:32*). If Adam was pure genetically, where did Shem,

Ham, and Japheth get their complexions? Additionally, where do we get different racial characteristics today?

Theory # 2 ~ Reconstructed Genes

Ancestral reconstruction (also known as Character Mapping or Character Optimization) is the extrapolation back in time from measured characteristics of individuals (or populations) to their common ancestors.

Reconstructed genes are the science of backtracking the genetic composition of ancient heritage and anthropology. However, it takes an evolutionary approach. ***"It is an important application of phylogenetics, the reconstruction and study of the evolution of relationships among individuals, populations or species to their ancestors. In the context of evolutionary biology, ancestral reconstruction can be used to recover different kinds of ancestral character states of organisms that lived millions of years ago."***

Regarding creation science, there are two distinct demarcations of genetic heritage: the lower order of creation (plants and animals), and the higher order of nature (human beings). There is an evolutionary strain to traits of plants and animals, meaning they take on natural selection—change over time based on environment and survival of the fittest. It says that among plant and animal species, a change in phenotype can alter genotype. However, when considering the higher order of creation, human beings, the phenotype does not change genotype because they are pre-determined along family lineage by the Creator.

According to the theory of evolution, plant and animal species that are strongest adapt to their environment. To survive along development cycles, those species will develop certain traits. The strong traits become the inheritance of the next generation. Does it mean that appearance (phenotype) changes with environment and conditions? Did the different races evolve in *Genesis 11* when the descendants of Noah migrated to different geographical locations? Did their environment and conditions change their appearance? Did their phenotype (appearance) reconstruct their genes (genotype)? Did they produce children who looked different from them?

Although there are mutations throughout genetic strains, as previously stated, we believe that the genetic lineage of human genes is fixed by our Creator. The factor that changes the genetic DNA is miscegenation. The environment does not reconstruct genotypes. **From a creationist standpoint, human beings did not begin with a *big bang* and evolved from plants to animals.**

Theory # 3 ~ Composite Genetics

We believe that the most logical conclusion, and the correct Biblical answer to the origin of the races, is in this third theory. God made Adam to look one way outwardly (phenotype) and put within him the composite genetic codes (genotype) for the Three Great Ethnic Families of the World, Shem, Ham, and Japheth, that came through their father, Noah, the eighth in line from Adam. The resulting diversity of humanity came from miscegenation, or the descendants of the sons of Noah crossbreeding, and their descendants crossbreeding.

God did not create a race; instead, He created ethnicities—different nations. When God stopped the construction of the Tower of Babel (*Genesis 11:9*), the descendants of Shem, Ham, and Japheth scattered across the earth. Those who spoke the same language and shared a similar appearance gravitated to each other and migrated to different geographical locations. God very carefully and providentially preserved the different ethnic characteristics in the three sons of Noah, noted by the proper Biblical designation of ethnic origins.

The conclusions concerning these theories come from our creationist point of view. Although there are genetic **mutations** in the human strain that can alter phenotype, we believe that God created all species and races and that the Bible is an accurate record of that creation. Some Christians may be evolutionary in their thinking. Although it's possible to think in evolutionary terms as a Christian, we find it difficult to reconcile evolution with creation. However, to be fair to those who are more evolutionary in their thinking, I have inserted a letter that focuses on evolutionary thinking as a Christian. A scientist from Oak Ridge, Tennessee, submitted the following letter during a racial reconciliation conference conducted in Oak Ridge, Tennessee during 1994:

Much as I appreciate and am enthusiastic about the approaches taken in the Agenda for Racial Reconciliation, I have to disagree quite strongly with the genetic approach in chapter four.

My first criticism is that I feel it weakens all the other arguments by its reliance on such stories as the creation story, Noah's story, etc., for its authenticity and its final impact. This may have meaning for those who are complete literalists in their understanding of the Bible, but for some of us who have a different understanding of what the Bible says and teaches, this makes us quite uncomfortable. It seems a bit far-fetched to rely on such early myths of creation, the flood, etc.—which contain much truth about God's relation to humankind—as historical facts from which we may draw obvious conclusions.

My second point is directed at the downplaying of the facts of evolution. Genetic genotypes are not immutable. Mutations take place all along the line, making for a different genetic makeup that can be passed on to succeeding generations. There is just too much evidence of species developing over many eons for us to ignore.

Thirdly, the argument that in one's lifetime, accommodation to one's environment cannot be passed on genetically to the next generation is quite true. However, when stretched out over millions of years, those with the ability to survive because of possible changes that have taken place in their genetic make-up will have a new genotype to pass to the future generations.

Another observation to be pointed out is what we detect in animals, birds, etc. Mammals, fowl, etc., most certainly inherit natural abilities, learned over generations, which are essential for their continued existence. These survival traits have undoubtedly become a genetic characteristic for each of them.

Please do not take these criticisms to mean that I disagree with what we are learning—and we are learning a lot, which hopefully will be taken back to our Church. It is only this rather doubtful item that has me somewhat concerned about an argument that weakens the whole.

—The Consummation of God's Eternal Plan in Noah's Prophecy—

The *Conclusion* is a biblical-historical panoramic view from ancient times, as described in the Book of Genesis, to the details of chapter seventeen from the perspective of biblical genealogy correlated with genetic science.

f Noah's prophecy reflects the fulfillment of God's eternal plan of salvation, which is carried out through the progenitors of the three major ethnic groups of the world: Shem, Ham, and Japheth. This demonstrates how God's sovereign will is manifested in the unfolding of predictive prophecy and history, using these groups as part of His divine purpose from whence Africans, Europeans, Indigenous Islanders and Inlanders, people of Latin descent, and Asians descended.

God's Temporary Purpose for American Slavery

Perspectives on Racial Reconciliation: In the process of racial reconciliation during the 1990s, considerable emphasis was placed on the idea that God had a temporary purpose for the challenging and negative effects associated with the history of slavery in America. These effects, which have been described as adverse, demoralizing, and diminishing, are an undeniable part of the nation's story. Despite efforts by some to censor or politically rewrite this history, it is important to recognize that history contains both the wrong and right sides.

Adding Footnotes to History: This perspective is not an attempt to erase or alter history, but rather to contribute a meaningful footnote that helps "right" the record. In the annals of history, all parties involved have the right to add their own cultural insights, much like the way Scripture provides commentary from distinct perspectives. The intention here is to offer a view that encourages disciples of the Lord to actively participate in reconciliation and restoration, ultimately working toward the fulfillment of God's promise.

Genesis 9:18-27–Noah and His Sons

The Descendants of Noah: After the flood, Noah's sons who emerged from the ark were Shem, Ham, and Japheth and their wives. Ham was the father of Canaan, who was born later. These three sons of Noah became the ancestors of all the people who populated the earth.

Noah's Vineyard and Ham's Offense: Noah began to farm the land and planted a vineyard, and by comparison of cultural norms, celebrated his family's settlement in the new land. He drank wine made from grapes, became drunk, and lay uncovered inside his tent. Ham, who was Canaan's father, saw his father's nakedness and told his two brothers who were outside.

Shem and Japheth Show Respect: Shem and Japheth took a garment, placed it on their shoulders, walked in backwards, and covered their father without looking at him, keeping their faces turned away so they would not see his nakedness.

Noah's Response: Blessings and Curses of His Sons

Noah's Response and Divine Providence: After awakening and discovering his youngest son's actions, Noah responded with both blessings and curses, reflecting the impact of divine providence on his family and their descendants. Noah declared, "Cursed be Canaan! He will be the lowest of servants to his brothers." This curse was directed toward Canaan, marking him as subordinate among his siblings.

Blessings for Shem and Japheth: Noah continued by blessing Shem, saying, "Blessed be the Lord, the God of Shem! May Canaan be his servant." This blessing not only acknowledged Shem's favored status but also reinforced Canaan's role as a servant to him. Furthermore, Noah pronounced, "May God enlarge Japheth; let him dwell in the tents of Shem and let Canaan be his servant." Here, Japheth is promised expansion and the privilege of sharing in Shem's blessings, while Canaan remains subject to servitude.

Meaning of Blessing and Curse: According to the sacred text's etymology, blessing is understood as bestowing a benefit, while cursing is the removal of a benefit and has nothing to do with the "dark arts." This principle is illustrated in the story of Adam, who lost the ease of farming after disobeying God's command regarding the tree of "knowledge of Good and Evil." Similarly, Eve lost the benefit of ease in childbearing.

—The Context of Noah's Prophecy—

The prophecy spoken by Noah was not triggered by his drunkenness or the actions of his youngest son, as referenced in the related biblical passage. Instead, Noah happened to be emerging from a drunken sleep when God chose to deliver a message to him, his sons, and his descendants. God's prophetic words to Noah and his three sons set the destinies for three major ethnic groups, descendants of each son.

Hereditary Consequences and Divine Foreknowledge: The behaviors of Noah's sons, described as "hereditary" acts, are considered to be passed down to future generations. The conclusion drawn, based on previous chapters and the sons' actions, is that God, in His foreknowledge, foresaw the choices their descendants would make by their own free will. Consequently, God proclaimed and decreed these outcomes, aligning them with His overarching plan of salvation—there was a purpose for their futures regarding God's end-time plan of salvation.

Exploring Historical Theories and Biblical Perspectives on Ethnicity

There has been speculation among some scholars that the earliest enslaved peoples may have descended from Canaanite populations who migrated into the interior regions of Africa. Although this theory remains conjectural, it deserves careful study to better understand what may have been God's temporary purpose for American slavery and its resulting consequences. This section aims to thoughtfully examine the theory and consider its broader implications.

Thesis Statement with Possible Prophetic Significance: In conclusion, it is worth considering the following thesis statement, which may carry prophetic significance: **The descendants of Ham—often associated with urban dwellers—and the descendants of Japheth—linked to seafarers—will unite at a pivotal moment in history. This union will spark a revival that draws the descendants of Shem—associated with nomadic peoples—toward Christ.** Such a moment would serve as a fulfillment of God's plan of salvation, as we have seen from the previous chapter.

Historians and sociologists commonly identify these three groups as races in the past, but race is not a category mentioned in Scripture. However, nations or ethnicities are mentioned throughout Scripture. Historically and genealogically, they are the progenitors of all ethnic groups worldwide. If one can believe in evolution, I don't see the difficulty in believing what Scripture says about humanity's ethnic and cultural transitions from ancient times to modern times.

Historical Classification and Modern Perspective: The old categorization of the three sons of Noah—Negroid, Caucasoid, and Mongoloid—was used as shorthand for Black, Brown, and White people. These terms were intended to represent all humanity by physical traits such as skin color and skull shape. However, modern science has thoroughly debunked these racial categories, showing they do not reflect the complexity of human genetic diversity.

Antiquated Descriptions

Negroid: Historically associated with Sub-Saharan African populations, described as having darker skin, woolly or frizzly hair, and broader nasal features.

- **Caucasoid:** Historically linked to populations from Europe, North Africa, the Horn of Africa, and Western Asia, with skin tones ranging from light to dark brown and varied hair textures.

- **Mongoloid:** Historically identified with populations in East, North, and Southeast Asia, as well as the Americas, often characterized by straight black hair, yellowish to brownish skin, and epicanthic eye folds.

These antiquated descriptions do not accurately reflect the true diversity and complexity found in humanity today, and they have been replaced by a modern understanding that emphasizes genetic variation rather than superficial physical traits.

Biblical Context and Migration: These truths bear out in Scripture concerning the "confounding of the languages" at Babel, and their subsequent migrations.

The Migrations of Shem, Ham, and Japheth After the Flood

The generations following the great flood were initially unified by a single culture, as stated in Genesis 11:1. The emergence of distinct cultures did not occur until after the dispersal that resulted from the confusion of languages at the Tower of Babel. During this early period, differences among people were not defined by racial characteristics such as skin color or physical features, so cohabitation among various clans proceeded without issue and existed with one language and culture. Genesis 11:1 provides a forward-looking perspective: *"And the whole earth was of one language and of one accent and mode of expression."*

The Journey from Mount Ararat to Shinar: After the floodwaters subsided, the Ark came to rest on Mount Ararat, which is located in the Eastern Anatolia Region of Turkey, between the provinces of Ağrı and Iğdır. This region is near the borders with Iran, Armenia, and the Nakhchivan exclave of Azerbaijan, situated between the Aras and Murat rivers. From Mount Ararat, the descendants of Noah's sons gradually traveled southeast to Shinar, an area in southern Mesopotamia corresponding to ancient Babylon. Today, this region is situated in southern Iraq, near the border with Saudi Arabia.

Dispersion at Babel and the Development of Cultures: Following the confusion of languages at Babel, the descendants of Shem, Ham, and Japheth were scattered across Africa, the Middle East, Indo-Europe, and Asia. The paths of their migrations gave rise to the various cultures that emerged in these regions.

Ethnicity is family orientation, and culture is an ethnic group of people adapting and adjusting to their geographical environments and developing different ways of living out of the human instinct to survive. When people are stripped of their culture, their instinct to survive is lessened. Culture is their total way of life, including appearance, dress, vocabulary, behavior patterns, and ways of thinking that are distinctly different from other cultures. These cultural differences are usually neutral and non-threatening to other cultures.

Migrations and Legacy of Shem's Descendants

Migrations of Shem's Descendants—Settlement Paths After Babel

According to Genesis 10:21-31, the descendants of Shem, Noah's middle son, migrated to various regions following the dispersion at Babel. Each of Shem's five sons and their clans established themselves in distinct territories. Lud and his descendants journeyed northwest, eventually settling in northern Turkey, in an area east of Syria along the Mediterranean coast. The lineage of Elam migrated to the southeast, occupying the region near the Mediterranean that is now part of Iran. Asshur and his group moved into central Iraq. Aram's descendants established themselves along the eastern Mediterranean coast in Syria. Meanwhile, Arpachshad's grandson, Joktan, led his family to the central and northern parts of Saudi Arabia.

The Lineage of Arpachshad: Ancestors of the Hebrews:
Within the lineage of Arpachshad, Shelah and Eber stand out as direct ancestors of the ancient Hebrews. From this line came Terah and Abraham, and it is from Eber's name that the term "Hebrew" is derived. This connection indicates that the earliest homeland of the Hebrew people was likely in central or northern Saudi Arabia. Additional migrations from Shem's line include Ophir, who settled along Saudi Arabia's eastern Red Sea coast, and Havilah, a grandson of Shem, who established his family between the regions of Sudan and Ethiopia.

Culture, Occupation, and Lasting Influence: Shem's descendants were drawn to Mediterranean climates, regions known for wet winters and dry summers. In these areas, they became shepherds and nomadic farmers, adapting their livelihoods to the environment. Today, the lands where Shem's descendants once settled are home to nations that continue to have a vested interest in the region. These nations seek possession of land that, according to tradition, was claimed by faith through Abraham. Jerusalem, central to this narrative, remains a focal point for God's end-time plan of salvation.

Migrations of Ham's Descendants

The travels of Ham's four sons, his grandsons, and their descendants are recorded in Genesis 10:6-20. Cush and his clan migrated to southern Egypt, and Cush became the father of Nimrod, a mighty figure on earth (Genesis 10:8). Phut and his descendants settled in Libya, near Egypt and the Mediterranean Sea. Canaan's group moved to the eastern Mediterranean coast, covering the regions of Syria and Jordan—today recognized as Palestine. There, Canaan became the ancestor of the Canaanites, including the Philistines. Havilah, born of the intermarriage between Shem's and Ham's families, migrated to the region between Sudan and Ethiopia.
Mizraim, representing Egypt, and his descendants also migrated with Cush into central Egypt. Cush's territory became Lower Egypt, while Mizraim's was Upper Egypt. Dedan, the son of Cush, settled in central Saudi Arabia, and Sheba, Canaan's

grandson, moved south of Saudi Arabia to the area now known as Yemen.

Ham's descendants settled in the hottest climates, including arid regions, dense jungles, and rainforests known as equatorial climates. Under Nimrod's leadership, they became urban dwellers and city builders.

Migrations of Japheth's Descendants

The migration paths of Japheth's seven sons, grandsons, and further descendants are given in Genesis 10:2-5. They established themselves along the coastlands of Indo-Europe. *"From these the coastlands of the nations were separated into their lands, everyone according to his language, according to their families, into their nations"* (Genesis 10:5).

From Babel, Gomer and his clan migrated to the area now known as Ukraine, adjacent to the Black Sea. Madia's group moved to the upper Iran by the Baku Sea coast. Javan settled in Greece, while Meshech traveled to northern Turkey along the Black Sea. Tubal migrated to southern Turkey, next to the Mediterranean. Gomer's son, Ashkenaz, continued east of Ukraine. Tarshish settled in Italy. Other descendants, such as Kittim, Elishah, Togarmah, and Dodanim, spread along the Mediterranean and Black Sea coasts.

Japheth's descendants lived in regions with a northern oceanic climate, featuring cooler, milder summers and wet winters. Naturally, they became seafaring nations.

Climatic Influence and Physical Complexion: The regions in which the descendants of Shem, Ham, and Japheth settled influenced their complexions and adaptation to particular climates. Egypt, named as "the land of Ham" in Psalms 105:23,17; 106:22 and 78:51, reflects Ham's association with the region. The names Shem ("dusky, or the like") and Japheth ("fair") suggest possible differences in complexion, while Ham is thought to mean "black," based on evidence from Hebrew and Arabic sources.

Miscegenation: Historical Perspectives and Modern Understanding

Definition and Historical Connotations: Miscegenation refers to relationships and marriage between different ethnic groups. Although the term has often carried negative or derogatory connotations, suggesting crossbreeding through cohabitation, its meaning and social implications have shifted over time.

Miscegenation in Ancient Societies: In the ancient societies formed during the migrations of Shem, Ham, and Japheth, the concept of miscegenation was regarded as a normal aspect of relationships and marriage. It was not viewed negatively but rather accepted as a usual path for forming familial and social bonds across different groups.

Modern and Theological Perspectives: From a contemporary standpoint, and in theological contexts referencing the "Eyes of God," miscegenation is considered a neutral term. It simply describes relationships between people from different ethnic backgrounds, without the negative implications that may have been present in the past.

Current Usage and Ethnological Insights: Today, the term "miscegenation" is used almost exclusively in historical discussions and is rarely applied to current populations. Importantly, the ethnological heritage and intermingling of nations described in history reveal that there is no such thing as a "pure" race. Instead, all people possess a blend of various ethnic descents.

From the previous chapter, we clearly see that multiethnic populations will be celebrated in God's Eternal Kingdom. But the harsh reality, due to historical preconditioning, the world at large will never fully accept multiethnicity.

The Historical Significance of Noah's Prophecy

Japheth

Japheth was the eldest son of Noah, as noted in Genesis 10:21. His name is associated with a fair or white complexion, which is attributed to the absence of the melanin hormone. This characteristic may have been a factor in the migration of his descendants to the colder, northern regions of Indo-Europe.

"From these the coastland peoples spread. [These are the sons of Japheth] in their lands, each with his own language, by their families within their nations" (Genesis 10:5).

Japheth is regarded as the ancestor of Indo-European or Caucasian peoples. Noah's prophecy regarding Japheth's actions after Noah's drunkenness reveals three key aspects concerning the destiny of the Caucasian people: ***Enlargement:*** According to Genesis 9:27a, God would "enlarge" Japheth. The Hebrew root of this word, when compared with other associations in Scripture, suggests economic prosperity. ***Dwelling in the tents of Shem:*** Genesis 9:27b prophesies that Japheth would "dwell in the tents of Shem." Studying the original language and comparing Scriptures indicates that this phrase refers to Japheth coming under the privileges of Shem's covenant relationship with God that later became the New Covenant associated with Christianity. ***Servitude of Canaan:*** Genesis 9:27c declares, "And Canaan shall be his servant." This prophecy means that Canaan would serve Japheth and his descendants, not just Shem, which can be seen in the history of slavery.

Noah's prophecy for Japheth and his descendants points to their destiny as seafarers or coast dwellers (Genesis 10:5). Indo-European people, therefore, would become pioneers in exploration due to their seafaring heritage. Exploration would become the primary means by which European people prospered, under the banner of "historical" Christianity, fulfilling the prophecy, "God shall enlarge Japheth." The Hebrew word for "enlarge" is also associated with "deceit," suggesting that Japheth's descendants would use deceit as a means of gaining wealth. Historically, exploration often turned into the exploitation of darker races around the world.

Noah's prophecy also indicates that Japheth and his descendants would come under Shem's covenant privileges, as stated in "he shall dwell in the tents of Shem." Shem's covenant, like others in the Bible, ultimately points to the New Covenant with God through Jesus Christ. Both Scripture and history suggest that Christianity, as Shem's covenant relationship with God, would become a means and tool for Japheth's descendants to prosper. European and American history may even be reflected in this prophetic verse, as slavery exploited by Christianity became a primary means by which Europeans attained wealth. However, the prophecy never foretold the inhumanity and atrocities of slavery as preordained by God. Remember, God in His omniscient foreknowledge foresees what human beings will do through free will and does not interfere. Rather, God works around and through human agencies with a plan for misguided human error. Coming up, you will see a summation of God's purpose and plan for the temporary nature of slavery.

Shem

Shem was Noah's middle son (Genesis 9:24; 10:2), and his name refers to an olive complexion. His family's ethno-geographical migrations are documented in Genesis 10:21-31. Shem is recognized as the ancestor of all Semitic peoples, who were known for their Afro-Asiatic language.

Noah's prophecy to Shem encompasses three aspects of his descendants' destinies: ***Covenant Relationship:*** Shem's descendants would enter into a covenant relationship with God. Genesis 9:26a states, "...Blessed be the Lord God of Shem." This prophecy was fulfilled through the Hebrews, descendants of Shem, who were identified by their geographical location (Genesis 10:21). ***Nomadic Lifestyle:*** Because of their covenant with God, Shem's descendants became nomadic people or itinerant farmers constantly seeking fertile land. ***Servitude of Canaan:*** Genesis 9:26b states, "And Canaan shall be his servant." This prophecy was fulfilled when Israel conquered and subjugated the Promised Land, the land of the Canaanites.

Shem's name and blessing refer to God's promise of land. After Abraham, the Jews became clans of nomads, moving from place to place in search of their Promised Land. To this day, Jews are considered wanderers.

Ham

Ham, the youngest son of Noah, is also referred to as the first son (Genesis 9:24). His name means black or dark, a reference to high melanin content in his skin, and his ethno-geographical migration to the hotter climates near the Torrid Zone. Ham represents all black or darker races of people. His actions during Noah's drunkenness are central to Noah's prophecy, which concerns two main aspects.

First, it was Canaan, not Ham, who was cursed. God had already blessed Ham (Genesis 9:1) and does not rescind His blessings. Canaan, the fourth son of Ham (Genesis 10:6), was cursed. Scripturally, blessing means certain privileges that lead to happiness, while a curse is the removal of such privileges. The meaning of a curse is illustrated in Genesis 3:17-19 and Genesis 3:23-24, when Adam lost privileges due to disobedience.

Due to misconceptions about Ham's curse, it is important to focus on Ham's blessing. Ham's blessing was for his people to become urban dwellers and civilization builders. This prophecy is exemplified by Ham's grandson, Nimrod, who became the first city-dwelling civilization builder after the flood (Genesis 10:7-10). Evidence from Scripture, science, anthropology, and archaeology supports the idea of civilization arising out of Africa and its ancient extended borders (Genesis 2:10-14).

The legacy of Ham to black people today is his blessing as urban-dwelling civilization builders, not Canaan's curse. There is ample historical evidence for the descendants of Ham serving as nation's infrastructure builders through the enterprise of slavery. Out of Ham's four sons mentioned in Genesis 10:6, all except Canaan continue to thrive today as great civilizations. Cush or Ethiopia remains a great kingdom; Mizraim or Egypt is a lasting dynasty; Phut or Libya persists in North Africa. The Canaanites' kingdom ceased, but their legacy as slaves may have continued during the age of exploration. Their kingdom became extinct, but not their lineage. So, were the first slaves descendants of Canaan, which exempted most people of African descent?

The second aspect of Canaan's curse is that his descendants would become slaves: "And he said, Cursed be Canaan; a servant of servants shall he be unto his brethren." (Genesis 9:25). The text notes that Canaan's descendants would be slaves to the descendants of Shem, to the descendants of Japheth. Historically and scripturally, both have been fulfilled through subjugation by the Israelites, and the latter beginning with the Portuguese, descendants of Japheth.

It is possible that Africans taken from West Africa into slavery by the Portuguese were descendants of the Canaanites. If so, their legacy as civilization builders continued. Slavery became the primary means of European economic expansion and played an instrumental role in building pre-industrial America.

Conclusion Thesis: The Objective of the Gospel is Redemption

Redemption, in its rudimentary meaning, is the act of buying back (liberating) people from the penalty, power, and presence of the effects of sin and death. From a natural standpoint, redemption requires a costly sacrifice to deliver people from spiritual oppression that keeps them in bondage to sin. That sacrifice is Jesus Christ and the cross of redemption that redeems people from evil corruption as a ransom. It signifies restoring what was lost and bringing people into a rightful relationship with God and each other, which is the objective of redemption.

God's Eternal Plan of Salvation grants immortality of transformed human nature into the likeness of Christ, with the central attribute of love for God and all believers in the Body of Christ. When we compare the eternal state of all believers to time, we see that the trajectory through time is a process of building unity among believers through the atonement of sin, which rescues them from their sins. It means that the oppressive effects of evil and hate are achieved in time before eternity.

Noah's perennial prophecy gives a snapshot of the trajectory from the roots of one culture and one language to disunity associated with historical ethnic and cultural division to embracing and celebrating those differences. Spiritual unity isn't outward uniformity.; it is an inward kinship to Christ. This trajectory traverses through the "Confounding" of the languages at Babel that led to ethnic cultural division, to uniting different ethnicities and cultures at Pentecost that will be ultimately fulfilled during the "Latter Rain" outpouring of God's Spirit that will unite the descendants of Shem, Ham, and Japheth during the transition from the "last days" to the "end times" that will be fulfilled in Revelation 7:9-10:

After this I looked and a vast host appeared which no one could count, [gathered out] of every nation, from all tribes and peoples and languages. These stood before the throne and before the Lamb; they were attired in white robes, with palm branches in their hands.

In loud voice they cried, saying, [Our] salvation is due to our God, Who is seated on the throne, and to the Lamb [to Them we owe our deliverance]!

That should be "Good News" for every believer. Now let's trace the perennial prophecy of Noah to see how it will happen.

Divine Spiritual Unity

Divine spiritual unity "in Christ" is the aim of the "gospel" in time, where God becomes "all in all," the basis of unity. I Corinthians 15:28, *"However, when everything is subjected to Him, then the Son Himself will also subject Himself to [the Father] Who put all things under Him, so that God may be all in all [be everything to everyone, supreme, the indwelling and controlling factor of life]."*

Therefore, besides salvation, building unity among different ethnicities and cultures is central to the gospel that becomes resisted spiritually among humanity. In that context of predictive prophecy, Noah's prophecy points out the roots, progression, and effects of division as having a temporary purpose through time in the plan of God.

This conclusion is designed to examine ethnic and cultural division as originating from demonic influence and unity being fulfilled by spiritual unity.

This conclusion turns to the concept of Noah's Perennial Prophecy to closely examine the underlying causes of prejudice and ethnic hatred that became a manmade concept of racism. According to the notes, these negative attitudes and behaviors were permitted by God for a purpose, as with Cain slaying Abel. The text explores the notion that, within the framework of "righteousness," hatred toward differences among people is often fueled by a desire to exploit those of different ethnicities, religions, and cultures, a human fault. This exploitation sets in motion a cycle in which those in power develop fears and phobias toward the very groups they seek to dominate.

The Role of Fear, Control—Historical Examples: As these fears intensify, they can evolve into mechanisms for controlling expanding populations. The experience of the Hebrews in Egypt exemplifies this dynamic. Pharaoh, witnessing the rapid growth of the Hebrew population, became fearful that their numbers would surpass those of the Egyptians. To prevent this, he imposed harsher labor and stricter oversight through taskmasters, as described in Exodus 5:1-18. This oppressive strategy reflects patterns later seen throughout history, including the tactics used by slave masters. Pharaoh's fear was rooted in the concern that the Hebrews could eventually rise in power and retaliate against their oppressors.

The Significance of "Servant of Servants"

The Enduring Impact of Slavery and Poverty: Slavery and poverty are universally recognized as deplorable conditions, and the final analysis presented here does nothing to lessen their severity or tragic legacy. Rather, this examination ends a biblical and historical exploration of both, revealing that these systems are not divinely instituted but are instead the result of human enterprise, created and sustained for economic advantage.

The Manmade Origins and Consequences: The evidence and reasoning in this work underscore that slavery and poverty stem from deliberate actions by people seeking material gain. These practices have left lasting scars on the descendants of those subjected to them, perpetuating cycles of hardship and broken relationships.

Divine Intervention and Restoration: Importantly, this analysis highlights the promise of divine intervention. At an appointed time, God will act to recompense the descendants of those who suffered under slavery and poverty. This intervention will serve to restore fractured relationships between the heritage of the victimizers and the victims, offering hope for reconciliation and justice.

Scriptural Foundation of Servanthood: Spiritually and according to Scripture, the highest position in God's Kingdom is that of a servant. This principle is clearly emphasized in Matthew 23:11: *"The greatest among you will be your servant."* There is consideration that early slaves may have been descendants of the Canaanites, a group known for their contributions as civilization builders. The ongoing legacy of black Americans suggests that they play an important role in God's ultimate plan of salvation. Anthony Evans, in his book *Let's Get To Know Each Other*, specifically in the chapter "The Black Church's Link to Africa," presents his perspective on God's purpose for slavery.

God's Purpose for Slavery in His Divine Plan: This perspective leads to a major conclusion regarding God's twofold, sovereign purpose for slavery. **First**, slavery was permitted by God not primarily to teach the ignorant slave the right way, but as exemplified by Cornelius in Acts 10:1-48, to recognize the slave's faith in the true God. Historically, the Catholic Church came alongside slave traders, with popes, religious orders (notably the Jesuits), and laity engaging in or authorizing the slave trade and holding enslaved people, particularly from the 15th through 19th centuries. Church leaders often justified this, particularly the enslavement of non-Christians and Africans, by citing biblical passages and arguing for the Christianization of the enslaved, rather than evangelizing them. Their introduction provided an opportunity for the slaves to discover Christ for themselves, the Mediator who would replace all sub-deities as the means of access to God. **Second**, slavery served as the means by which God would introduce the true meaning of His justice to American culture, which had neglected this aspect of Christ's character, instead, and for the sake of economic advantage, used violence and war as a means of civilizing the heathens. As hard as this pill is to swallow, history bears out this truth.

Justice, Righteousness, and Restoration: Reflecting on Anthony Evans' statement about justice, Scripture suggests that God's righteousness will be revealed in America when white Americans participate in restoring black Americans. Isaiah 32:16-17 foretells this restoration: *"Then justice will dwell in the wilderness, and righteousness (moral and spiritual rectitude in every area and relation) will abide in the fruitful field. And the effect of righteousness will be peace [internal and external], and the result of righteousness will be quietness and confident trust forever."*

God's righteousness in America will be demonstrated through reconciliation. The reconciliation between black and white Americans, along with restoration in urban and rural communities, will result in justice. Isaiah 32:1 declares: *"Behold, a King will reign in righteousness, and princes will rule with justice."*

The Fulfillment of "Servant of Servants"

Although much of Biblical prophecy centers on Israel, the Middle East, and neighboring nations, the plight of the world's poor also holds significance in relation to Christ's return (James 5:1-11). A large portion of African Americans in inner cities experience poverty comparable to Third World conditions.

Servant of Servants ultimately finds its fulfillment when Black Americans are restored. This restoration is believed to also include poor rural residents of non-black heritage, and poor people as a whole. Then, forthwith, as described in chapter 17, this will lead to the Nation of Israel and Jew populations, who

were former slaves, to recognize Jesus Christ as the
The revival brought about by the restoration of Black
is envisioned as igniting spiritual awakening throug
world, described metaphorically as "streams in th
(Isaiah 35:1,6).

Ultimately, God's purpose for slavery and its a
suffering is to use black Americans as a pivota
facilitating the salvation of the Jews and the restorati
twelve tribes of Israel. When black people in Thii
nations and black Americans living in similar conditic
to Christ in significant numbers, it signals that salva
redemption are near. In summary, the descendants
(Urban Dwellers) and Japheth (Seafarers) will unite at
moment in history, sparking a revival that will c
descendants of Shem (Nomadic people) to Christ, fulfill
plan of salvation.

Biblical Prophecy and the Significance of Pover
most Biblical prophecy focuses on the Nation of Is
Middle East, and neighboring nations, the cond
impoverished people worldwide are also significant t
return (James 5:1-11). A majority of African American
inner cities are experiencing poverty and conditions co
to those found in Third World countries.

When the last Gentile comes to Christ, then all Jewi
will turn to Christ as the Messiah. ***"I do not want y
ignorant of this mystery, brothers, so that you m
conceited: Israel has experienced a hardening
until the full number of Gentiles has come in. A
Israel will be saved..." (Romans 11:25,26a)***
Gentiles seem to be in the Third World and living
World conditions. If that is true, our inner cities
rural communities are targets for mass evange
revival that will be the key to Christ's return.

None of the things mentioned can happen
reconciliation between races. It is time to get busy
ministry of reconciliation.